Cheese		
hard, grated	4oz/115g	1 cup
soft (ricotta, etc)	1oz/25g	2 tablespoons
Chick peas	8oz/225g	1 cup
Coconut, desiccated	3oz/85g	1 cup
Currants	6oz/170g	1 cup
Dried fruit (apricots, pears, figs, dates, etc)		
whole	5oz/140g	1 cup
chopped	3oz/85g	½ cup
Flour		
(wholemeal)	4oz/115g	1 cup
Fresh fruit, chopped	5oz/140g	1 cup
Grains	8oz/225g	1 cup
Hazelnut kernels	4oz/115g	¾ cup
Honey	12oz/340g	1 cup
Jam, raw sugar	6oz/170g	½ cup
Leeks, sliced	4oz/115g	1 cup
Lentils/split peas	5oz/140g	¾ cup
Macaroni, raw	4oz/115g	1 cup
Margarine see butter		
Mushrooms		
whole	2oz/55g	1 cup
chopped	2oz/55g	¾ cup
Noodles, raw	5oz/140g	1 cup
Nuts	1oz/25g	3 tablespoons
	2oz/55g	½ cup
	3oz/85g	⅔ cup
	4oz/115g	¾ cup
	5oz/140g	1 cup
	8oz/225g	1⅔ cups
Oatmeal	4oz/115g	1 cup
Oats, rolled	4oz/115g	1 cup
Olives	4oz/115g	1 cup
Onions, chopped	6oz/170g	1 cup
Parsley, chopped fresh	1oz/25g	1 cup
Pasta shapes	1½–2oz/45–55g	1 cup
Peanut butter	1oz/25g	¼ cup/2½ tablespoons
Peanuts, raw	4oz/115g	¾ cup
Potatoes		
diced	6oz/170g	1 cup
cooked and mashed	8oz/225g	1 cup
Raisins	1lb/455g	3 cups
Rhubarb, chopped	1lb/455g	4 cups
Rice, brown		
raw	8oz/225g	1 cup
	1lb/455g	2 cups
cooked	6oz/170g	1 cup
Sesame and sunflower		
seeds	5oz/140g	1 cup
	1lb/455g	3¼ cups
Spinach, raw		
coarsely chopped	1lb/455g	10 cups
cooked or defrosted	8oz/225g	1 cup
Sugar, raw cane	6oz/170g	1 cup
Tomatoes		
chopped	1lb/455g	2⅔ cups
puree	3oz/85g	⅓ cup
TVP mince	4oz/115g	1 cup
Yeast		
dried	½oz/15g	1 tablespoon
fresh	1oz/25g	2½ tablespoons
	2oz/55g	¼ cup

LINDA MCCARTNEY'S HOME COOKING

LINDA McCARTNEY'S HOME COOKING

Linda McCartney

Arcade Publishing · New York

Little, Brown and Company

To my husband and children who, like me, love animals and enjoy cooking.

My thanks to Peter Cox for all his help and research in making this book possible.

FIRST U.S. EDITION 1990

ISBN 1–55970–097–1
Library of Congress Catalog Card Number 90–80670
Library of Congress Cataloging-in-Publication information is available.

Published in the United States by Arcade Publishing, Inc., New York, a Little, Brown company

10 9 8 7 6 5 4

Designed by Fielding Rowinski

Published simultaneously in Canada by Little, Brown & Company (Canada) Limited

PRINTED IN THE UNITED STATES OF AMERICA

WOR

CONTENTS

Introduction 1

My Kitchen 3

Thinking About Food 6

The New Age of Food 11

A Cook's Companion 14

Essential Utensils 20

Choosing and Using Vegetables 22

Nutritious Nuts and Seeds 32

Fruit 35

Glorious Grains and Legumes 40

Helpful Herbs and Spectacular Spices 44

Growing Your Own Goodness 48

Soups 51

Snacks, Appetizers and Light Dishes 61

Salads 70

Main Courses 80

Vegetable Specialties 134

Sauces and Sundries 143

Desserts, Cakes and Cookies 152

Index 167

PUBLISHER'S NOTE

The author of this book, Linda McCartney, is American by birth but has made England her home for the past twenty years. Virtually all the ingredients contained in this book are available in both the US and in the UK. Many of the meatless dishes call for the use of TVP. For those not familiar with this product, TVP is textured vegetable protein, a common meat substitute available in health-food stores throughout the United States, and even in many supermarkets. TVP can be found in a variety of forms: flavored, unflavored, minced and in chunks. In the frozen-foods section of most health-food stores there are even ready-made products shaped and flavored to resemble sausages, bacon, patties and fish fillets. Linda McCartney and her family have been cooking and eating vegetarian for many years, partly for nutritional reasons, but also out of their profound respect for animals. These are her tried-and-true recipes, which she has used to good effect with her own family through the years.

INTRODUCTION

I was lucky enough to grow up in a family of food lovers. We rarely had fancy meals but they always tasted good. I used to spend a lot of time hanging out in the kitchen, partly because I liked to be around food, but also because I loved to watch my mum preparing a meal often without measuring or weighing any ingredients. She just seemed to know instinctively what was right.

I like to think I'm a person who picks things up easily and those hours I spent hanging around the kitchen have served me well. They've given me a natural feeling for putting together a meal without spending hours poring over recipes.

There is, of course, one main difference between my cooking and the food I was brought up on – I don't use any meat but everybody seems to say it tastes as good as, if not better than using (to put it bluntly) dead animals.

Which brings me to the reason I've written this book. Partly as a way of handing down my recipes to my family, but most importantly because I want to encourage all those people who so often say to me: 'I'd like to cook without using meat but I don't know where to begin', or 'How do you fill that gap on the plate where there's usually a piece of lamb or beef?' My response is simple – there are quiches, pastas, salads and many wonderful new soya protein foods that taste so much better than meat!

And to those people who complain: 'I'd love to be a vegetarian but my family would never allow it', I suggest you try a few of my recipes – without mentioning there's no meat – and see how much they enjoy them!

We stopped eating meat many years ago. During the course of a Sunday lunch we happened to look out of the kitchen window at our young lambs gambolling happily in the fields. Glancing down at our plates we suddenly realized that we were eating the leg of an animal that had until recently been gambolling in a field itself. We looked at each other and said 'Wait a minute, we love these sheep – they're such gentle creatures, so why are we eating them?' It was the last time we ever did.

Some people find it easier to cut out meat gradually, supplementing their diet with chicken and fish. We chose not to take this route – a decision which was reinforced a few weeks later when we found ourselves stuck behind a truck packed tightly with beautiful white hens. As it turned into the chicken processing plant a few miles ahead, we imagined the fate in store for those poor hens and felt we had acted wisely.

There are people who try to justify eating fish by saying they have no feelings. Well, you watch a fish gasping for breath as it's pulled out of the water and then try and tell me it has no feelings! Anyway, with the amount of pollution in our poisoned rivers and seas, I'm surprised that *anyone* wants to eat fish. But that's another story. . .

I think a lot of people are rather afraid of cooking. I've met so many people who say: 'Oh, I could never cook that!' when more often than not it's just been a bunch of really good food thrown together – and doesn't it taste good! It's a shame that so many people shy away from the kitchen because it can be an artistic and creative place. And rewarding too – it's great to prepare a meal that is well received.

I don't think you have to be a particularly talented person to be a good cook. It helps enormously, of course, if you enjoy cooking, but even if you don't I hope this book will encourage you to have a go – and maybe you'll find you start to get some unexpected pleasure out of it!

To tell you the truth, I'm a real peasant cook. My cooking has never been about following recipes in a book, and it's been a challenge to translate these instinctive methods into hard and fast rules. For example, if I'm making a stew I *never* weigh the carrots, potatoes, and onions. I simply say: 'that looks the right amount' and in they go. If you like a particular herb, or if you like garlic, onions or potatoes, then add more of what you like to my recipes – don't be afraid to make a few changes to suit your own taste. That's what cooking's all about!

The important thing, I believe, is to have a really good time cooking. Don't be too serious, and – most of all – don't be 'precious'.

I spend a lot of time in our kitchen. I find it the cosiest, friendliest place in the house. It's not something my American upbringing prepared me for, but now that I live in England it's become very important to me. It's a great place to nurture a happy harmonious family and to spend time with friends, chatting over a cup of tea.

I've put down a lot of my favourite recipes here and I really hope you find them as easy to make as I do. They're very popular with everybody I know, and I hope they'll become favourites of yours as well. I haven't written this book in order to be acclaimed as a great cook – like everyone, I've had my share of disasters in the kitchen. I'm simply doing it for the animals.

Linda McCartney

MY KITCHEN

We all hang out in my kitchen. It's full of warmth and friendliness – cosy and snug in winter, but cool and calm in summer. It is a basic but very comfortable kitchen, as I think all kitchens should be. We only have a few labour-saving gadgets to help with food preparation – I like to do most things by hand, because we have a lot more fun doing it, and because you get to appreciate the textures and smells more. The family all lend a hand, which makes every mealtime a real family occasion.

I think cooking should be *fun*, because that's the best way to pass on all the tricks and skills from one generation to the next. If you learn about good food from your mum and dad, then you're set for life, and won't go out and eat hamburgers and other rubbish. So here are a few tips for welcoming your family into the kitchen, and a few more tips that will encourage them to join in with the cooking.

BABIES

When babies are ready for solid foods, I recommend offering them right away a variety of vegetable purees. It takes three-to-five minutes to cook most vegetables, then a few seconds to puree them after they are drained. They may be combined. You may preserve little containers in your freezer for later use.

VERY YOUNG CHILDREN

Children between the ages of one and three are intensely curious. They always want to be 'where the action is' – so give them something exciting to do, like shelling peas, peeling sweetcorn or peeling bananas. Simple, safe tasks like these are great fun and are very rewarding for a youngster.

Most raw foods are very colourful and interesting to look at, so give your child a crayon and some paper and ask them to draw the cabbages, carrots, peppers and so on. They can post their masterpieces to a granny or stick them to the refrigerator door!

Tell a story about the foods you are using. If you don't know the real history, tell a magical tale to get the child really enthusiastic about each food. This can also encourage children to eat foods they are unfamiliar with.

Wash the children's hands and arms up to the elbows, tie back their hair and let them touch the unprepared food. Then let them know what each food is – a potato can be very interesting when you are allowed to study it for the first time! The child cannot harm anything, and you needn't give them 'messy' foods such as eggs or liquids.

YOUNG CHILDREN

Children between the ages of four and seven are determined not to be left out of anything, so I always try to offer them something interesting to do before they have a chance to feel excluded! Wash the child's hands and arms, tie back their hair and seat them at the table. Then give them a job that lets them use at least one kitchen utensil (make sure you show them how to use it properly). For this age group, the utensil should be very safe, no matter how it is used. A wooden spoon, rolling pin, small hand whisk or pastry cutter are good examples. Make sure that the job the child is given is real, however. Mixing dry ingredients in a large bowl or whisking a salad dressing are good starting points.

There is a huge difference between what a four-year-old can do and what a seven-year-old can do. Children like to feel successful in whatever they do (don't we all?), so never give an 'impossible' task to a child: a four-year-old may feel challenged when learning to use a whisk, while a seven-year-old may find that cutting pastry or filling and decorating sticks of celery is a more appropriate job. But try swapping these duties, however, and you'll see that one is suddenly too difficult and the other far too easy – boredom would follow shortly! Give careful consideration to the child's age and personality before you allocate tasks.

If the child doesn't actually want to help in the practical aspects of cooking, then I suggest you involve them simply by talking. Explain what you are making, talk about the ingredients and why they are used in this way and show, by example, the importance of hygiene. Always try to make it sound like fun and an adventure!

Home cooking includes a whole variety of skills, some more enjoyable than others. Let your child do some washing up (not sharp knives and heavy pans) to learn this very basic skill. They needn't dislike it if you don't tell them it's not *your* favourite!

On the more artistic side, why not let children of this age design a table setting? This could easily become a project that goes on for a few days or a week: they can make place mats out of coloured paper, napkin rings out of cardboard tube, even a paper flower centre-piece for the table. Then let them lay the table for each evening meal so that they gain a sense of form and fun.

A whole variety of kitchen tasks are suitable for this age group. Here are just a few: scrubbing vegetables, squeezing lemons, cracking eggs, brushing up the spilled flour on the floor, measuring and weighing ingredients, setting the timer, finding the right pots and pans, greasing the baking dish, washing the rice.

PRE-TEENS

Children from eight to twelve years of age are capable of learning more responsible tasks. Their co-ordination is better, their attention span is usually rather longer and they have had time to learn the basic elements of hygiene and safety. Children of this age are really fun to work with in the kitchen – provided they are not pushed too hard. Some in this age group might be trusted near a hot stove, but I would *never* leave them alone with one. Closely supervise them as you both add measured ingredients to a pan, or slowly stir a sauté. Teach them how to guard their movements when they are near the protruding handles and mixing spoons that line a cooker. Show them how to use oven gloves safely, and strongly emphasize the potential dangers of fires, burns and spillages. Make sure they understand that if they really want to cook, they will have to *prove* that they can be conscientious and alert in this very responsible adult situation.

Some of the very simple peeling, chopping and slicing tasks can be learned at this age. You will have to select the precise tasks according to the maturity and previous 'record' your child has with these implements. For instance, a nine-year-old child could be given a small knife (not sharp) and allowed to slice the beans diagonally while you chop onions next to them. Don't leave the child alone, and don't ask them to cut carrots or parsnips – they are too hard and require too much force and a larger knife.

Use your ingenuity to come up with new ways of performing standard kitchen tasks so that a child can try them. For instance, fresh herbs can be safely, cleanly and easily chopped by placing the washed herbs in a one-pint cup or bowl. Then use the kitchen scissors to cut the herb, over and over again, until the desired fineness is achieved. This is entirely safe and keeps all of the herbs where you want them – not on the floor!

Many of the shows of strength and balancing acts so important in cooking may be learned at this age. Use of colanders, salad spinners, hand graters and sieves, for instance, or pouring from a small pan to a gravy boat, may be explained and demonstrated in detail until the youngsters are ready to try one or two techniques for themselves.

Children in this age group may safely learn to carry the completed dish from work-top to table starting first with cold dishes and graduating to hot dishes. Teach them, too, how to place the food on the table so that it is safe and attractive.

Once each week, help a child of this age to serve the meal on to each plate. You can begin to teach them how to arrange the food according to colour and texture and, also, how to judge the appropriate size of portions.

Not so much fun, but still part of the process, ask children of this age to help clear up the table and the work-top after the meal is completed. Safety, hygiene and a sense of order are all reinforced in this activity.

TEENS

Youngsters from twelve years old up to the middle teens are usually wonderfully capable, especially if you have taught them well during the previous years. They should be familiar with all of the elements of hygiene and safety, and you should have introduced them to the basic skills necessary to use the oven, cooker, and other kitchen tools and utensils. Make sure that your children know how to read a recipe, and encourage them to prepare at least one dish each week using a new recipe. I suggest you stay close at hand, perhaps reading or doing some work at the kitchen table – in case any queries arise and so they don't feel abandoned.

Demonstrate how a complete meal is put together by helping children of this age to plan a menu. Then teach them how to organize the various tasks so that all the components of the meal are ready at once. This is a difficult skill for some people to learn, no matter what their age, so allow yourself and your children a few attempts before you expect perfection.

Encourage children of this age to gain expertise in at least one area of cooking. For instance, bread-making, cakes, soups and salad dressings are each impressive skills that will help your child gain confidence and prestige – especially if you praise them in company.

Children of this age sometimes love to make up their own recipes. This could be the start of something rather special – like a cookbook!

MEN

Let's face it – most day-to-day home cooking is still done by women. But that doesn't mean that it *should* be – or always will be. So here are some tips to entice a reluctant spouse into the kitchen. . . First, try putting them in charge of the 'kitchen garden' (it doesn't matter if this is only on your windowsill or porch). Once they've grown some food, encourage them to take part in its preparation. . . Dad's Special Vegetable Curry, Tomatoes Stuffed with Cottage Cheese and Basil, Leeks Vinaigrette, or Green Beans Savoury are all dishes that men can supervise, from the garden to the table!

Men often seem to enjoy the 'technical' processes in the kitchen – for example, bread-making. We never used to have homemade bread in our house, until there was a bread strike a few years ago. Paul went to the local baker and asked him for some live yeast, came home and made the most incredible bread, and he's been making it ever since. We all adore it, and there's nothing that smells more wonderful in the house than fresh bread baking. Pickles, marmalade, sauces, dressings, jams and even home-made wine are all ideal for men to get involved with.

Even if your man simply sits reading the paper while you cook, encourage him to read it in the kitchen! At the very least, he'll realize just how much time and effort goes into making his meal, and what a wonderful time you can have doing it!

Ask your man to encourage the children to pick up some kitchen skills – even if it's only how to sweep and wash up! This will help to prevent the children from growing up unskilled and with the wrong attitudes. It will also give your man and the kids a chance to be together in a family atmosphere.

Don't push your luck, but if possible, arrange things so that one meal per day (or week, at the very least) is his sole responsibility. This gives you a break so that you truly enjoy the meals you do make. It also gives him the chance to develop his own style and, er, expertise! (Well, it gives him the chance to practise!) A lot of men I've met love cooking, and are very good at it.

Most important of all, have fun. Enjoy the whole process of preparing, presenting and eating your food. I promise you it will be tastier, healthier and infinitely more satisfying!

THINKING ABOUT FOOD

Not so long ago, people never used to be concerned about the food they bought. If it was advertised on television, and if they could find it in the supermarket, then they bought it – even though it may have been packed full of all sorts of unhealthy ingredients. I suppose some people still behave rather like this – they'd rather not know where the food they buy comes from, nor how it was produced, what it really contains nor if it ever had a mother! But sometimes, you can't escape finding out facts that perhaps you'd rather not know. Do you remember when we started to see items like these in the newspapers and on television?

'Diets high in saturated animal fat double your risk of dying from heart disease'

'The Great Fish Scandal – seafood goes uninspected as bacteria, viruses, toxins, effluent and parasites in fish cause disease in thousands of people every year'

'Hormones and antibiotics given to farm animals can cause cancer, deformities and other diseases in humans'

'Battery hens suffer in overcrowded cages and endure horrific treatment in slaughterhouses'

Everyone's seen shocking news items like these, but some people still manage to turn a blind eye. Each time I see the latest scandal, I'm astonished that people know so little about the way their food is produced. The important question is: what can we, as concerned consumers, really do about it?

Well, I believe that the food we eat should be **good for us**, and **good for everyone and everything** involved in its production. I also think it's good to bring my children up to appreciate good food, and to realize that not everything advertised on television is automatically good for them, or for other creatures either. This means that there are certain types of food that I just won't buy. Here is my 'blacklist' – as the many recipes in this book prove, you can eat extremely well without including any of these undesirable items on your shopping-list:

WHY YOU DON'T NEED MEAT

Reasons: High in unhealthy saturated animal fat. Often contaminated with antibiotics, hormones and other drugs not stated on any label. Involved in thousands of serious cases of food poisoning every year. Scientists have shown that people *not* eating these products suffer far less from cancer, heart disease, diabetes, hypertension, and other diseases. Meat production is very cruel, also very wasteful of our world's precious food resources (did you know that over half the world's grain production is fed to animals, not humans?).

WHY YOU DON'T NEED FISH

Reasons: The pollution of our seas is at a peak with untreated sewage, pollution from heavy metals (mercury, cadmium, lead, zinc and sometimes plutonium, strontium etc), bacteria and viruses, parasites and intestinal worms. None of us would willingly swim in this mess, so why should we eat fish that have been exposed to it all their lives? Also, millions of dolphins, seals and other marine life are butchered every year by indiscriminate large-scale fishing, not to mention the fish themselves.

WHY YOU DON'T NEED ADDITIVES

Reasons: Food colourings are present simply to make food more enticing – not for any good nutritional reason. Some of them have been linked to hyperactivity, and others to cancer. Some preservatives and anti-oxidants may also produce severe adverse reactions.

NOW HERE'S THE GOOD NEWS

So what can you eat to make sure you're getting a really wholesome and humane diet? Well, it's not difficult at all. This book is packed full of quick and tasty recipes that you can use – all of them tried and tested by me and my family. Every day, I try to ensure that we eat a balanced diet consisting of lots of fresh food, at least one dish high in protein, and a variety of other foods that are particularly high in essential vitamins, minerals and nutrients. Here is a simple guide to the most common types of nutrients, and some suggestions as to where they may be found.

PROTEIN

Protein is often described as the building block of life, because it helps build muscles, blood, skin, hair, nails and our internal organs, as well as helping to create enzymes, antibodies and hormones. Next to water, protein is the most plentiful substance in the human body. A deficiency of protein in the diet is rarely seen in the West, or anywhere where people are eating varied and regular meals. For a long time it was thought that the more protein you ate, the better. However, it is now becoming clear that too much protein in the diet may be harmful, and it has been associated with degenerative diseases such as osteoporosis (softening of the bones through calcium loss). When you think about it, mother's milk, which is without doubt our most 'natural' food, only contains a small proportion of protein – less than a third of the protein that is found, for example, in cow's milk. High-protein foods include soya products, beans and legumes, whole grains and seeds. Dairy produce is also a rich source of protein, but be careful not to rely too heavily on it in your diet, because much of it (but not low-fat or skimmed milk) contains significant amounts of saturated fat. Here are some naturally high-protein foods from the plant kingdom:

GRAINS	LEGUMES	NUTS
Whole wheat	Soya beans	Sunflower seeds
Pasta	Soya products	Sesame seeds
Bread	Kidney beans	Tahini
Oats	Peas	Cashew nuts
Rye	Lentils	Almonds
Brown rice	Bean sprouts	Hazel nuts
Barley	Peanuts	Coconuts
Millet	Chick peas	Walnuts

WHY YOU DON'T NEED ANIMAL FAT

A balanced diet will contain some fat. The important thing to remember is that your *overall* fat intake should not be too high. This means that when you eat a dish which contains a high proportion of fat, remember to balance it by eating food that is correspondingly low in fat (such as salads or fruit). Also, remember that saturated fat – the type that is found in animal produce, such as milk, eggs and cheese – is much less healthy than either polyunsaturated or mono-unsaturated kinds, which are found in plant foods and oils. If you need to cut down on your fat intake (and many of us do), first reduce your consumption of saturated animal fats, then replace other fat-rich foods in your diet with foods that are high in carbohydrates and low in fat – such as pasta, potatoes, bread, vegetables and legumes.

CARBOHYDRATES

Carbohydrates provide energy for the body, and can be divided into 'simple' or 'complex' types. Simple carbohydrates are present in sugar, honey and fruit, and provide 'instant energy'. Complex carbohydrates (sometimes called starches) are found in vegetables, fruits, grains, seeds and nuts, and provide a slower, more sustained source of energy – many athletes now stoke up on complex carbohydrates (such as pasta and potatoes) before a big event, to provide them with a continuing source of energy. Foods rich in complex carbohydrates are much less fattening than foods high in fats, and are a very important part of a healthy diet.

FIBRE IS ONLY PRESENT IN PLANT FOODS

There is no fibre in meat, fish or dairy produce. Fibre is essential to good digestion because it helps the intestines function properly, so preventing constipation and helping the body to absorb nutrients from food. There is considerable evidence to show that diets that are low in fibre are associated with cancers of the colon and rectum, heart disease, obesity and varicose veins, so this is another reason why a healthy diet always includes plenty of fresh fruit and vegetables.

VITAMINS AND MINERALS

Small quantities of vitamins are necessary for growth and maintenance of health throughout your life. Vitamins do not supply energy, but they *are* essential for the proper functioning of all the body's systems. There are two basic forms of vitamins: water-soluble and fat-soluble. Water-soluble vitamins are not stored for any period in the body (excess amounts are simply excreted), and so they must be taken daily in your diet. They are easily destroyed by cooking and food processing, so fresh food is likely to be the highest-quality source of most water-soluble vitamins. Fat-soluble vitamins are also destroyed by heat, light, air and cooking. They are stored in the fatty tissues of your body, so excess doses may build up and eventually cause toxic reactions. You do not need to take great quantities of them on a regular basis, since your body uses its store of these vitamins as and when it needs them. In recent years, vitamin pills have become a multi-million pound industry. However, no pill can duplicate the very delicate relationship that exists between different vitamins in nature, and taking mega-doses of synthetic vitamins is never preferable to getting a good supply of natural vitamins from a well-balanced diet.

Every tissue in the body contains minerals and every bodily process and action requires minerals to be present in adequate supply. Some minerals – such as calcium, potassium and magnesium – are present in relatively large amounts in the body, but others (called trace minerals) are only present in very small amounts. A varied diet, with plenty of fresh food, will provide you with all the vitamins and minerals you are likely to need.

Vitamin A

Vitamin A is a fat-soluble vitamin which is essential for the continuous repair and replacement of cell tissues throughout your body. An excellent vegetable source of vitamin A is carotene, which is a plant pigment (present in carrots and many yellow- or orange-coloured vegetables). Carotene is converted in the human body into vitamin A (retinol), which is stored in the liver, kidneys, lungs and eyes. Cooked vegetables are often higher in usable vitamin A than raw ones, because the plant cell membranes are destroyed during cooking, thus making more carotene available for our bodies to utilize. However, high-temperature cooking will tend to destroy or degrade it. Best sources are carrots, spinach, broccoli and other leafy vegetables.

Vitamin B Complex

This collection of water-soluble vitamins includes thiamin, riboflavin, folic acid and niacin. They work to maintain the health of your nervous system and your circulatory system. Many of them can be found in yeast products (brewer's yeast, or yeast extracts),

and whole-grain cereals are another good source. Other foods rich in B vitamins include wheatgerm, nuts and seeds, eggs, milk and soya products.

Vitamin C

Vitamin C is another water-soluble vitamin that strengthens blood vessels and provides resistance to infection. Citrus fruits are an excellent source of vitamin C, and other good sources include red and green peppers, bean sprouts, potatoes, spinach, cabbage, broccoli and brussels sprouts. Your need for vitamin C may increase with age, since the body has a greater need to regenerate its collagen (connective tissue). Cigarette smoking will rob your body of vitamin C, and a dirty environment – such as the urban pollution that most of us now have to put up with – may also increase your need for this vitamin.

Vitamin D

This has been called the sunshine vitamin, because the sun's rays act on a fat contained in our skin and convert it into vitamin D. Vitamin D deficiency is therefore more common in northern regions of the world, and results in failure to absorb calcium and phosphorus, causing faulty formation of bone (rickets). In your diet, this vitamin can be obtained from fortified products (such as margarine) or dairy products.

Vitamin E

Vitamin E is a fat-soluble vitamin which protects red blood cells, improves their capacity to transport oxygen and prevents impaired flow of blood through clotting. It enhances the action of other major nutrients by preventing them from breaking down before your body can use them (this is called oxidation, therefore vitamin E is an anti-oxidant). The main sources are cereals and vegetable oils, including wheatgerm, sunflower oil, soya oil, and most nuts and seeds.

Calcium

Everyone knows that calcium is necessary for the development of strong and healthy teeth and bones. However, many people who eat a typical junk food diet could be at risk from calcium deficiency. Calcium is present in milk, cheese, soya products, dark green leafy vegetables, dried fruits, sea vegetables (such as kelp and kombu), almonds, molasses and a great many other delicious foods – but it is not present in the kind of snack food that many young people are, unfortunately, inclined to eat. This is one more reason to prefer nutritious home cooking to expensive and unhealthy fast food.

Iodine

Iodine is a trace mineral which helps the thyroid gland to grow and function. It's easy to get enough iodine if you eat mushrooms, sea vegetables, sea salt or iodized table salt, and sunflower seeds.

Iron

Lack of iron is the one of the most common nutritional deficiencies in the West and, once again, the fundamental cause is a poor basic diet that relies too heavily on highly processed junk food. Iron combines with protein in the body and, when further combined with copper, creates haemoglobin. Haemoglobin is the red colouring of your blood and supplies oxygen to all your body tissues. Iron also helps many of the vitamins and minerals do their work and builds your resistance to infection and disease. Foods containing vitamins C and E help the body to absorb iron in the diet, and the use of iron cooking utensils may also provide a boost to iron availability. The main sources of iron in the diet are bread, flour and other cereal products, potatoes and green leafy vegetables, and in particular, prune juice, rolled oats, brewer's yeast powder, dried apricots, raisins, plain chocolate and broccoli.

Magnesium

Magnesium helps your body to process carbohydrates, and plays a part in the development of bones, teeth, muscle and nerves. It is supplied in a healthy diet by nuts and seeds, fresh green vegetables, fruit, whole grains and molasses.

Phosphorus

Phosphorus works with calcium to develop bones and teeth and to maintain them in good repair. This mineral is important to the contraction of muscles – even those you don't see, such as the heart – and is used in nearly every function that your body performs. Phosphorus is generally found in protein foods such as dairy produce, nuts and seeds, whole grains, beans and lentils. You need to have calcium and vitamin D in adequate supply to ensure that phosphorus will be absorbed from your diet. A high-fat or high-sugar diet will reduce the amount of phosphorus you are able to absorb and should therefore be avoided.

Potassium

Potassium works together with sodium to keep the fluid (water) inside and outside the cell walls in balance. Your heart, nerves, kidneys and skin especially rely on an adequate supply of potassium, but all metabolic processes require it to be present in balance with sodium. Magnesium helps maintain correct levels of potassium. Potatoes and bananas provide excellent sources of potassium; oranges, sunflower seeds and green, leafy vegetables are also good sources.

Zinc

Zinc plays an important role in digestion and the absorption of vitamins, and also has a beneficial effect on fertility, growth and healing. Yeast products, grains and seeds are tasty foods with useful quantities of zinc.

A QUICK GUIDE TO HEALTHY EATING

Years ago, our mothers used to think that the only way you could get enough protein, vitamins and minerals was by eating meat. But times have changed, and today we know from many scientific studies that people who *don't* eat meat are, in fact, better nourished and healthier than those who still eat flesh foods. The proof of this is all around us – meat-eaters are known to suffer much more from diet-related diseases, such as coronary heart disease, various cancers, diabetes, high blood pressure, and other modern-day killers. In fact, in one study, scientists found that meat-eaters spend on average *five times longer* in hospital than vegetarians do.

Even so, some people may still be worried about getting the right nourishment when they decide to go meat-free. But there's no need to be. All you have to do is to make sure that every day you eat some food from each one of the three food groups listed below, and you're well on the way to eating a diet which is far healthier than the average.

1 Grains and Seeds

Include a mixture of whole wheat (such as bread) and some beans or legumes. Good sources of energy and protein. Add some nuts and seeds from time to time for variety and extra nutrition.

2 Vegetables and Fruit

The fresher the better – naturally low in calories but high in vitamins and minerals. Great for quick snacks. Eat one 'raw' meal a day.

3 Dairy Products

Go for low-fat products, such as skimmed milk. Helps your body to absorb all the protein contained in other plant foods such as wheat and beans.

THE NEW AGE OF FOOD

I love to have friends and family around for a weekend barbecue. For me, a barbecue makes a welcome break from the usual routines of cooking, and with a little luck, the men do most of the cooking anyway (have you noticed how men always seem to take over at barbecues?). Paper plates and disposable knives and forks are a must on these occasions, because no-one wants to spend half an hour doing the washing up after a lazy afternoon spent eating, chatting and generally relaxing.

Whenever we have friends over for the first time, I know in advance that there will be one or two puzzled looks and glances before the afternoon's over. Eventually someone always says:

'Linda, this is great food, but I didn't think you ate meat. Have you changed – or are you just barbecueing it for us?'

At this point I smile, and say:

'Actually, there was no meat at all in it!'

For the entire afternoon, they've been thinking that they were eating sausages, burgers and kebabs made from meat, marinated in a really tasty barbecue sauce. In fact, they have been eating the most exciting, and perhaps the most revolutionary, development in food this century.

For several years now, the manufacturers of meat products have been using Textured Vegetable Protein (known as TVP) to extend their products – in other words, the sausages hanging in the butcher's shop window may actually contain one-third or more vegetable protein. So most meat-eaters are already eating more vegetarian food than they realize! Now, some enterprising food manufacturers have gone further, and produced the *perfect* sausages and burgers – but without using *any* animal meat at all. This is the sort of 'meat' I use on my barbecue, and it is so identical to butcher's meat in flavour and texture that I'm not surprised that so many of my friends think we've gone back to eating it!

There are so many varieties of vegetable burgers, sausages, mince and chunks available now (*see picture on pages 18–19*) that you're really spoilt for choice. But why should *you* consider buying it? Firstly, it's much cheaper and healthier than butcher's meat. Textured vegetable protein (TVP) is actually *higher* in protein than most meat. At the same time, it's *lower* in fat, has no cholesterol, no nasty gristle – and the really good news is that it has *fewer* calories – so it's

ideal for slimmers! Sounds pretty good stuff, doesn't it? Well it is! Something else I very much like about TVP products is that they're so clean and fuss-free. Preparing meat is so messy and unpleasant – just the touch of it is so disgusting sometimes, and it really *feels* like the dead flesh it is. And as for gutting a fish, or sticking my hand inside a chicken or turkey – forget it! Also, of course, TVP will store indefinitely on the shelf or in the freezer – something that meat won't do. And it's actually *easier* to cook with too – just try any of the recipes that use it in the Main Courses section of this book, and you'll see what I mean.

SOME COOKING HINTS. . .

When I cook vegetable burgers, sausages, TVP chunks and TVP mince I find they taste their best if they're lightly sautéd in oil before being further cooked or rehydrated. Sautéing them with chopped onions or mushrooms also gives them a delicious flavour. Ready-made burgers, sausages and schnitzels can be cooked just about any way without being damaged – they're much, much more resilient than butcher's meat in this way. Some of my recipes specify one packet TVP chunks, or 4 cubed vegetable burgers. If you use ready-made burgers instead of the TVP chunks, use less liquid in the recipe. Just as when cooking meat, the key to producing a tasty dish really lies in the flavouring. By itself, meat really has next to no flavour – as Paul says, if you want to know what meat really tastes like, just bite the inside of your mouth! Cooking tasty TVP successfully is just the same as cooking meat, because it's the seasoning and the sauce that makes it really mouthwatering. You can buy TVP chunks and mince that has already been flavoured – it is available in beef flavour, ham flavour, or natural unflavoured chunks or mince. Choose the one you like best.

WHERE CAN I GET MY PROTEIN?

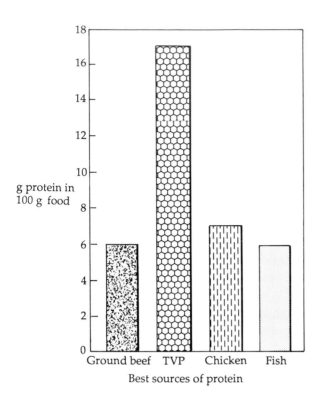

Best sources of protein

Some people still believe that protein is only available from meat, but as you can see from this chart, TVP provides much more protein than beef, chicken or fish.

Supermarkets

Morningstar Farms®
  Breakfast Links
  Breakfast Patties
  Breakfast Strips
  Grillers®

Health Food Stores

Worthington®
  FriChik®
  Veja-Links®
  Vegetarian Burger
  Vegetable Skallops
  Prime Stakes
  Stripples®
  Stakelets®
  FriPats®
La Loma®
  Linketts®
  Big Franks
  Dinner Cuts
  Vege-Burger
Natural Touch®
  Okara Patties
  Dinner Entree
  Lentil Rice Loaf

WHERE TO FIND THE NEW FOOD

More and more supermarkets are catering to the growing demand for non-meat protein foods by adding health and nutrition sections. The Morningstar Farms® line of meat substitutes can be found in most frozen breakfast sections of supermarkets across the United States. Also, many health food stores in all areas of the country carry an excellent selection of soy, wheat and tofu based products ranging from 'hot dogs' to 'steaks' . . . but without any meat or meat by-products.

One hectare of land could produce :

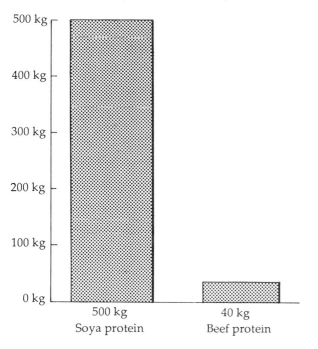

A protein machine in reverse

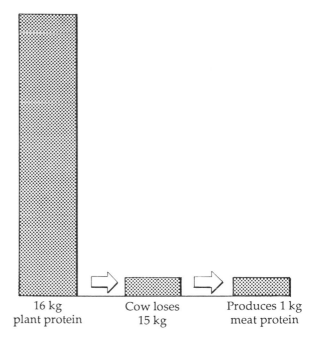

A TALE OF TWO FOODS – WHY TVP IS BETTER FOR ALL OF US

When you think about it, it makes better sense to use high-quality vegetable protein – such as soya beans to feed humans directly rather than to feed animals. Did you know that enough grain is already grown in the world to feed every man, woman and child on the planet? But over *half* of our total grain production is bought for use as a feedstuff for meat-producing animals, thus implicating meat production in human hunger. Here's how it works:

THE TRUE COST OF A HAMBURGER

One hectare (roughly two and one-half acres) of rain forest supports about 800,000kg of plants and animals. When the same land has been cleared and used for grazing for cattle, it will produce at most 200kg of meat a year – which is enough flesh to make about 1,600 hamburgers. This makes the *true* cost of a hamburger to be half a metric ton of rain forest for each burger – something to chew on.

A Cook's Companion

Cooking is easy and fun! Some people may disagree with me, but I know from my own experience that making good, tasty food in your own kitchen can be hassle-free, highly creative and very, very gratifying. It's a great shame that some people allow themselves to be intimidated into believing that cooking is somehow an 'expert's' territory where ordinary folk shouldn't dare to intrude. Rubbish! You don't need a degree in domestic science to be a good cook. In fact, the greatest cooks I've ever met have all been self-taught people who have developed their skills mainly through their love of good food. That's really the key to success in the kitchen. Now of course, it helps to know some of the basic skills, and it helps to be familiar with some of the most common words and techniques you're likely to come into contact with. So here are a few fundamental points about some of the methods and expressions you'll encounter in the following pages.

Bake: To cook with a dry heat, as supplied by an oven, using a pan, dish or wrapping. So, for instance, baked potatoes may be wrapped in foil, while cakes and breads are baked in their respective tins.

Baste: This involves replacing moisture in a food while it is cooking in an oven or under a grill – pouring a sauce over it, for example. Basting is usually done at regular intervals during the cooking time.

Beat: Just as it sounds, this is a vigorous movement with a fork or spoon so that an ingredient, or mixture of ingredients, is brought to a smooth consistency.

Blanch: Food is usually blanched in boiling water, but it may be blanched in hot oil if it is to be eaten immediately. The water is brought to a brisk boil, and the food is lowered into the water and then quickly removed. This technique is often used before freezing vegetables, in order to slow the action of the enzymes contained in the food, which helps to preserve the colour, texture and flavour until it is eaten.

Blend: This is a careful mixing of ingredients to the point when they lose most or all of their individual characteristics. The term is usually used in reference to wet and dry ingredients being 'blended' together.

Boil: A liquid, usually water or stock, is brought to a temperature of 212°F, at which point it bubbles noisily and gives off steam. You may be asked in a recipe to bring a liquid to the boil or, just occasionally, to boil an ingredient in water or stock. For instance, when cooking beets the water is boiled (use enough to cover the beets), the beets are added to it, and the water is brought back to the boil and maintained at that temperature until the beets are cooked. Other techniques, such as steaming, are now increasingly used to retain as much goodness in the vegetables as possible.

Braise: This is a technique that helps to keep the flavour and texture of a food. First brown the food quickly in hot fat, then cook it slowly in a covered dish using very little liquid. The second part of the process may be done in the oven or on the stove top.

Casserole: The word 'casserole' refers both to the oven-proof dish and the meal that it contains. A casserole should remain covered throughout its cooking time, and is usually cooked slowly on a low heat. Many casseroles are covered in a breadcrumb or cheese topping.

Chop: To cut food into small pieces. The basic requirements are a blade and a board. Some people chop by holding the tip of a knife down on to the board and lifting and lowering the heel of the knife. Others lift and lower the whole knife – some with frightening speed and accuracy! Eastern cooks sometimes use a curved blade with two handles which they simply rock back and forth over the food. In today's kitchens, most chopping tasks can be greatly speeded up by using a food processor, with a variety of blades.

Coat: To cover a food with a sauce, batter or other liquid.

Cream: To mix butter or margarine in a bowl with flour or sugar until a light, smooth consistency is reached.

Deep-fry: To deep-fry food with the least absorption of fat, start with a flat-bottomed pan and fill it no more than one-third full with vegetable oil. Make sure the pan is broad enough to allow the food to move around, and use a wire basket or slatted spoon to lower and lift the food. Now heat the oil to approximately 375°F. If you don't have a thermometer, you can test the temperature by dropping a very small amount of batter or piece of bread into

14

Vegetable Curry (*p 132*)

the hot fat. Count to sixty and remove the food. If it is browned and crispy within this time, then go ahead and begin frying.

Make sure the food to be fried is in small pieces and that it is dry (use a clean towel to dry it). This especially applies to raw foods, which are often quite moist. A batter, though moist, does not cause the same degree of bubbling and splash that a moist vegetable does, so if in doubt coat with a batter.

Don't let the oil smoke – that will spoil the oil and the taste of your food.

Don't start frying until the oil is hot enough, otherwise your food will be very greasy – it will hold a lot of oil in its crust or batter.

Fry only small amounts at any one time. If you add a lot of food at once, the temperature of the oil is reduced too much and the result will be soggy, oily food. For this same reason, do not attempt to deep-fry foods that are frozen or colder than room temperature.

Lower the food gently into the hot fat to avoid splashes and the possibility of the oil catching fire.

Let the oil heat up again before adding the second batch of food and, while it is doing so, use your slatted spoon to remove any bits of batter or food.

Fold in: To combine a very light food, such as beaten egg whites or whipped cream, with a heavier food, such as white sauce or batter. The folding motion used to combine them is slow and gentle – too brisk a movement would break down the light food and the dish would be likely to fail.

Garnish: The process of decorating dishes with small, colourful pieces of food or herbs. Sprigs of parsley or mint and wedges of lemon or tomato are examples of commonly used garnishes.

Glaze: In this technique, the food is coated with a liquid that leaves it looking shiny. A combination of melted butter and sugar is a common type of glaze.

Grill: A dry heat is applied to one side of the food you are cooking. Most of us use the broiler on our ovens and this is usually above the food. But barbecued food is actually grilled too, although the heat is under the food. Controlling the speed of cooking is normally done by moving the food nearer to or further from the heat.

Marinate: Here the food is soaked in a marinade (often a mixture of oil, wine or vinegar and seasoning). This tenderizes the food, and adds flavour. In some cases, such as pickling, marinating also acts to preserve a food.

Parboil: The food is lowered into boiling water and partly cooked for no more than two-thirds the length of time it would take to cook it completely. The cooking process is finished in another way.

Presentation: I love the aesthetic appeal of cooking – the smell, touch and taste. I think as long as food is presented in an appealing, mouthwatering way, you

don't need a lot of extra decoration or garnishes. Here are some simple tips to help you to cook your food so that it continues to appeal until the last portion has been served.

To retain their shape, steam your foods instead of boiling them. This is a particularly good technique for potatoes, rutabagas and other root vegetables.

Sauté or stir-fry for preference, using very little oil heated to a high temperature. Foods such as leeks, green beans, thinly sliced carrots and chopped celery are delicious when cooked in this way. They keep their shape, colour and slightly crisp texture – and it's healthier, too.

When making a casserole-type dish it is useful to arrange the foods in layers in the baking dish so that the colours and textures are alternated. This method creates visual interest if the dish is glass, or when individual portions are served. The moisture and flavour of each individual food should be carefully alternated so that all the layers complement each other. For instance, the more moist foods should be placed above the drier foods; and the more powerful flavours, such as garlic, should be placed under gentler flavours, such as potato. In this way each food will contribute to the final, successful blend of flavour, colour, texture and aroma.

Pressure cooker: A pressure cooker relies on the food being cooked by steam generated under high pressure. It is very quick, especially for dried beans or peas and other food that normally takes a long time by other methods. For instance, cooking chick peas on the stove top will take three hours, but in a pressure cooker it will only take twenty minutes (the beans must be pre-soaked in both cases, but this can be done overnight or while you're away at work). The nutrients lost to cooking are kept to a minimum in pressure cooking and, if you don't open the pressure cooker, the seal keeps the cooked food sterile for some time.

Puree: A food is cooked until tender, then passed through a hand sieve, blender or food processor to make a smooth pulp.

Roast: Food is cooked in an oven, usually uncovered, with an accompaniment of fat to moisten and brown it.

Roux: To make a roux, melt the butter and stir an equal amount of flour into it to make a thick, smooth paste. The paste is your roux. When you add liquid to it, you begin to make a sauce.

Sauté: A small amount of oil is brought to a high temperature in a frying pan, skillet or saucepan. The food is added to the oil and turned constantly until it is browned.

Scald: This is usually applied to milk, and involves heating it to the point just before it begins to boil.

Simmer: Cooking soups, stews and other foods surrounded by liquid at a temperature that causes 'lazy' bubbles to appear on the surface. The liquid is often brought to the boil first, then the heat is reduced and the mixture allowed to simmer gently for a longer period of time.

Steam: In this method, food is cooked from the steam of boiling water or stock. There are many steaming techniques to try. A double-boiler uses steam, as does a universal, or French, steamer. Puddings are steamed by surrounding them with boiling water, and pressure cooking is also based on steam. It is a particularly healthy way to cook vegetables.

Stew: This is a very slow method in which the food is cooked in liquid, such as a sauce or gravy. The pot is kept covered all the time the stew is cooking. The oven or the stove top may be used.

Stir-fry: Quite similar to sautéing, stir-frying means that the food will be ready to eat when you have finished the process. Stir-frying is strongly associated with the wok, a special curved pan from the Orient. Very little oil is used, and the cooking time is brief so that the food doesn't shrink and its nutritional value is kept high. The frying food must be agitated continuously until it is cooked to a tender-crisp texture.

Whip: Using a swift, sharp beating movement to add air to a food such as cream or egg. A firm or stiff consistency is often achieved. An electric beater is frequently used to speed this process.

Whisk: The same method as whipping, though whisking does not usually achieve the same degree of stiffness. Egg and milk are often whisked together to form a light, airy, frothy mixture.

Worthington prosage links
Textured Vegetable Protein/Artificial Sausage Flavor

Protein Rich
Completely Meatless
No Preservatives

10 LINKS
NET WT. 8 OZ.

KEEP
FROZEN

PROTOVEG
SIZZLES
SMOKED BACON FLAVOUR

Contains no meat or animal fat
175 g pack (makes over 1 lb)

Worthington **wham**
MEATLESS HAM
VEGETABLE PROTEIN SLICES

Worthington **BOLONO**
VEGETABLE PROTEIN SLICES/ARTIFICIAL BOLOGNA FLAVOR

COMPLETELY MEATLESS · RICH IN PROTEIN · NO PRESERVATIVES

ORIGINAL FLAVOR
Fantastic Foods

MADE WITH
OATS
AND OTHER
WHOLE
GRAINS

Nature's Burger
MEATLESS
BURGER
MIX

NET WT. 10 OZ (283.5 g)

· No Cholesterol
· No Preservatives
· No Artificial Colouring

tivall
Vegetarian Burger

· No Cholesterol
· No Preservatives
· No Artificial Colouring

tivall
Vegetarian Sausage

· No Cholesterol
· No Preservatives
· No Artificial Colouring

Vegetarian Schnitzel

Lightly seasoned, shaped and breaded vegetable protein in a crispy crunch coating.

This food contains the essential nutritional requirements, whole protein, carbohydrates, vegetable oils, minerals and vitamins.

600 grams
This package contains 6 persons.
PRODUCT OF ISRAEL.

Keep frozen Until Ready to Use

Love burger

Original

fritini
Vegetable Pattie Mix

No Cholesterol · All Natural · High Protein

NET WEIGHT
7 OZ / 200 g

OPEN AND POUR

WORTHINGTON
GranBurger

VEGETABLE
PROTEIN GRANULES
ARTIFICIAL BEEF FLAVOR

CONTAINS NO MEAT

USE LIKE
GROUND
BEEF!

MAKES
OVER 1.5
POUNDS

NET WT. 10 OZ.
(283 GMS)

Morningstar

Cholesterol Free
Breakfast Strips
Artificial Bacon Flavor
Textured Vegetable Protein

PROTOVEG Menu
5 Grain BURGAMIX
A VEGETABLE BURGAMIX WITH BLENDED WHOLE GRAINS

REALEAT
VEGE BURGER
All Natural-All Vegetable

DIET ADE
FOOD

Vegetarian
JERKY MIX

GRANOSE
Vegetarian
Spicy Links

GRANOSE
SAUSALATAS

FRIMIX
GRAVY POWDER

GRANOSE
Vegelinks
Wheat protein frankfurter sausages in brine

WORTHINGTON
Veja-Links
Vegetable Protein Links
Artificial Food

GRANOSE
SAUSFRY

Vegetarian **Fillets** **Worthington**
A Vegetable Protein Product/Artificial Fish Flavor

stakelets Worthington

stakelets striipples

stripples WORTHINGTON

This selection of exciting non-meat products shows what variety is now available through supermarkets and health-food stores.

Products shown here include: sausage links; Sizzles and Stripples (non-meat bacon); Wham – tastes just like ham; Bolono – better than Bologna; Fillets and Stakelets and vegetarian gravy mixes.

ESSENTIAL UTENSILS

There's a labour-saving gadget to do just about everything in the kitchen these days (except for actually eating the food – my family does that!). Don't be misled – most of these devices aren't indispensable, and you may find that by the time you prepared them for use, and cleaned up afterwards, you haven't really saved much time. One thing that *is* absolutely essential is a good set of pots and pans – choose correctly, and you'll get a lifetime's wear out of them. Let's talk first about the various materials used to make pots and pans and why some are better than others.

Aluminium: Inexpensive, easily available. However, a high intake of aluminium has been associated with senile dementia, and using aluminium pans could increase your consumption of this metal. Replace all those aluminium pots and pans that you already have in your cupboards – one at a time if necessary – until your utensils are aluminium-free.

Cast-iron: Solid, heavy, should be kept well oiled to prevent rust. One of the oldest cooking materials used by the human race. Cast-iron pots can take on quite a personality over the years, just like old friends! They transfer heat very evenly whether placed over a high or low flame. Cooking in cast-iron pans can actually boost the iron content of the food you eat. Must not be dropped, since cast-iron is brittle and may fracture.

Copper: Expensive, pretty, needs regular polishing. Not a very useful material. Copper can deplete food of its vitamin C content.

Enamel: There are two basic types of enamel pans: a lightweight metal such as aluminium or stainless steel that is covered in enamel, or a heavy cast-iron pan lined or completely covered with enamel. As you might expect, the first type is less expensive than the second and tends not to be so long-lived. Enamel is non-porous so the foods that come into contact with it are not altered in any way. These pans are especially useful for foods that discolour when cooked in iron (I find barley and apple sauce can suffer in this way), or if you make your own jams and pickles.

Ovenproof glass: Versatile, easy to clean, fuel-efficient. Most of these dishes can be used both in the oven, and on the table as a serving dish. Some can also be used on the stove top (check to see that they say 'fireproof' and not just 'ovenproof'). I find

this material is best used for casserole dishes, individual baking dishes and pie dishes. Pay particular attention to the style and positioning of the handles when you buy them. Be sure to let them cool slowly as they break easily if the temperature changes too quickly.

Non-stick pans: My favourites. These are useful for people who wish to use very little oil or water when cooking. Be sure to use wooden or plastic spatulas on this surface – metal utensils will scratch the non-stick surface and ruin the pan. It is handy to have frying pans, a milk pan and one or two saucepans made from this material.

Porcelain or earthenware pots: Great for the oven. These come in every shape, size, colour and design and are generally used in the oven, rather than on the stove top. They include ramekins, souffle, casserole, pie and flan dishes, individual-sized baking and custard dishes, stew pots, loaf 'pans', roasting trays . . . the list could go on and on. I love the look and feel of these pots and use them whenever I bake something for a long time. As with glass, let these pots cool down gradually or they will break.

Stainless Steel: Easy to clean – doesn't rust, but also easier to burn the food. Don't leave your food in them for longer than you have to (not overnight, for instance) as the metal may taint the food. Stainless steel is especially good for cake and loaf pans, baking trays, double-boilers and kettles. Knives are also best made out of stainless steel.

PRINCIPAL POTS AND PANS

Here are the basic requirements for a well-equipped kitchen – in addition, I find a cast-iron griddle, a wok and an omelette pan very useful from time to time.

3 frying pans – small, medium, large
3 saucepans – small, medium, large
1 double-boiler with approximately 6 inch base (optional)
1–3 roasting dishes – small, medium, large
2 pie dishes – 9 inch diameter
1 large tart and flan dish
2 loaf pans

2 round cake pans – 8 or 9 inch diameter
2 large, deep casserole dishes
1 medium or shallow casserole dish
1 pressure cooker (optional)

EQUIPMENT FOR FOOD PREPARATION AND STORAGE

There are dozens of utensils and little gadgets that are fun to use and will make some tasks easier. These range from butter curlers and melon scoops to decorative tomato cutters and lattice-work rolling pins. You can collect such utensils together over a period of time, but they aren't essential to the recipes included in this book. To be honest, I find that many of these gadgets get pushed to the back of my kitchen drawer and forgotten. I often get the same results without the gadget – and I don't have to wash it up afterwards! If you do enjoy them, though, I recommend that you display your 'bitty' kitchen equipment as much as possible. For small utensils like those I have just described, a revolving tray placed in one corner of your work surface is space saving and practical, yet out of the way until you actually need something from it.

The tools that follow will be your constant companions in the kitchen, and will enable you to undertake almost any task you are ever likely to attempt. Optionally, I would also include a pastry cutter, a mortar and pestle (it may be old-fashioned, but it's lovely to look at!) and some time-saving equipment such as an electric blender or food processor and an electric toaster.

can opener
cheese grater (one with different-size holes on the various surfaces is most useful)
chopping boards – wooden: one for bread, two for vegetables
colanders
garlic crusher
kitchen scales
kitchen scissors
kitchen tongs
knives: bread knife, vegetable peeler, paring knife, chopping knife and slicing knife
lemon squeezer
mats on which to place hot dishes
measuring cups – at least 1 pint capacity
measuring spoons with both metric and imperial measurements
mixing bowls – small, medium, large
oven gloves
pastry board – marble is best
plastic or other refrigerator/freezer storage containers

pudding basins – 2 pints each
rolling pin – wooden or glass
sieve
soup ladle
spaghetti ladle
spoon - large slatted
storage jars for flours, sugar, grains, beans, lentils and other dry ingredients
universal steaming baskets (also called French steamers, these adapt to fit any size pan)
vegetable scrubbing brush
whisks – large and small
wire cooling racks
wooden mixing spoons and spatulas – all sizes

The Mighty Microwave

The microwave oven is used in more and more homes as a time-saving alternative to conventional cooking. However, it isn't *always* faster to use a microwave – for example, many vegetables take just as long in a microwave oven as they would to boil or steam on the stove top, and legumes cook just as quickly in a pressure cooker. The real advantage of microwave cooking is when you use it in conjunction with your freezer. Many recipes in this book are suitable for freezing and later re-heating using your microwave oven, and this is an excellent way to enjoy first-class home cooking when you can't really spare the time to do it all from scratch. It combines all the advantages of fast food with all the taste of home cooking!

Here's a tip: when you're cooking a favourite dish you know you'll want to eat again, make twice the normal amount, and freeze half of it for later use.

Microwave cooking is very different to cooking with a standard gas or electric oven. The food is actually heated 'from the inside' – the microwaves make the water molecules inside the food you're cooking vibrate so rapidly that heat is produced, thus creating steam and cooking the food. This is a fundamentally different form of cooking, and it means that food will not brown properly (unless you have a dual-type oven) so it isn't a good method to choose for roasting or baking.

Some hints – never use any metal containers or metal foil in a microwave oven, and preferably use only those dishes which are classified by the manufacturers as 'suitable for use in a microwave'. Try to ensure that the food is about the same depth in the dish – variations in thickness may mean that parts of the food may be over- or under-cooked. Since quite a lot of water-vapour is generated during cooking, let your food stand for a few minutes after taking it out of the oven to allow condensation to disappear.

CHOOSING AND USING VEGETABLES

Acorn Squash

When to buy: From July to the end of September.

What to look for: Test for a hard rind that, when tapped, gives a slightly hollow sound. The rind should also have a deep colour, either solid green or striped, and should be free from blemishes and bruises. Most acorn squash weigh between 2 and 10 lb. Old or very large ones may prove too tough.

How to store: In a cool, dry place. The best way is on a slatted shelf or hanging in a net so that the air is free to circulate round it. Acorn squash will keep in this way for up to 3 months.

How to prepare: Wash the squash and slice it in half. Scoop out the seeds and stringy pulp and discard.

The squash may be left in two halves and stuffed or baked as it is, or it may be sliced or cubed. It may also be steamed, sautéd, stewed or boiled. Both a microwave and a pressure cooker may be used. The flavour of acorn squash is rather bland, so it relies on other flavours used in the dish.

Good source of vitamin C.

Artichoke

When to buy: All the year round, though fresh, locally grown artichokes are available from May to July.

What to look for: Tightly spaced leaves in a plump, closed globe. The colour should be bright green, although it is normal for brown spots to appear on the outer leaves. The size of the globe does not affect the flavour or quality.

How to store: Will keep in the refrigerator for 1–2 weeks.

How to prepare: Use non-iron utensils to avoid discoloration. Trim the stalk away even with the base of the globe. Remove the small leaves near the base and slice away the top inch of the artichoke.

Artichokes may be eaten raw or cooked in a variety of ways – including baking, sautéing, microwaving, pressure cooking and frying. However, the simplest method is to steam or boil them until a leaf may be pulled away without effort. Then serve one globe per person with a small bowl of sauce and leave them to eat it leaf by leaf! The heart of the artichoke is particularly delicate and tender, but avoid eating the thistle-like portion of the centre. *Good source of vitamin C and folic acid.*

Asparagus

When to buy: Most of the summer.

What to look for: The spears should be 6–8 inches long to avoid woodiness, and about the thickness of your thumb. Each spear should be firm, straight and pale to dark green. White asparagus is available, but it has been 'forced' by growing it in the dark. The tip of each spear must be a tight bud. A loose bud indicates either that the asparagus is not fresh, or that it was too old when picked.

How to store: Keep the spears cool and moist. Wrap the stalk ends in a damp towel or place the bundle upright in a small amount of cold water. In the refrigerator, keep the spears in a plastic bag with holes in it. Do not prepare the spears until just before you wish to use them.

How to prepare: Trim the stalk end of each spear. If the stalk appears slightly woody, cut all of this portion away. Scrape off the coarse peel of each spear.

Asparagus may be eaten raw, or you may cook it by steaming the spears until tender, baking, deep-frying or microwaving them. To stir-fry asparagus, slice it diagonally into short pieces and cook it quickly over a high heat.

Good source of vitamins A and C.

Aubergine (Eggplant)

When to buy: All the year round. Locally grown aubergines are best from late July to early October.

What to look for: Firmness and a smooth, shiny skin. Aubergines should not have any brown blemishes – their skin should be a deep, even, purple colour (occasionally you will see white ones, which explains their alternative name of egg-plant). Gently press the aubergine at its flowering end to test for firmness. A very soft feel indicates that it may be over-ripe.

How to store: In a cool but not cold place. Refrigeration is not ideal and, in any case, aubergines should be used within two days of picking.

How to prepare: Wash and trim the flowering end. If

the aubergine is young, it may be chopped without peeling. If it is slightly larger and older, it may be tastier if peeled, seeded, and sprinkled generously with salt then left to drain for 20–30 minutes in a colander (this will draw out any bitterness). Rinse it well under cold water and pat it dry with paper towels.

Aubergines may be boiled, steamed, baked, sautéd, fried, grilled or microwaved.

Avocado

When to buy: All the year round.
What to look for: An evenly coloured, unbroken skin. If the skin is broken, do not buy the avocado. If dark bruises appear on the skin, the flesh will also appear bruised and so will be unsuitable for some dishes. Test the ripeness of an avocado by cradling it in your hand with the narrow portion resting on your fingers. Gently grasp the avocado and allow your fingers to press the very tip of the narrow end. The avocado is ripe, or very nearly so, if this portion feels slightly soft and tender.
How to store: In a warm place until ripened to the desired degree.
How to prepare: Usually eaten raw. Slice the avocado in half along its length and gently pry apart. Remove the stone from the centre and discard (or try to grow it!). Fill the hollow in each avocado half with dressing or stuffing and serve with a salad. Alternatively, spoon the flesh in to a bowl and mash with other ingredients into a paste or dip. You may also peel the avocado halves, slice the flesh and arrange it on a plate of salad.

Use an avocado as soon as possible after it is cut or it may discolour. Pouring lemon juice over it preserves its colour for a short time. Avocados are also sometimes cooked in a casserole or soup.
Good source of vitamins A, B6 and C, thiamin, riboflavin, folic acid and niacin. They also contain a considerable amount of fat.

Beans, Dried (also Dried Peas and Lentils)

See Legumes, p.41.

Beans, Green

When to buy: Most tasty when in season, from June to October, but available frozen all year round.
What to look for: Choose them for their crispness – they should snap easily, the pod should not be leathery or wrinkled, and they should look and smell new.
How to store: Try to eat them as soon after picking as possible, or store them in a cool place, loosely

wrapped in paper or a perforated plastic bag. Green beans may be frozen for use in the winter months.
How to prepare: Wash them in cold water. 'Top and tail' French and runner beans by trimming the ends away and peeling the string back if necessary (if they are quite young, they may not have a string to pull). Young and tender beans may be left whole, or you may prefer to slice them diagonally into 1 inch pieces. Broad beans are removed from the pod and the pod discarded.

Steam or boil beans until just tender – if you cook them too long they will lose their colour. Green beans may also combine with other ingredients to be stir-fried, baked or microwaved.
Good source of protein, vitamin B6, thiamin, folic acid, fibre, potassium, calcium and iron.

Beets

When to buy: All the year round. In-season beets are available fresh from June to November.
What to look for: Small to medium beets are best. They should have an intact skin and feel quite firm and smooth. If the greens are still attached, these should be crisp. The tap root should be intact.
How to store: In a cool, dry place. If the greens are attached, keep them in the refrigerator for up to one week. If the greens are not attached, the beets may keep longer. Commercial growers and gardeners sometimes store them in their growing place over the winter, lifting them as they are required.
How to prepare: Do not cut the beet. Scrub it well without damaging the skin, then trim the greens away to a short distance from the beet.

Beets may be eaten raw, grated into a salad, pickled, stewed or made into a soup. To cook, boil the roots whole in water that just covers them. When they are tender, trim the root and stalks away, peel and slice or cube as required.
Good source of vitamin C, folic acid, fibre and potassium.

Broccoli

When to buy: All the year round. In-season broccoli is available fresh from November to June.
What to look for: The stalks should be thick and firm but not woody. The heads should be dense, compact buds that are not flowering. Broccoli may be either deep green or purple in colour, but do not use yellowing broccoli.
How to store: In a refrigerator for a maximum of one week. However, broccoli loses its texture and freshness quickly and should, ideally, be used on the day of cutting or purchase.
How to prepare: Wash in cold water and trim away

any woody pieces of stalk. Cut the stalks into florets or quarter each stalk to make thin pieces.

Broccoli raw or steamed loses none of its colour and flavour and it may be added to a stir-fry with great success. Deep-fried broccoli is rich and delicious; it may also be microwaved.

Good source of vitamins A, B6 and C, riboflavin, folic acid, calcium and fibre.

Brussels Sprouts

When to buy: November to May.

What to look for: Firm, bright green heads no bigger than a chestnut. The outer leaves should be green, tight-fitting and whole.

How to store: In the refrigerator or a cool, dry place for no more than 3 or 4 days. Brussels sprouts may be frozen.

How to prepare: Remove the outer leaves and cut a cross in the bottom of each sprout.

Boil or steam them whole for approximately 12 minutes, according to their size. A cooked sprout should have a tender outside and a slightly crisp inner 'bite'. In addition, they may be stir- or deep-fried so that they keep most of their natural crispness. Occasionally, brussels sprouts are cooked until they are quite soft, then mashed with potatoes, carrots or other vegetables to make a soufflé, filling or soup.

Good source of vitamins A, B6 and C, thiamin, folic acid, potassium, iron and fibre.

Cabbage

When to buy: All the year round.

What to look for: Firm outer leaves. Depending on the type of cabbage you are buying, the head should be either hard (as in red or green cabbage) or squeezable but crisp (as in savoy or chinese cabbage). Avoid cabbages with yellow outer leaves or a light, leathery feel – they are not fresh.

How to store: In a refrigerator or cool place for no more than 7–10 days.

How to prepare: Wash and trim the outer leaves.

Use cabbage raw in salads, either shredded or finely chopped. It may also be boiled, steamed, pickled, sautéed or baked. Some recipes call for the whole leaves to be parboiled (until just tender) and wrapped around a filling. Select crisp but not tough outer leaves for this purpose.

Good source of vitamin C and folic acid.

Carrots

When to buy: Available all the year round.

What to look for: Most important are firmness and a deep, bright orange colour. A perfect shape is not essential to a good carrot, but avoid those with serious skin blemishes or deep cracks. If you purchase them with the leaves attached, these should be green and fresh-looking, not brown and wilted.

How to store: In a cool, dry place for up to 2 weeks. A refrigerator is ideal. Carrots may be frozen.

How to prepare: Scrub and trim the carrots. Peel them if desired, especially if they are not organically grown.

Carrots may be eaten raw in whole, chopped or grated form. They are excellent in all forms of cooking – boiled, steamed, stir-fried, baked, in soups, stews and sautés. They may be cooked in the microwave as well.

Good source of vitamins A and C, thiamin, potassium and fibre.

Cauliflower

When to buy: All the year round. However, cauliflower is a cold weather plant and is at its best when fresh from October to April.

What to look for: A white or cream coloured head with dense clusters of florets. These should be free of the dark speckles that indicate an old cauliflower. A fresh head should be heavy and the surrounding leaves crisp and light green, not yellow.

How to store: In the refrigerator. Do not allow the head to become moist as this will encourage mould. Cauliflower may be frozen.

How to prepare: Peel away the outer leaves, trim the thick stalk from the centre and wash the head. Cut or break the cauliflower into florets, or leave it whole.

It may be cut into individual florets and eaten raw with dips and sauces, or it may be steamed, boiled, stir-fried or microwaved. Cauliflower is excellent dipped in batter and deep-fried.

Good source of vitamins B6 and C, folic acid and potassium.

Celery

When to buy: All the year round, though at its best from late summer to early winter.

What to look for: A crisp, firm bunch. Squeeze the bunch and it should make a slight squeaking noise. Any soft or rubbery stalks indicate old celery. The small leaves should be bright green, not wilted, and slightly aromatic when rubbed. The celery stalks should be pale or deep green.

How to store: In a refrigerator for up to one week. Beyond this time the celery begins to wilt.

How to prepare: Separate the stalks. Trim the rough

bottom and the top, fine leaves away. Wash each stalk in cold water and drain.

Eat celery raw with dips or chopped into salads. It may also be boiled, steamed, sautéd, baked and microwaved.
Good source of vitamin C, potassium and fibre.

Corn on the Cob

See Sweet Corn.

Cucumber

When to buy: All the year round. Locally grown cucumbers are best from May to September.
What to look for: Small to medium diameter with a good, deep green colouring. A cucumber should be firm, those that are allowed to get too thick are often soft and seedy inside. A perfectly shaped cucumber is not necessarily a good cucumber. However, most commercially grown cucumbers are very straight – which can make them easier to use.
How to store: In a cool, but not cold place. Refrigeration is not always ideal. They do not keep beyond one week.
How to prepare: They may be simply washed, sliced and eaten raw in salads and dips. Or you may peel them and even remove some of the seeds. Salting for 20–30 minutes removes the occasional bitter taste. Rinse them in cold water afterwards. Cucumbers may also be pickled, steamed, sautéd, baked or deep-fried.

Garlic

When to buy: All the year round.
What to look for: Firm bulbs that have dry outer skins. They should not be purchased once they begin to sprout again – usually in early spring. Do not buy bulbs that have soft or powdery patches.
How to store: In a cool, dark, dry place. The refrigerator is not an ideal storage place, whereas a dry spice cupboard or airy larder is. Garlic was traditionally kept in a braid or in nets that hung in the open. These methods allowed dry air to circulate round the bulbs and prevented mould and sprouting.
How to prepare: Separate the bulb into cloves. Peel the clove and either chop it finely or crush it into the dish you are making.

Garlic may be eaten raw in small quantities, or added to sautés, soups, stews and casseroles. It may be baked, boiled, fried or even steamed.

Leeks

When to buy: From early February to October.
What to look for: A bright green leafy top. Do not buy those with yellow leaves. The lower part of the leek should be firm, pale and aromatic. A rubbery or tough lower section indicates age.
How to store: In the refrigerator or other cool place for up to 5 days. Remove any yellow or withered leaves first, however.
How to prepare: Trim the root end first, then the tips of the leaves. Cut the leeks either along their length into quarters, or in rounds using a diagonal slicing motion. Place the sliced leeks into a bowl of very cold water and wash them vigorously. Remove them into a colander and rinse them under running cold water. Leave to drain.

Leeks may be used raw in salads, or steamed, boiled or microwaved (whole or sliced). They are excellent in sautés, stir-fries and as a braised dish. Deep-fried leeks, dipped in batter, have a delicate onion flavour.

Lentils

See Legumes, p.41.

Lettuce

When to buy: All the year round. The variety available fresh and locally grown will change according to the time of year, but may include cos (romaine), Webb or cabbage (round). More unusual varieties are also widely available, such as oakleaf and lollo rosso.
What to look for: The most important feature is the colour and texture of the leaves. The variety of lettuce will determine whether the leaf is crisp and pale green or soft and dark green. Whichever variety is chosen, however, the leaves should have a bright colour without brown or yellow patches. They should be erect, not wilted, and not at all rubbery when torn.
How to store: In a cool, dark place. A refrigerator is excellent, and you can buy special containers to store lettuce so that it remains fresh. Loose-leafed lettuces only keep a day or two, crisp heads, such as iceberg, may keep up to one week.
How to prepare: Discard any yellowed or blemished leaves. Wash the lettuce in very cold water and drain it well. A salad spinner is useful for drying lettuce.

Use the leaves whole, sliced or torn as a bed for other foods or as part of a salad. A classic French dressing over a perfect lettuce is a simple and elegant starter or accompaniment to any meal.

Mushrooms

When to buy: All the year round.

What to look for: Firmness and a dull, unblemished surface. Mushrooms that have begun to 'sweat' should not be used. There are a number of varieties on the market, each with its own shape, size and colouring, so other criteria for selection vary according to the mushrooms you use.

How to store: In a cool, dry place. If stored in the refrigerator, keep the mushrooms in their paper bag (never in a plastic one). Use as soon as possible after purchase.

How to prepare: Trim the stalks or remove them entirely. Clean the mushrooms by peeling them or wiping the heads with a damp cloth. Mushrooms absorb moisture rapidly, so it is best not to rinse them under water unless the dirt is stubborn.

Mushrooms may be eaten raw or cooked in sautés, soups, stews and casseroles. They may be microwaved, deep-fried in batter, stuffed and baked or grilled. Experiment with the great number of varieties on the market to enjoy the versatile nature of mushrooms.

Good source of riboflavin, niacin, potassium and iron.

Okra

When to buy: All the year round, though slightly easier to find from May to September.

What to look for: Firm, bright green pods. Each pod may be 3–7 inches long and should pop slightly – like a pea pod – when opened. Do not buy wilted, dull-looking or shrivelled pods.

How to store: In a cool, dry place. A cool cupboard is sufficient, though a refrigerator can be used. Use okra as soon after purchase as possible, and always within 3 days.

How to prepare: Wash the pods and slice the thick end of each one away.

Try not to cook okra in a cast-iron pot as it may discolour. It may be deep-fried, microwaved, stewed, boiled or steamed. A very successful way of cooking okra, however, is to sauté it over a very hot flame until it is just tender. Then add the okra to the dish you are preparing. This method prevents the sticky liquid in okra from ruining the dish but, instead, adds flavour and texture.

Good source of vitamins A, B6 and C, thiamin, folic acid, potassium, calcium and fibre.

Onions

When to buy: All the year round. Spring onions (scallions) are in season from March to October.

What to look for: A firm, dry, unblemished skin. A soft feel to the onion or a patch of brown, damp skin indicates an onion that is beginning to go off. Avoid purchasing onions that have begun to sprout. Spring onions have bright green tops and a firm, white bulb.

How to store: A refrigerator is not ideal – instead, hang the onions in a net bag in a dry, airy place. In these conditions, onions will keep for several months. Spring onions are intended for use within one week of lifting.

How to prepare: Cut the top and bottom from each onion and remove the papery peel and the fine inner membrane. Slice or finely chop the onion, frequently rinsing your hands and knife under cold water to reduce the sting from the onion. Use onions (particularly spring onions) raw or in virtually any form of cooking. They are incredibly versatile and enhance the flavour and texture of any savoury dish.

Parsnips

When to buy: Best from October to March.

What to look for: Firmness and a small to medium size. Very large parsnips can be quite woody and unpalatable. A skin that is free from blemishes is ideal though parsnips are easily bruised during transport. Avoid roots that are cracked and very discoloured.

How to store: In a cool, dry place. A refrigerator is useful, provided the parsnips do not become moist as this quickly creates mould. A dark, cool and airy cupboard is an excellent store. Use them within one week of purchase.

How to prepare: Scrub the parsnips. Peel them or scrape away the fine hair roots and trim the top and tail away. Leave parsnips whole, slice them in half along their length, or chop them into chunky rounds with a diagonal cut.

Parsnips may be boiled, steamed, fried, microwaved, pressure cooked or added to soups, stews, casseroles and other baked dishes.

Good source of vitamin C, folic acid, potassium, calcium and fibre.

Peas, Dried

See Legumes, p.41.

Peas

When to buy: Frozen available all the year round. Fresh available from May to October.

What to look for: Bright green and rather rotund pods. The pod should snap open easily and the peas should taste juicy and sweet. Do not purchase pods with a leathery feel.

26

Corn Bread Mexican Style (*p* 63)

Of course, canned or frozen peas are always available. Buy only those free from colouring, sugar, and other additives.

How to store: In the refrigerator or other cool, dry place. Try to use fresh peas within 1–2 days of picking or purchase. Peas may be podded and frozen.

How to prepare: Snap open the pod and run your thumb down the inside to release the peas. They may be eaten raw in salads or cooked in a variety of ways: microwaved, pressure cooked, steamed or boiled with a little mint, added to a stir-fry or baked in a stew or casserole.

Good source of vitamins A, B6 and C, thiamin, protein, riboflavin, folic acid, niacin, potassium, iron, zinc, and fibre.

Peppers (Green, Red and Yellow)

When to buy: All the year round, though fresh locally grown peppers are available from June to September.

What to look for: A glossy, undamaged skin. Peppers should be firm, without wrinkles, brown patches or cracks.

How to store: In a cool but not cold place. Use peppers as soon as possible after purchase and always within one week.

How to prepare: Wash the peppers under cold water. Slice them in half and remove the stalk and the seed head.

Leave the pepper halves intact, stuff them and bake, or slice or chop into smaller pieces. Peppers may be eaten raw in salads or with dips and pâtés. They may be sautéed, stir-fried, dipped in batter and deep-fried, grilled, microwaved, steamed, boiled or added to casseroles, soups and stews. Don't over-cook them, as they may lose their texture and much of their colour.

Good source of vitamins A, B6 and C, thiamin, iron and fibre.

Potatoes

When to buy: All the year round. Local 'new' potatoes are often available in midsummer, though imported varieties are available as early as March.

What to look for: Firmness and an unblemished skin. Potatoes should never be used if they are sprouting or green in colour – both indicate changes that make them less digestible.

How to store: Always in the dark and cool. Potatoes kept in the light begin to sprout and turn green and should not be used. In cool, dry storage potatoes will keep for up to 2 months.

How to prepare: Scrub them with a brush and cold water. Leave them unpeeled if possible (especially if they are new or organically grown), then bake them whole, slice or chop them into required size. Keep cut potatoes in cold water until you are ready to use them, to prevent them greying.

Potatoes are very versatile. They may be baked (puncture them with a fork to stop them exploding), boiled, steamed, microwaved, deep-fried, pressure cooked or used in a variety of ways in casseroles, stews and soups.

Good source of vitamins B6 and C, thiamin, niacin, potassium, iron and fibre.

Radishes

When to buy: Spring and summer for fresh, locally grown. Imported varieties are available all the year round.

What to look for: Firmness and a small to medium size. Very large radishes can be hollow and rather woody or dry. An unblemished skin and a good colour are also criteria for selection, and any leaves still attached to the radish should be bright green and not wilted.

How to store: In a cool place or the refrigerator for up to one week. However, it is best to use radishes as soon as possible after purchase or picking.

How to prepare: Wash them and trim the root and greens away. Serve sliced, quartered or whole. Radishes are best raw in salads or with dips and pâtés.

Rutabagas

When to buy: All the year round, though fresh, locally grown rutabagas are available from November to April.

What to look for: Firmness. The skin should not be rubbery, bruised or blemished. Rutabagas vary greatly in size – from a few ounces to a pound or two. Select them on the basis of how fresh their skin appears.

How to store: In a cool or cold place. In your kitchen, they should be used within a week of purchase. In a cold, dry cellar they may keep for up to 2 months.

How to prepare: Peel away the thick skin. Then use your strongest arm to chop or slice the rutabaga into the size and shape required.

If you prefer, simply grate the rutabaga into a big winter salad and eat it raw. Otherwise, cook rutabagas in any way you like, although they don't hold up to deep-frying very well. A rutabaga turns a rose-gold colour when cooked.

Good source of vitamin C, thiamin, potassium, calcium and fibre.

Spinach

When to buy: Fresh, locally grown spinach is available from May to October. Imported, frozen and canned spinach is available all the year round.
What to look for: A firm leaf with even, dark green colour. Yellow, brown edged or wilted leaves should be discarded. Frozen or canned spinach should be free from artificial additives.
How to store: In the refrigerator for up to 2 days. Ideally, spinach should be used the same day it is purchased or picked.
How to prepare: Wash very well in cold water. You may need to change the water two or three times to clean away all the dirt. Drain the spinach, or even dry it with a clean tea towel. Trim away the coarse or tough stalks, then use the spinach whole or sliced into wide strips. Young spinach may be eaten raw in salads, or cooked in soups, stir-fries or sautés. It may be boiled, steamed, microwaved or pressure cooked, or dipped in batter and deep-fried. Spinach may also be baked in casseroles and lasagne.
Good source of vitamins A, B6 and C, iron, folic acid, thiamin, riboflavin, potassium and calcium.

Sweet Corn

When to buy: From July to September. Frozen and canned sweet corn is available all the year round.
What to look for: When buying corn on the cob, look first at the husk and corn silk. The husk should be green – dark green on the outer husk and pale green nearer the corn. The silk should be glossy and slightly moist near the corn, darker and drier as it hangs over the top of the husk. The kernels should be plump and moist. Any dimpling of the kernels, especially near the centre of the cob, indicates an old cob.
How to store: In the husks in a cool place. However, it is best to eat the corn as soon after picking or purchasing as possible.
How to prepare: Peel the husk and silk away from the corn. Rinse the corn, then drop the whole cob into boiling water and boil for 6–8 minutes, until the kernels turn golden. Serve immediately with butter and salt. Alternatively, the kernels may be scraped away from the cob using a sharp knife. They may then be steamed, stir-fried, stewed, baked, pressure cooked or microwaved in any number of dishes.
Good source of protein, vitamin C, thiamin, folic acid and niacin.

Sweet Potatoes

When to buy: From September to February, but they are imported all the year round.
What to look for: Firmness and plumpness. The potato should feel heavy for its size, implying a moist, fresh vegetable. Avoid those that have soft patches or grey, shrivelled areas. The colour, size and shape of sweet potatoes varies greatly and does not determine their quality.
How to store: In a cool, dry place they will keep up to 2 months. A refrigerator is not ideal – a dark cupboard is better.
How to prepare: Scrub each potato and trim off any blemishes. They may be peeled before or after cooking, or not at all.

Microwave and pressure cooker are speedy ways of cooking sweet potatoes, but their flavour improves when they are baked (remember to puncture them with a fork), stewed, sautéed, boiled or fried.
Good source of vitamins A, B6 and C, riboflavin and potassium.

Tomatoes

When to buy: All the year round. They are grown just about everywhere in the world, either in the open or under glass. If you don't like the fresh ones this month and only want them for cooking, buy them canned.
What to look for: Fresh tomatoes should be firm, unbruised and of a deep, even colour. Some varieties are naturally yellow but most should be a deep red colour as the pale ones have less flavour. Avoid buying split tomatoes.
How to store: At room temperature or in a cool, not cold place. A refrigerator is not ideal as the cold reduces their flavour. Use tomatoes within 7 – 10 days if they are red. If they are green, ripen them in a dark, slightly cool place.
How to prepare: Wash, remove the stem and core and slice or chop them. Tomatoes may be eaten raw or cooked in any way you choose. They quickly lose their shape when cooked, however. To remove the skin of a tomato, lower it into boiling water for one minute, then remove, drop into cold water, cut the skin and peel the tomato. Alternatively, pierce the tomato with a fork at the stem end. Hold the tomato over a low flame, turning slowly, until the skin pops. Remove from the flame and peel the skin away.
Good source of vitamins A and C.

Turnips

When to buy: All the year round, though fresh, locally grown turnips are available from October to March.
What to look for: Firmness. An old turnip will appear slightly too small for its skin. Most turnips

have a fairly smooth skin that is a combination of white and purple or mauve. They have most flavour when they are small to medium in size.

How to store: In the refrigerator or a cool, dark place for 7 – 10 days.

How to prepare: Scrub them first, then trim the tops and tails away. Peel away the skin and chop or slice as desired.

Like rutabagas, turnips may be eaten raw and are delicious grated into a winter salad or coleslaw. They may be cooked in any way: from boiling or steaming to microwaving and deep-frying. They hold their shape and texture well throughout the cooking process.

Good source of vitamin C.

Watercress

When to buy: All the year round.

What to look for: A deep, dark green colour. The leaves should be crisp and slightly glossy: Yellow or wilted leaves indicate an old bunch and you won't get much flavour or nutrition from them.

How to store: With the stems in a jar of cold water or in the refrigerator for one day. However, it is best to use watercress as soon as possible after buying it.

How to prepare: Separate the bunch and wash the stems in very cold water. Drain the cress or spin the water off, then trim away the thick, woody or tough stems. Use watercress, either in large, whole stalks or coarsely chopped into a salad, soup or dressing.

Good source of vitamins A and C, thiamin, riboflavin, potassium and calcium.

Zucchini

When to buy: From May to early October.

What to look for: A slightly glossy skin. If the skin looks drab and leathery, the zucchini is not fresh. When you squeeze the zucchini it should be firm, without soft patches or bruises. A zucchini is much smaller than an acorn squash, though they are both from the same family. Select those that are small to medium in size to get the best flavour and texture.

How to store: In a cool place for up to 3 days.

How to prepare: Wash the zucchini and trim both ends away. If using large zucchini, peel them (optional), slice them in half along their length, then sprinkle a little salt over the cut surfaces. Leave the salt to work for 20–30 minutes to remove any bitter flavour, then rinse.

Cut the zucchini into fairly thick slices or chunks and cook them in any way you wish. They are very tasty sautéd, baked, grilled or steamed. A microwave or pressure cooker may also be used, or you can combine zucchini with other foods in casseroles, stews, soups or stir-fries.

New Potato Salad (*p 76*)

Nutritious Nuts and Seeds

Nuts and seeds are concentrated storehouses of nature's goodness, and should be used either as a nutritious snack food, or to give protein, texture and body to almost any meal. Store them in airtight containers. Nuts supply important quantities of B group vitamins, vitamin E, calcium, copper, iron, magnesium, phosphorus, potassium and zinc. Most of them are also rich in unsaturated fats (a few also contain some saturated fats) so – as with all foods – beware of unlimited over-indulgence! You can roast most nuts at home to give them that 'just cooked' taste, or chop them in a food processor and sprinkle over main courses and desserts for extra taste and nutrition.

Almonds

The almond is one of the oldest nuts, mentioned in the Bible, and first grown many centuries ago in Russia. They can be eaten freshly cracked from the shell, or blanched in hot water for a couple of minutes, then peeled to reveal the white, tasty flesh. Their subtle flavour complements many desserts, and when flaked and lightly toasted they can be tossed into a salad for protein and colour. Almonds are rich in healthy mono-unsaturated oil. They are cultivated in Mediterranean countries and also in California.
Good source of protein, riboflavin, potassium, calcium, iron and zinc.

Brazil Nuts

As the name suggests, brazil nuts come from South America, where they are native to the valley of the River Amazon. High in calories and oils, they should be used sparingly to add bulk and chewiness to any light meal.
Good source of thiamin, calcium and zinc.

Cashew Nuts

Surely one of the finest and most delicious of nuts, the cashew has a flavour that is distinctively and exquisitely rich. Originally grown in Brazil, most cashews now come from India or Mozambique. Cashews can be finely chopped or ground, and

mixed in to savoury baked food, such as meatloaf, to give a very special flavour.
Good source of protein, iron and zinc.

Chestnuts

Chestnuts are particularly attractive to the health-conscious cook because they are very low in fat. 1 oz of roasted chestnuts only provides about ½ g of fat – less than one per cent of your recommended daily allowance! As a foodstuff, they are versatile and adaptable – you can roast them by the fireside; you can use the puree in a soup, casserole or filling; you can add sugar or honey to make a delicious sweet sauce or dessert; or you can buy them as *marrons glacés* to decorate and flavour a favourite cake or pudding.
Good source of vitamin C.

Cob Nuts

See Hazel Nuts.

Coconuts

You can buy whole coconuts from most supermarkets and greengrocers – choose only those whose milk can be heard inside when you shake them, and which are undamaged (unpunctured) on the outside.

To drain the milk, pierce two of the soft 'eyes' and stand the nut over a cup or jug. The milk can be used to give a rich, smooth taste to soups, stews, curries and sauces. Smash the coconut and extract the white flesh from inside (if you don't want to use all of it, hang half of the nut outside in the garden and watch the birds enjoy themselves!). The white 'meat' can be used raw as a delicious snack, toasted, or grated into curries and rice dishes to give them an exotic flavour. The flesh can also be bought dried and grated (desiccated) and is used in cakes and biscuits.

Coconut oil, coconut butter and creamed coconut are all names for the fat that is extracted from this useful nut. It is the world's most widely used vegetable oil, used to make margarine, soap, shampoo, candles and many other items. In cookery, the oil gives a rich, creamy texture to any dish, but beware – it is one of the few plant oils that is high in saturated fat.

Filberts

See Hazel Nuts.

Hazel Nuts

Hazel nuts, cob nuts, and filberts are very similar to each other in taste and appearance. They can be eaten fresh (you can find them in some greengrocers in early autumn), dried, or cooked in dishes. They can be ground, sliced or chopped, and are used to flavour both sweet and savoury foods, particularly nut roasts, burgers and muesli. On their own they make a most nutritious snack.
Good source of thiamin, vitamin B6 and calcium.

Peanuts

Packed full of protein, peanuts are also a useful source of some B group vitamins, whilst being high in polyunsaturated and mono-unsaturated fats and low in saturated fats. They are highly versatile and can be eaten raw, roasted with salt, as peanut butter, or tossed into salads, rice dishes and curries.
Good source of protein, thiamin, niacin and zinc.

Pecan Nuts

Pecans originated in North America, but in recent years have become increasingly available in European shops and supermarkets. Rather milder and sweeter than walnuts, pecans make a tasty snack food on their own, although my personal favourites are pecan cake and chocolate and pecan nut cookies!
Good source of thiamin and zinc.

Pine Nuts

Pine nuts are harvested from the cones of certain species of pine trees. They do not store well because they tend to go rancid quite quickly, so should be bought just before you intend to use them. They have a light and attractive flavour, and may be used to garnish many dishes, including salads, omelettes, and fruit salads. I particularly like using pine nuts in Cauliflower Gratin and Tabouli Salad, and to add some body to a rich Christmas Pudding. Pine nuts are also an indispensable part of Pesto, one of the most delicious pasta sauces ever invented! Try lightly browning a handful of pine nuts in a frying pan, and tossing them into any rice dish or omelette.
Good source of protein, thiamin, iron and zinc.

Pistachio Nuts

Pistachios are grown in the Mediterranean region, and also in some parts of the United States. They are generally eaten as a snack, and are high in iron. Though usually green in colour, you can sometimes find red ones in the shops, although they may have been artificially coloured.
Good source of protein, thiamin, potassium and iron.

Poppy Seeds

Poppy seeds are generally sprinkled over bread, although they can be used in curries, cakes and other desserts for their thickening properties as well as their flavour. They have a mild, slightly nutty taste and are a pretty blue-grey in colour.

Pumpkin Seeds

Pumpkin seeds are a particularly good source of iron, zinc and some of the B group vitamins. Just 1 oz of pumpkin seeds will provide you with about a quarter of your daily iron requirement! Since they are rather large, they are perhaps best used either ground or chopped. They can be incorporated into rice dishes, salads, and roasts or burgers.
Good source of protein, iron and zinc.

Sesame Seeds

Sesame seeds are nutritious, versatile and cheap. They are a good source of many of the B group of vitamins, and are high in calcium, iron and zinc. I like to toast them lightly and sprinkle them over a wide variety of dishes, breads and salads. You can buy sesame seeds ground up to make a paste called tahini – use it for flavouring, or mix it with cooked chick peas, olive oil and lemon juice to make the Middle Eastern pâté called Hummus. Another Middle Eastern dish, a sweet called halva, is also made from sesame seeds. It is truly mouth-watering – you can buy it from most supermarkets and health food shops.

Sesame oil can be used in salad dressings, but should be bought and used fresh since its delicate flavour is lost quite quickly.
Good source of protein, thiamin, vitamin B6, calcium, iron and zinc.

Sunflower Seeds

Sunflower seeds are high in certain vitamins in the B group, and also high in polyunsaturated fat. They make an excellent snack, either fresh or roasted, and can be added to salads, roasts or muesli.

Sunflower oil is very popular for cooking, and is particularly good for salads and dressings. The first pressed oil is the best.

Good source of protein, thiamin, iron and zinc.

Walnuts

Walnuts are generally sold either dried or pickled, although they can also be eaten fresh from the tree. Dried walnuts are a useful ingredient in many items, particularly salads, snacks, breakfast cereals and desserts.

Walnut oil is a delicious variation on olive oil for salad dressings – but make sure, once again, that you buy it fresh! Pickled walnuts are a delicious savoury treat, and make a great accompaniment to cheese and cheese dishes.

Good source of thiamin.

FRUIT

You'll always find bowls of fruit around my kitchen. They not only provide colour and decoration, but also make tempting snacks for children and adults, instead of highly processed and unhealthy sweets. Since so much fruit is so easily available nowadays, I tend to buy small amounts regularly. Most popular types of fruit are available all the year round now, although it is still worth buying fresh, locally produced fruit in season for extra freshness and flavour. Most fruit is very high in vitamin C, and has useful amounts of other vitamins and minerals as well. Fruit is also one of the few tremendously good sources of natural fibre, which we all know is good for us. Here are some of my favourite fruits, with some hints designed to help you choose the very best available.

Apples

There are thousands of varieties of apple, but sadly, only a handful of them ever reach the supermarket or greengrocers' shelves. One of the most widely available types is the Golden Delicious, although this is, perhaps, one of the least flavoursome. Granny Smiths have a bright green colour, with a firm texture and a rather sharp taste. Cox's Orange Pippin is usually quite small, with a variegated colour, but possesses one of the most intriguing and distinctive tastes of all. Other varieties to experiment with, whenever you are lucky enough to see them in the shops, include Crispin, Russet, James Grieve and, for cooking, the Bramley.

Apples are incredibly versatile. I use them not just as a sweet or dessert, but also in savoury dishes such as Zucchini with Apples, Madras Onion Curry and Maine Sauerkraut.

Apricots

Finding ripe apricots is not always easy, because they have a very short summer growing season, are often picked unripe, and frequently fail to ripen subsequently.

For cooking, dried apricots are often preferable, because they are usually picked when ripe and dried in the country of origin, to preserve most of their flavour and sweetness.

Bananas

One of the most widely eaten fruits in the world, bananas are available everywhere, all year round. Bananas are almost always cut from the tree well before they ripen, and are often seen still green in the shops. Bananas bought in this state will continue to ripen at home, and should be eaten when the skin has turned completely yellow and is perhaps flecked with a few brown spots. Bananas that have completely ripened, and whose skin is either brown or even black, may still be bought and used (in cooking or to make a gorgeous milkshake with either skimmed milk or soya milk).

Bananas are very valuable nutritionally, being low in calories and fat and high in vitamin C and some of the B group vitamins, with useful amounts of potassium. They should never be refrigerated.

They can be fried and served with a little lemon juice or cream, or used to flavour any number of sweet or savoury dishes, including, of course, fruit salads.

Dried bananas make a good snack food, when mixed with nuts and fruit.

Blackberries

Blackberries, also known as brambles, are related to raspberries. Ideally, you should try to sample before buying, because even the most attractive blackberries may, once tasted, prove to be bitter and without any deep flavour. Picking blackberries from the countryside is a wonderful way to spend a Saturday or Sunday afternoon in autumn, but beware – avoid those grown by roadsides or within industrial areas, since they are likely to be heavily contaminated with pollutants such as lead.

Blackberries are an excellent ingredient in an autumn fruit salad, and make great jams and pies. They also contain useful amounts of the B group vitamins and calcium.

Blueberries

Blueberries are an American fruit, increasingly seen in British supermarkets and greengrocers. They are a tasty accompaniment to pancakes, muffins and ice cream, or as a special ingredient in breakfast cereals and muesli. They can also be used as pie fillings, or, when turned into a sauce, make a tasty topping for cheesecakes.

Cherries

I love cherries! They range in colour from yellow through red to black. In taste, they tend to be either sweet or sour (Morello cherries are probably the best-known bitter ones, and are used to make jams and other preserves).

The best way to judge the ripeness of cherries is by trying one – with your greengrocer's permission! They will keep well for several days at room temperature, and will freeze quite well too.

Currants

Black currants and red currants are closely related, and are available from July onwards.

They are excellent sources of vitamin C, and also contain some potassium and calcium. Black currant juice is a traditional children's favourite, but do try and find one that has not been heavily sugared.

Black and red currants are generally cooked in tarts, pies and jams. Make sure you 'top and tail' them first.

To make black currant jelly, put 1 quart of cleaned black currants into a saucepan with ½ cup of water and boil until pulped. Sieve, remove the pulp, and add 3 cups of preserving sugar for every quart of liquid. Boil until it starts to thicken, then pour into pots and tightly cap.

Figs

Figs are rich in some of the B group vitamins, as well as potassium and calcium. Dried figs are also rich in iron. Fresh figs sold in Britain are often not completely ripe, and therefore lack the flavour and sweetness found in truly ripe fruit.

Fresh figs are best eaten raw, rather than cooked, since dried figs are much cheaper and are more suitable for cooking. Fresh figs make an exotic and original dessert, accompanied by yoghurt or some fine cheese.

Gooseberries

A traditional English fruit, it is sad to say that the gooseberry has been increasingly difficult to obtain in recent years. It is sometimes possible to find gooseberries that are suitable for eating raw, but generally they need to be cooked with sugar to remove the tart flavour – they make great pies and a great sauce.

Grapefruit

Often used as an appetiser or a pleasant accompaniment to breakfast, grapefruit can be served imaginatively by cutting in half, lightly sprinkling with brown sugar, butter or maple syrup and browning under the broiler for a minute or two.

Grapes

My favourites are seedless Concords. Like apples, there are thousands of varieties of grape, with colourings that range from green, through red to purple. Muscat grapes have a particularly mellow flavour, and seedless grapes are increasingly popular because of their sweetness and ease of use. Some grapes have particularly thick skins, which are not to everyone's taste, and can sometimes impart a slightly bitter taste.

Grapes are available all the year round, because many of them are now grown in commercial greenhouses. Grapes should be bought just before they are ripe, so that they can be eaten at home at the ideal moment. When choosing grapes, make sure that you examine the grapes towards the centre of the bunch to ensure that they are not squashed or damaged.

To make grape marmalade, take the grapes off the stem, put them in a saucepan without any water, and heat while stirring occasionally. When the seeds separate from the rest of the pulp, strain it to separate the fine pulp from the skins and seeds, which you should throw away. Measure the filtered grape puree back into the saucepan, and add an equal amount of preserving sugar, then simmer for about 30 minutes, and pour into glass jars. This can be seasoned with a little ground cinnamon or lemon peel, and is delicious on toast for breakfast.

Kiwi Fruit

Just a few years ago, it was nothing more than a wild, uncultivated berry found in New Zealand. Today the kiwi fruit (or Chinese gooseberry as it is sometimes called) is sold all over the world. A remarkably rich source of vitamin C, the kiwi fruit is also high in fibre and low in calories.

Buy them when they are slightly soft to the touch, and either scoop them out with a spoon, or peel and slice them thinly and use them to garnish any appropriate dish, particularly fruit salads.

Lemons

We use tons of lemons. Lemon juice may be used in place of vinegar in most recipes, including French dressing. Lemon juice will also stop some foods (such as bananas, apples, peaches and avocados) from discolouring quickly.

The skin of the lemon is important because it provides 'zest' which is, in fact, the essential oil of the lemon.

Do not buy lemons that are excessively green. Also, if you tend to use the skin, do make sure that the lemon is very carefully washed to remove any trace of chemicals. A dash of lemon juice is great on certain vegetables, such as spinach, asparagus and broccoli.

Mangoes

Mangoes are often found on supermarket shelves and, when ripe, are yellow or red in colour. Although they can be used in cooked dishes, they taste so luscious and tropical that they are probably best used as a fresh dessert or treat.

The mango is an astonishingly rich source of vitamin A and vitamin C.

The central stone is very difficult to cut through. Therefore it is best to slice the mango into fairly thin sections around the stone.

Melons

There are many different varieties of melon, but my favourites are watermelon and honeydew melon. Canteloupe melon is quite small, with orange flesh, and has an extremely high vitamin A and vitamin C content. The honeydew melon, on the other hand, has virtually no vitamin A but a reasonably high vitamin C content.

Melons are usually served as an appetiser or as a dessert, and may be sliced or cut in half and filled with port, grapes or cottage cheese. A touch of ginger, or even salt and pepper, can also add flavour.

When choosing a melon press gently at the stalk end – a ripe melon will give slightly all the way round the stalk.

Watermelons are increasingly popular, and because of their size provide enough food and fun for a whole family. Choose watermelons that sound slightly hollow when rapped with the knuckles.

Nectarines

My family loves nectarines. They are similar to peaches, but with smoother, thinner skins. They should be bought nearly ripe, and may be placed on a window sill at home for a day or two to ripen to perfection. Do not, however, buy green fruit or ones which may have been kept in cold storage, since they will never ripen properly and simply go mushy.

The rich flavour of nectarines complements most types of cheese, and they make an ideal ingredient in any fruit salad.

Oranges

Navel oranges are the greatest to eat. Seville oranges are very bitter and only used with a sweetening agent, mainly in marmalades. Other members of the orange family include jaffas, blood oranges, tangerines, clementines and ugli fruit. They are all suitable for use in fruit salads or as a snack food by themselves. Fresh orange juice is a real treat.

To make a delicious orange sauce suitable for serving with any savoury dish, take the juice and rind of one orange, and combine with 4 tablespoons of tahini (ground sesame seeds) and 2 tablespoons of soy sauce. Heat gently, stirring, until the sauce is thick.

Peaches

Peaches, in common with many other yellow-coloured fruit and vegetables, are good sources of vitamin A. Choose peaches that are plump to the touch, nearly ripe, and whose skin is unbroken. Reject any with the skin slightly loose or shrunken.

Peaches and cream are, of course, a traditionally English delicacy. Also consider lightly frying small portions of chopped peaches, and tossing them into any rice dish to give a delicious tropical flavour.

Peaches are generally best between May and September, although they are available in some shops all the year round. White peaches are a special treat.

Pears

Locally grown pears are usually available from September onwards, and should be bought slightly under-ripe, so that they can ripen at home on a window sill or in a fruit bowl. It is best not to keep them in the refrigerator.

Pears that are slightly past their peak, with tinges of brown, can still be used to cook with, providing the skin has not been broken.

Pears can turn brown rather quickly when sliced, and this can be unsightly in dishes such as fruit salads. A useful tip to prevent this happening is to dip them quickly in lemon juice.

The William pear is perhaps the best for cooking, although Conference are also suitable and keep their shape beautifully when cooked. Both are good raw. For fruit salads and eating as a dessert or with cheese, a ripe Comice melts in the mouth.

Pineapples

To select a good pineapple, first ensure that it is not damaged, and that the colour is not predominantly green. Then try pulling out one of the leaves from the centre of the fruit. If it detaches easily, the pineapple is ready to eat. Otherwise, it needs a few days storage in a sunny place. A ripe pineapple smells scented.

You can hollow out a pineapple and use it as an exotic container for other types of food such as ice cream, or even a sweet curry. A sprinkling of lemon juice and sugar is enough to turn it into a first-class dessert all by itself.

Plums

There are a great many varieties and flavours of plums, but in essence, they can be divided into the sweeter ones and the sour ones. Sour ones, such as damsons, should be cooked. Either stew with sugar or turn into exquisitely flavoursome damson jam (allow about 2 cups sugar to every 2 cups fruit, slowly bring to the boil without adding any further liquid, then simmer for about 45 minutes and pour into glass jars).

Eating plums, such as Victorias, should be bought when they have just started to ripen, and are plump and slightly soft to the touch, but before they become too mushy. The exception to this rule is the Greengage, which should be bought when very soft, as otherwise it has a sharp, tart flavour.

Raspberries

Raspberries are available from midsummer to autumn, and you should choose locally grown fruit (because they don't travel well) that are clean and juicy.

A bowl of raspberries, with a little sugar and cream, make a gorgeously simple sweet after a rich meal.

You can freeze raspberries, although they are likely to become rather mushy when defrosted, and should probably be used for flavouring sorbets or ice cream.

Rhubarb

Rhubarb always needs to be cooked before being eaten. Choose young stalks where possible, since more mature ones have less flavour and become rather stringy. The leaves are poisonous and must not be eaten.

Stewed rhubarb, with sugar and lemon juice, makes a quick and tasty dessert.

Strawberries

Strawberries are synonymous with the British summer – strawberries and cream at Wimbledon, or on a lazy Sunday afternoon picnic.

When buying strawberries, always check the quality of those underneath the top layer in the container, to ensure that they are not squashed, unripe or musty. Although large strawberries look delicious, smaller ones are usually much more flavoursome.

There is a period of a week or two every summer when most strawberry plants produce fruit, and at this time the prices fall sharply. This is the right time to buy them in bulk to make your own strawberry jam. Wild strawberries, if you can get them, are really special.

Devilled Eggs (p 63)

GLORIOUS GRAINS AND LEGUMES

GRAINS

Buckwheat

Roasted buckwheat is much underrated as a useful grain. In fact, it makes a tasty alternative to rice in many dishes. It is rich in minerals and B group vitamins, and has the advantage of being low in calories.

To cook roasted buckwheat, wash it thoroughly, and then place it in a saucepan with about twice its volume of water. Bring to a slow boil and season with salt (or a teaspoon of yeast extract), then reduce the heat and simmer until all the water has been absorbed. Serve with a selection of stir-fried or boiled vegetables.

Bulgur Wheat

Bulgur wheat can be used interchangeably with cracked wheat to produce dishes such as tabouli salad. In many countries it is used as a substitute for rice, and can be mixed with small chopped vegetables or nuts and raisins to produce a most appetising side dish.

Bulgur wheat should be cooked in the proportion of 1 cup of bulgur to 2 cups of water, brought to the boil, and then simmered for 10–15 minutes, until all the excess liquid has been absorbed. As a final touch, add some finely chopped and sautéed onions and any other finely chopped vegetables you care to. Season with salt and pepper and serve either as a side dish or as an accompaniment to pies or curries, or cold with salads.

Couscous

Couscous is an exotic North African dish, which is quick and easy to make. Steam 2 cups of couscous grains for about 30 minutes, then transfer them into a mixing bowl, add a few tablespoons of oil and mix thoroughly to break up any lumps. Then chop a selection of vegetables together (carrots, tomatoes, garlic, leeks, etc). Place the vegetables with a little water, tomato puree and seasoning in the bottom of a large pan, and put the couscous grains in a steamer on top. Cover and cook for about 30 minutes, until the vegetables are tender. Serve together.

Oats

Oats are increasingly popular at the moment, because they have been shown to lower cholesterol in the blood. Porridge can be made like this: combine 2 cups of rolled oats or oatmeal with 4 cups of water, bring to the boil and simmer for about 15 minutes, stirring constantly to prevent sticking. Flavour with salt, brown sugar or honey and serve with milk or cream if desired. Some people soak the oatmeal overnight in cold water, and say that it greatly improves the taste. At the other end of the scale, instant porridge is of course made in a matter of a minute or two.

Besides porridge, oats can be used as an ingredient in bread (for example, Irish Brown Bread), to make oatcakes, as a base for many varieties of muesli, or as a crumbly topping for sweets and savouries.

Rice

There are many different types of rice available in supermarkets, health food shops and ethnic groceries, so it is well worth experimenting and finding one type that you and your family really like. Of course packet rice, such as Uncle Ben's, is the easiest and quickest to prepare, and virtually guarantees you perfect results every time.

Rice is generally divided into either long grain (which tends to stay separate when cooked) and short-grain (which generally sticks together – great for rice puddings). The vitamin and mineral content of brown rice is high, because little has been removed from it, apart from the indigestible outer shell. White rice is brown rice that has been further processed to remove more of the outer layers. Polished rice has been processed further still, and has fewer nutrients left in it. Basmati rice is a long-grain variety that is often used in Indian cooking, and has an attractive nutty smell to it.

To cook white rice: put 1 cup of white rice in a saucepan with 2 cups of water. Bring to the boil, then turn the heat down to a low simmer, and cook until all the water has been absorbed.

To cook brown rice: 2 cups of brown rice makes approximately 6 cups of cooked rice, which is usually enough to serve 4-6 people. Measure the rice into a mixing bowl and cover with cold water. Wash it thoroughly, drain the water and repeat this process three times until the water is fairly clear. Drain the rice and tip into an iron pot. Cover the clean rice in the pan with 4 cups of water. Cover the pan and place over a high flame. Bring to the boil, then reduce the flame to a low simmer and cook for approximately 50 minutes, or until the water is completely absorbed. Don't stir the rice at this point, or it may become sticky. If it is still too firm at the end of 50 minutes, boil the kettle and add a little boiling water to the rice. Cover again and cook for another 10 minutes. Brown rice takes longer to cook than white rice because it is a whole grain.

See also Wild Rice.

Wheat

Perhaps the most important grain in the history of the human race, wheat can be processed into an enormous range of foodstuffs, including pasta, bread, all types of baked products, breakfast foods and biscuits. When wheat is processed, the husk (also called bran) is removed, leaving the kernel. At this stage, it is called whole wheat.

Further processing results in the production of white flour, which mainly consists of the starch and gluten surrounding the central wheatgerm. Gluten is the springy, spongy substance in wheat that helps bread to keep its shape once it has risen. Wheatgerm itself can be bought separately, and is a good source of vitamin E, protein and fibre.

'Hard' types of wheat, such as durum wheat, are rich in gluten and are particularly suitable for making semolina, pasta and other processed wheat foods. Soft wheat types tend to be used for flour milling.

Wild Rice

Wild rice is quite different from other types of rice, although it can be cooked and used in much the same way. It has a delicious, flavoursome taste and is often regarded as a real gourmet food. Originally grown and harvested by American Indians, much of it is still harvested from the wild, which accounts for its high price. Wild rice makes a classic accompaniment to any really special meal, such as Asparagus Casserole with Sour Cream, Mushrooms and Onions in Sherry, or New Orleans Okra. For an extra special touch, mix it with lightly toasted almonds, thinly sliced fried mushrooms, or small slivers of garlic and

ginger. I often mix wild rice with white rice to give a great texture and appearance to any rice dish.

LEGUMES

Dried Beans, Peas and Lentils

When to buy: All the year round.

What to look for: The beans should be dry, with no obvious signs of damp or mould.

How to store: Keep them in a dry, preferably cool place. A tightly covered container is better than a sack or bag.

How to prepare: Pick out any unsightly beans and the occasional small piece of stone. Wash the beans in cold water two or three times using a rubbing movement with your hands to really scrub them. Drain the water away each time and, finally, cover them with fresh, cold water and leave them to soak for a minimum of 4 hours. (Soaking overnight or while you are out at work is a handy time.) Drain the soaking water away from the beans and discard it. Decide whether you will pressure cook the beans or cook them slowly in a covered pot.

In a covered pot, cover the beans with fresh water and place over a high heat. Bring the water to the boil and cook furiously for 10 minutes. Then reduce the heat and simmer until the beans are tender – up to 3 hours, depending on the type of bean you are cooking. To test for tenderness, put one bean in your mouth and press it with your tongue against the roof of your mouth. If the bean squashes easily, it is cooked, if not then continue to simmer.

A pressure cooker is tremendously useful for cooking beans. Wash and soak your beans as usual, then place them in the pressure cooker with cold water just covering them. Close the pressure cooker, place over a high heat and bring to pressure. Cook at pressure for approximately 10–30 minutes, depending on the bean.

Bean	Covered Pot Cooking	Pressure Cooker
Aduki beans	30 minutes	10 minutes
Black-eyed peas	45 minutes	15 minutes
Borlotti beans	1 hour	20 minutes
Broad beans (dried)	1½ hours	30 minutes
Butter beans	1½ hours	30 minutes
Chick peas	1½ hours	30 minutes
Continental lentils	45 minutes	15 minutes
Green peas (dried)	45 minutes	15 minutes
Haricot beans	1½ hours	30 minutes

Bean	Covered Pot Cooking	Pressure Cooker
Lima beans	1 hour	20 minutes
Mung beans	30 minutes	10 minutes
Pinto beans	1½ hours	30 minutes
Red kidney beans	1 hour	20 minutes
Red lentils	20 minutes	–
Split peas	30 minutes	–
Soya beans	3 hours	1 hour

Whichever method you choose, do not add salt, vinegar, lemon juice, bicarbonate of soda or any sauce or dressing until the beans are cooked to the tender stage. Once they are tender, you may finish cooking them with other ingredients, if desired.

Red Kidney beans can cause food poisoning when undercooked. They are harmless when they have been soaked and cooked for an adequate length of time.

Most beans are good sources of protein and fibre, low in fat, and rich in minerals such as potassium and iron.

Aduki Beans

Grown mainly in Japan and China, these beautiful little beans have a light, fresh taste and are ideal for soups, stews and curries.

Broad Beans

Fresh broad beans, if selected young enough, make a tasty and healthy side dish to any main course such as meatloaf, burgers or chili. Fresh beans can also be pureed. Dried, they make an excellent addition to soups, stews and curries.

Butter Beans

Also known as lima beans, butter beans blend easily with almost any dish, and have an attractive tender texture.

Chick Peas

Chick peas are amongst the most versatile of all legumes, and have a uniquely delicious taste. They are available either dried or canned. The canned variety, although generally lacking some of the flavour, are much more convenient to use if you've forgotten to soak them overnight.

Often used in Middle Eastern dishes such as couscous, falafal and hummus, chick peas can also be added to most types of main courses. As an ingredient in a fresh salad, they add flavour, texture and nutrition. They are very high in protein, the B group vitamins, potassium, calcium, iron and zinc.

Flageolet Beans

Flageolets are small kidney beans, grown in France, and used in stews and casseroles. They are a pretty green colour and will add interest to almost any dish.

Haricot Beans

Highly nutritious beans which contain more protein than meat. In Britain, haricot beans are known to millions of people as baked beans. Like most other legumes, haricot beans are supremely versatile, and can be used (after being cooked) in a vast range of hot or cold dishes – so experiment for yourself!

Kidney Beans

Widely available in cans, kidney beans (sometimes just called red beans) are an ingredient in several of the Mexican dishes that are amongst my favourites. But you can also use a can of kidney beans in just about anything savoury, to add colour and taste and to bolster the nutrition.

Lentils

There are many different types of lentils, including brown lentils, red lentils, green lentils and split (orange or red) lentils. Very high in protein and minerals, most lentils need to be soaked, although red split lentils can be cooked from their dry state to make a nourishing Indian dal in about 20 minutes. Lentils go well in thick wintry stews; they are also equally at home in a bean-based salad, covered in tangy French dressing.

Soya Beans

A truly remarkable bean, long recognized in the Orient, but only recently becoming well known in the West. After cooking, soya beans can be used to enormously increase the protein content of many types of food, and an increasing range of soya bean-based oriental products – such as soya milk, tofu and soy sauce – are now appearing on our supermarket shelves. Soya flour, too, is worth keeping in the kitchen, as it is very high in protein, and a small amount added to any flour mixture will greatly increase its nutritional value.

Baked Macaroni Cheese (*p 84*)

HELPFUL HERBS AND SPECTACULAR SPICES

HERBS

I adore using *fresh* herbs! Their flavours and aromas are more tantalising, and they blend better with the food I'm cooking. I try to have one or two varieties growing in my garden or on my kitchen window sill all the year round, because I love looking at them – they're an important part of the living kitchen. You may also be lucky enough to live near a local greengrocer who stocks little bundles of fresh herbs all the year round – they often have the more exotic types that don't grow locally.

Dried herbs are useful as a stand-by, because they're always available. When using them, remember that 1 tablespoon of chopped dried herbs will taste as strong as 2 tablespoons of fresh herbs – their essential oils are concentrated, and their effect on a dish is often surprising.

Never buy dried herbs if they smell musty – also, check that they have a good strong colour. Parsley, for instance, should be a bright 'forest green' colour. If it is grey, then it has been dried too harshly and many of its properties will have been lost. Some herbs, such as rosemary, are naturally greyish when dried and you should rub a little between thumb and forefinger to test that the essential oils are still strong.

Store dried herbs in a dark cupboard or corner of your work top, preferably in airtight dark glass or earthenware jars. Always measure the required amount of herbs away from the steam of a simmering pot to prevent the moisture being absorbed into the stored herb. Give the herb a minute or two to blend into the food you are making, then use your sense of smell to determine whether to add more. Cooking with herbs is a fun and fascinating way of developing your own personal style in recipes, so enjoy yourself by experimenting with various herb combinations.

Basil

One of my favourites in taste and smell! Many greengrocers sell little pots of fresh basil in the spring and early summer. With careful use, you can keep two or three of these growing and supplying you until the late autumn. This is a strongly flavoured herb, so you don't need very much in any one dish.

Basil is most strongly associated with tomato dishes, salads and that old favourite of mine, pesto – an Italian sauce for pasta. Do try to find fresh basil if you can – there's nothing like it!

Bay Leaves

If you have a patio or sheltered corner of the garden, you can grow your own bay tree in a large earthenware pot. The leaves are used to flavour sauces, stews and soups. They sharpen the flavour and aroma of a dish, and thus stimulate your appetite. Single leaves are sometimes used to garnish a dish.

Chives

Chives are part of the onion family, and have a subtle onion flavour. I use them in salads and salad dressings, in sour cream sprinkled on to baked potatoes, in omelettes and clear soups.

Dill

Both the seed and the weed, or leafy part, are used. The weed is used sparingly in salads, dressings and sauces, and I use the seed (and the weed) in pickling. The wonderful clean flavour of dill is quite unique in the world of herbs – it has a faintly liquorice flavour. I love dill!

Garlic

That famous bulb that people either love or hate! Fresh garlic pulls apart into separate cloves and you will find that recipes usually call for 1 – 3 cloves (but even that amount is optional). The cloves are peeled, and then either chopped very finely or crushed – either will do. Garlic powder and garlic granules are sold in the spice section of most supermarkets. Garlic – in any form – is exceptionally versatile and may be used in sauces, dressings, casseroles, stews, eggs dishes, pasta dishes and salad dressings.

Marjoram

This herb has a strong flavour that adds a 'bite' to food. It is usually used in company with thyme and is best in dishes that include eggs, cheese, oils and strong-tasting ingredients. Onions, spinach, cabbage, aubergines and zucchini squash are further examples of foods that are complemented by this herb. It may be grown in your garden but is usually used in dried form.

Mint

Who doesn't know the flavour of this wonderful, refreshing herb? Apart from its cooling use in homemade lemonade and iced tea, it adds its fragrance to steamed or boiled peas, beans and potatoes – two or three leaves will do for a pan full of vegetables. I use it fresh most of the time as I find the dried herb has a slight sharpness. Experiment with the many varieties such as spearmint, peppermint and applemint – to name a few, and use the young, tight leaves as a garnish for cold soups, salads and drinks.

Mixed Herbs

This is a pre-mixed blend of dried herbs stocked in most supermarkets. It is sometimes sold as 'mixed sweet herbs' and is usually a blend of parsley, thyme, marjoram, oregano and bay. Use in stews, soups and baked vegetable loaves.

Oregano

I tend to call oregano the pizza herb. The tomato, onion, cheese and mushroom combination in a pizza topping is a perfect background for this herb as it helps to unite the flavours of these strong ingredients. But don't stop there! Eggs, beans and pasta – and their sauces – are all enhanced with a light sprinkling of oregano.

Parsley

Next time your restaurant meal appears with that familiar sprig of green tucked in one corner, eat it! Parsley is rich in vitamin C and, when eaten fresh, helps to clean the palate ready for the next course. It is an exceptionally versatile herb and I would say that it is probably impossible to use too much or to use it incorrectly – it seems to go with everything. So if you are just beginning to use herbs in your cooking, start with parsley.

The dried herb should have a strong green colour and may be used generously in soups, stews, casseroles and other cooked dishes. The fresh herb is easy to grow and always better than the dried herb in salads, sandwiches, dips and spreads.

Rosemary

This is a strong-flavoured herb with an aroma that is slightly reminiscent of eucalyptus. It may be used fresh or dried in stuffings, stews, casseroles, egg dishes, white sauces and with winter vegetables.

Sage

This has a unique flavour, one that has become famous through sage and onion stuffing. Sage is truly excellent with all lentils, legumes and cheeses. It is best used sparingly, whether fresh or dried, and may be included in some tomato sauces.

If you cannot obtain the herb fresh, select the dried herb cautiously. Sage must never smell musty and, though it has a natural grey-green colour, it shouldn't appear very dusty and grey.

Tarragon

A favourite of mine! Used lightly, it will add a clean and delicate sweetness to a sauce, dressing, omelette, marinade or salad. You can grow all the tarragon you will need in a very small, sunny patch in your patio or garden.

Thyme

A herb that helps in the digestion of rich and fatty foods, so it is often used in cheese and egg dishes. It is good both fresh and dried and should be used sparingly, as its flavour can be overwhelming if too much is added. Thyme is often combined with other herbs, such as parsley, oregano, sage, rosemary and basil when a soup, stew or casserole is being cooked. A little is sometimes used alone in vegetable dishes or sauces when a slightly spicy flavour is desired.

SPICES

Caraway

This is a crescent-shaped seed that adds a clean flavour to cabbage dishes such as coleslaw and sauerkraut, onions and – of course – breads. It has a strong flavour, so should be used sparingly. Try chewing a pinch of caraway after a meal, to freshen your breath and clean your palate.

Cayenne

This reddish-orange spice is a member of the capsicum, or pepper, family of plants and is half way between mild and hot (see Chili Powder and Paprika). It is ground from the dried red pepper pod and should be used a pinch at a time to create a subtle rather than a too powerful effect. It is used in barbecue, tomato and cheese sauces as well as some egg dishes.

Chili Powder

Also a member of the capsicum family, chili is considered the hottest of the peppers. The darker red this powder is, the stronger and hotter is its flavour. It is used cautiously in Mexican food, sauces, dressings, casseroles (such as Chili con Carne), relishes, chutneys and in some egg dishes.

Cinnamon

This is the bark of a tree which is dried and sold in strips or ground into a powder. It is a sweet, aromatic spice that is a versatile favourite for cakes, cookies, puddings, fruit dishes and hot drinks. It may be used alone or in combination with other spices, such as cloves or nutmeg. Experiment with the amount used because it has a definite flavour and does not need to be used lavishly.

Cloves

Consisting of the dried bud of a tropical tree, cloves are sold as little spikes or in powdered form. It is a strong, aromatic spice that should be used carefully, since its flavour can easily overwhelm other flavours in a dish. I use it in pies and fruit dishes. It is good in combination with cinnamon or nutmeg in cakes or cookies.

Cumin

This tiny seed has a powerful and unmistakable flavour and aroma. It is used in curries, stews, soups, chutneys and breads. It is best purchased whole, as it retains more of its flavour in this form. Then, depending on the recipe, you can either sauté it whole in a little oil, or grind it yourself with a small mortar and pestle. Use cumin sparingly until you are familiar with its flavour.

Curry Powder

This is a blend of spices that goes well in an Indian dish. At least one of the capsicum family (chili, cayenne, paprika) is included as well as turmeric, ginger or allspice and possibly dried garlic. It is great fun to make up your own curry powder when you have become familiar with a number of different spices – an excellent challenge for your sense of smell! Otherwise, buy small quantities of the various brands on the market until you find one that suits you.

Ginger

Fresh ginger looks rather like a shiny Jerusalem artichoke – it is best used in oriental dishes, or grated into relishes, chutneys, salads and fruit dishes. It is sometimes used to enhance root vegetables – just grate a little over the vegetables in the final few minutes they are cooking. Ground ginger is used sparingly in cakes, cookies, Indian or Chinese dishes and some sauces and dressings.

Mixed Spice

This is a blend of spices that is sold in most supermarkets. It is made up of coriander, cinnamon, caraway, nutmeg, ginger and cloves and is used predominantly in breads, cakes, cookies and other sweet or semi-sweet dishes. I find it is useful to have a little of this product in the cupboard for those times when I don't feel like mixing my own spices.

Mustard

This is a strongly flavoured black or yellow seed that may be used whole, ground into a powder, or ground and mixed with liquid into a paste. The seeds are often added to pickles, sauces or dressings where they add a subtle bite to the mixture. Once ground, the seeds may be mixed with other spices and sprinkled into egg or cheese dishes or, more commonly, made into a paste. The liquid used may be water, vinegar or wine, and each of these greatly affects the final outcome of your mustard. Generally, a tangy but mild flavour is of most use, though mustard can be made into a very hot paste.

Nutmeg

Though this spice is usually purchased as a reddish brown powder, it is made from the kernel of a fruit and you may occasionally see it in this form. If you do, you'll notice a deep red, vein-like casing around it: this is mace, another spice with a flavour closely resembling nutmeg.

Nutmeg is a strong spice and should be used sparingly in cakes, cookies, fruit dishes, milk dishes and in some vegetable dishes. Familiar examples are apple sauce, custard, eggnog and glazed vegetables – you can also serve fresh melon with a sprinkling of nutmeg.

Paprika

Paprika is the mildest member of the capsicum family of peppers, after chili and cayenne. It is purchased dried and powdered, and may be used in goulash, in egg, milk or cheese dishes, and in some dressings and sauces.

Pepper

Not related to the capsicums, which are also called peppers. I always use black pepper out of personal preference, and I prefer to grind my own as and when I need it. That means that I buy peppercorns rather than ground pepper, and use a pepper mill to grind them. Pepper loses its fresh taste quickly once it has been ground. Use pepper in almost any savoury dish to put the final edge on the taste of each ingredient.

Salt

We need some salt in our diet, but only a small proportion of the amount most of us take in already. Too much salt in the diet can create health problems so we should keep our salt intake to a minimum: I find that seasoning food with salt at the table (rather than during cooking) can reduce the amount we use. I always use sea salt as it usually contains other minerals and trace elements such as iodine.

Sometimes I use celery salt, garlic salt or sesame salt, which are simply mixtures of salt and celery seed, dried garlic or sesame seed. You can make your own salt mixture using spices, seeds or other dried herbs, then store your creation in a moisture-proof container or salt cellar.

Turmeric

Though a member of the ginger family of plants, turmeric has nothing like the sharpness of ginger. It is slightly bitter, slightly sweet and only faintly aromatic. It adds a delicate aroma to foods when it is cooked with them and provides a beautiful deep yellow colouring. I use it in rice, egg and milk dishes as well as curries, chutneys and, occasionally, a salad dressing.

GROWING YOUR OWN GOODNESS

You know, there is nothing to compare with the sheer pleasure of eating fresh food straight from your own kitchen garden. If you live in a city and don't have your own vegetable garden or allotment, you can still grow your own food. You don't have to spend hours every week knee-deep in muck – simply do as I do, and start cultivating the patio or kitchen window sill right now! It's easy, fun and produces the best (and cheapest) food you're ever likely to find. Even young children can plant and look after a window sill garden. Here are some of my family's favourites.

Basil

You can buy young plants from most greengrocers in the early spring. Place the pot (or pots) on your window sill in good sunlight, keep them well watered and pinch out the young leaves often for use in cooking. This helps the plant stay bushy and healthy and keeps you well stocked with fresh basil. Basil grows to a height of only 9–10 inches and has very pretty, delicate leaves. This herb is an annual and you will need to buy new plants each year.

Bay

This is really a tree which can eventually grow to quite a size. However, it is usually sold in an earthenware container and trimmed to keep a maximum height of 3 feet, with a round, ball-shaped head of leaves only 12–18 inches across. It needs a patio or balcony in good light, a little water and not too much disturbance. This plant is long-lived if you either feed it or give it new soil each year. Pick one or two leaves at a time for use in cooking.

Bean Sprouts

Those rock-hard beans and dried legumes you buy in supermarkets can be turned into crisp, succulent green vegetables in just three or four days – all on your own window sill or draining board! Bean sprouts are rich in nutrients and, because they are eaten fresh, lose very little goodness during cooking. You can eat bean sprouts raw in salads, steamed, stir-fried or deep-fried in a spring roll. Here's how to start:

First, decide which beans you wish to sprout. The most common, and the sort you are most likely to have tasted already, are sprouted mung beans. Others include alfalfa seed, soya beans, chick peas, wheat berries, whole lentils (not split) and fenugreek seeds. Each of these has its own unique flavour and texture, so you can experiment to find those that you and your family prefer best. All of these seeds and beans are easy to buy at supermarkets or whole-food shops.

When you have chosen the seeds or beans you wish to sprout, find a glass jar that holds at least 1 pint of water. Rinse it and measure 3 tablespoons (no more!) of seeds or beans into it. Cover them with three or four times their volume of water and leave to sit overnight.

In the morning, drain all the water away from the swollen seeds or beans. Cover the jar with a fine piece of cheesecloth, kept in place with a rubber band round the neck. Shake the jar so that the seeds settle along the side, then rest the jar on its side on your window sill or draining board. Bean sprouts do not need direct sunlight or, indeed, much light at all to grow.

In the evening, pour a good quantity of water through the cheesecloth on to the beans. Swirl the water gently round (to avoid breaking off the tender sprouts), then drain it away again. Place the jar on its side again and leave it overnight. Continue in this way for three or four days rinsing the sprouts morning and evening.

Taste the growing sprouts after two or three days. When the sprouts are the taste and length you find most appealing, pull them gently from the jar, place them in a large bowl, cover them with cold water and wash away the husks of the beans.

Lift the sprouts from the water and drain them in a colander. Use them immediately in sandwiches, salads, spring rolls and stir-fries.

Hint: Start a new batch of beans or seeds every day so that you always have some fresh ones available. If you have a vegetable juicing machine, add some fresh sprouts to your juices to increase the nutrient content.

Chives

I like to grow more than one clump of this herb, which is part of the onion family but resembles grass. The leaves grow to about 6 inches tall and, if allowed, blossom into pretty, round heads of purple flowers. You can grow chives in little pots on your window sill all the year round, or on your balcony or patio for about eight months of the year. They need regular watering, good light and occasional feeding. Use a pair of kitchen scissors to cut chives for use in salads, soups, stuffings, dips, dressings and spreads. Cut the chives about 1 inch from the base of the plant so that new shoots will grow.

Marjoram

Also called pot marjoram. It is best to grow this herb from seed, though you may be able to buy a young plant from a nursery or greengrocer. Marjoram is a very aromatic plant which I find especially pleasing in my window-sill collection. Plant it in a fairly coarse mixture of compost and grit and water it regularly, but not often. Marjoram loves direct sunlight. Trim the vertical shoots away for use in cooked foods, especially those that are slightly heavier in flavour such as stews, casseroles and bakes.

Mint

Grow this in its own separate container or it will take over all the other herbs! Mint will grow quite easily in just about any situation, but it likes to have some sun and some shade each day, a little water each day and a feed once each year. It grows vigorously and retains a nice, bushy shape if you keep taking the new shoots away. I grow the spearmint and peppermint varieties, but you could try apple mint, variegated mint and even pineapple mint.

Mustard and Cress

With very little trouble and a window sill you can grow your own mustard and cress for use in sandwiches, salads and garnish. Here's how:

Buy mustard and cress seeds at your local health food shop or seed merchant, then invest in one or two shallow seed trays.

Spread some ordinary compost into the seed tray and press it down firmly. Using cress or mustard alone, or a mixture of the two, spread the seeds thickly over the compost and water them well with tepid water. Do not cover the seeds with soil.

Put the tray in a black plastic bag or place a piece of cardboard over the top, and put in a warm place for about two days.

When the seeds have germinated, remove the cover and gently water them with a fine spray. Keep the seedlings well watered, and in a warm place in good light as they grow.

After 10–14 days, the tiny plants will be ready to eat. Use the kitchen scissors to cut them near their base so that a bit of stalk and the compost is left behind. Use the mustard and/or cress immediately as it will not keep.

Hint: An area of cress approximately 4 inches square is usually sufficient to meet the needs of a small family for one day. An average-sized seed tray (8 x 14 inches) can therefore grow a six-day supply of cress. For a constant supply of this delicious and versatile plant, begin processing a new batch of seeds every six or seven days.

Parsley

No kitchen should be without it! Even if you have only one small window sill, you should devote some of it to growing parsley. It may be grown all the year round, using as large a container as you can manage. It is a beautiful, bright green with tightly curled leaves and a faint aroma. It needs plenty of watering, moderate light and regular pruning to encourage new growth and keep it shapely.

Thyme

This herb really thrives when grown in pots on a window sill. It loves warmth, direct sunlight and coarse compost, all of which seem to strengthen its aroma and flavour. I find it doesn't require very much water – just two or three times each week in summer – and needs a careful hand when trimmed. This comes naturally after a few attempts, because fresh thyme is so strong you don't need much in your food to make an impact. Try the ordinary garden thyme, or be adventurous and grow pots of lemon or caraway thyme as well. Let the plant flower in midsummer, then prune the flower heads away to keep the plant shapely.

SOUPS

I've always loved soup. It's infinitely adaptable, and is just right for *any* occasion. In the winter soup can be a meal in itself, and in the summer a cold soup is deliciously refreshing. Soup also has a very sensual appeal, with its smells, colours and flavours. Most of my favourite soups are amazingly easy and quick to make – and they rarely, if ever, go wrong. Soup is so economical, as well – any extra left over (there isn't, often!) will keep very well for the next meal. In fact, many of these soups will benefit from standing for a few hours or so before serving. Soup is probably the original convenience food – have as much of it as you want, any time you're hungry! A bottomless pot of soup on the stove is my idea of the way family kitchens *ought* to be, and it means you're always prepared for any last-minute visitors who happen to drop by unannounced.

Avocado and Dill Soup

This is a cold soup, perfect for dinner parties or summer picnics. Chill it and serve garnished with a little chopped dill or chives.

> 2 large ripe avocados
> 1 cup sour cream
> 2 tablespoons finely chopped fresh dill
> 1½ cups cold vegetable stock
> 1 teaspoon soy sauce
> salt and freshly ground black pepper to taste
> a little chopped dill or chives for garnish

Cut the avocados in half, extract the stones, scoop out the flesh and place it in a blender. Add the rest of the ingredients and blend for 1–2 minutes until smooth. Chill for 20 minutes, garnish and serve.

30 minutes to make
Good source of vitamin A, B group vitamins, potassium

Avocado and Green Chili Soup

This is a spicy chilled soup – serve garnished with chopped chilies or fresh parsley. Serves 4-6 people.

> 2 ripe avocados
> 2½ cups milk
> 1 4oz can green chilies in brine
> 1 medium onion, chopped
> salt and freshly ground black pepper to taste
> 2 tablespoons lemon juice
> 2 tablespoons sherry
> chopped chilies or fresh parsley for garnish

Cut the avocados in half, extract the stones, scoop out the flesh and puree in a blender. Add the remaining ingredients to the blender and puree until a very even consistency is reached.

Pour the mixture into a serving bowl, garnish and serve immediately. Alternatively, you can pour the soup into individual bowls and chill them.

10 minutes to make
Good source of vitamin A, B group vitamins, vitamin C, calcium

Vegetable Soup (p 58)

Bisque of Mushroom

A rich and flavoursome hot soup, best garnished with chopped chives and slivers of mushroom. Serves 6-8 people.

4 cups medium mushrooms
1 medium onion, chopped
2 cups vegetable stock or water
7 tablespoons butter or margarine
6 tablespoons plain flour
2 cups milk
1 cup heavy cream
salt and freshly ground black pepper to taste

for the garnish (optional):
chopped chives
slivers of mushroom

Set 4 of the mushrooms aside, then chop the rest finely. Place the onion with the chopped mushrooms in a saucepan and cover with vegetable stock. Cover and simmer for 30 minutes.

Meanwhile slice the 4 remaining mushrooms and brown them in a frying pan with 1 tablespoon of the butter.

Melt the rest of the butter in a pan. Slowly whisk the flour into the butter to produce a smooth mixture with no lumps. Then heat the milk and whisk it into this mixture. Bring to the boil, stirring constantly, and simmer for 2–3 minutes.

Add the mushroom and stock mixture, the sautéd mushrooms and the cream. Stir well and season to taste. Pour into bowls, garnish and serve immediately.

40 minutes to make
Good source of protein, vitamin A, B group vitamins, calcium

Bortsch Soup

This is my personal variation on the traditional rich Russian, peasant soup. It can be served hot or cold.

1lb beets
2 medium potatoes (about 4oz when mashed)
1 medium onion, chopped
2 tablespoons lemon juice
salt and freshly ground black pepper to taste
2 cups vegetable stock or water
¾ cup sour cream

for the garnish:
4 tablespoons freshly chopped chives or parsley
sour cream (optional)

Cook the beets until tender, then peel and slice. Boil the potatoes and mash them.

Put the cooled beets, mashed potato, chopped onion and lemon juice in a blender or food processor and puree. Add salt and pepper, vegetable stock and sour cream and puree for a further 1 minute.

Place the soup in the fridge and chill for 1 hour, then pour into individual serving dishes and sprinkle a little chopped chives or parsley on top to garnish, follow with a dollop of sour cream if desired.

1 hour 40 minutes to make – including chilling
Good source of vitamin A, B group vitamins, vitamin C, potassium

Broccoli Cream Soup

Another delicious cold soup, perfect for summer or winter, refreshing and nourishing.

1lb broccoli
1 large onion
2 sticks celery
1 large carrot
½ cup macaroni
1½ cups vegetable stock or water
salt and freshly ground black pepper to taste
1 cup light cream

for the garnish:
¼ cup sour cream

Chop the broccoli, onion, celery and carrot into cubes, and simmer them with the macaroni in half the vegetable stock for 15 minutes. Then place in a blender and liquidize.

Add the seasoning, the remainder of the vegetable stock and the light cream, and blend again.

Pour into a cold bowl and place in the refrigerator to chill for 1 hour. Serve with a little sour cream in the middle of each individual bowl.

1 hour 20 minutes to make – including chilling
Good source of vitamin A, B group vitamins, vitamin C

Carrot Cream Soup

Carrots like you've never tasted them before! Smooth, rich and tasty, this chilled soup should be served with a garnish of chopped parsley sprinkled on top.

1½ cups carrots, finely chopped
1 medium onion, finely chopped
2 sticks celery, finely chopped
2 tablespoons butter
2½ cups vegetable stock or water
¼ cup white rice
salt and freshly ground black pepper to taste
1 cup light cream

for the garnish:
4 tablespoons chopped fresh parsley

Sauté the carrots, onion and celery in the butter, stirring constantly for 10 minutes over a low heat. Then add the vegetable stock and rice and bring to a gentle boil.

Simmer, covered, for 20 minutes or until the carrots and rice are tender, then remove from the heat and allow to cool for 10 minutes. Season to taste.

Pour the soup and half the cream into a blender and puree until smooth.

Transfer the soup into a large serving dish and stir in the rest of the cream with a wooden spoon. Chill for 1 hour. Garnish with the parsley and serve.

1 hour 45 minutes to make – including chilling
Good source of vitamin A, vitamin C

Cream of Celery Soup

A light and creamy soup, superb for a quick, nourishing snack.

3 tablespoons butter or margarine
8 sticks celery
1 tablespoon plain flour
2 cups milk
salt and freshly ground black pepper to taste
1 cup light cream

Heat the butter in a large saucepan, then chop the celery into cubes and add to the pan. Stir over a medium heat for 5 minutes until the celery becomes translucent.

Sprinkle the flour over the celery, then gradually add the milk and seasonings. Bring to the boil, stirring constantly, then simmer over a low heat for about 20 minutes. Puree the soup. Finally stir in the cream and gently reheat before serving.

35 minutes to make
Good source of protein, vitamin A, B group vitamins, calcium

Cream of Tomato Soup

Freshness is the essence of this soup, since it must be served as soon as it has been made. You've never tasted tomato soup so good!

1½lb ripe tomatoes, quartered
1 large onion, chopped
2 sticks celery, chopped
½ cup vegetable stock or water
2 tablespoons butter or margarine
1½ tablespoons plain flour
2 cups milk
½ cup heavy cream
salt and freshly ground black pepper to taste

Place the vegetables and stock in a large saucepan and simmer them gently for about 15 minutes, until very soft. Then either sieve the mixture, or puree in a blender and sieve afterwards to remove any pulp or seeds.

Melt the butter in a saucepan. Sprinkle the flour over the butter and whisk together until a very smooth paste is formed. Heat the milk and gradually add it to the paste, beating after each addition to make a smooth sauce. Simmer gently for 4–5 minutes.

Add the cream and seasoning to the sauce and, just before serving, combine the sauce with the pureed vegetables and mix thoroughly. Serve immediately, otherwise the soup may separate or curdle.

40 minutes to make
Good source of vitamin A, vitamin C, calcium

Delicious Watercress Soup

A hot soup for those misty autumn days, best served garnished with chives.

4 tablespoons butter or margarine
2 medium onions, chopped
1 clove garlic, crushed
2 medium potatoes, cubed
2 bunches watercress, chopped
2¼ cups vegetable stock or water
salt and freshly ground black pepper to taste
1½ cups milk
½ cup light cream
2 egg yolks, beaten

for the garnish (optional):
chives

Heat the butter in a large saucepan and lightly fry the onions and garlic for 2–3 minutes. Then add the potatoes and watercress and sauté them gently for 5 minutes, covered.

Add the vegetable stock to the pan, cover and leave to simmer for 15 minutes. Cool, and puree in a blender.

Pour the mixture back into the pan and add the seasoning. Mix in the milk, cream and egg yolks, heat gently for a few minutes to cook the egg yolks, then serve.

1 hour to make
Good source of vitamin A, vitamin C

French Carrot Soup

A delightful variation on a traditional favourite, this soup can be served hot, but may also be chilled and served cold with a spoonful of heavy cream stirred into each serving. For 4–6 people.

4 tablespoons butter or margarine
1 large onion, chopped
2 cloves garlic, crushed
2 medium potatoes, chopped
2½ cups carrots, shredded
2¼ cups vegetable stock or water
1 teaspoon sugar
¼ teaspoon ground nutmeg
salt and freshly ground black pepper to taste
4 teaspoons heavy cream (optional for cold soup)

Melt the butter in a large saucepan and sauté the onion and garlic in it. Add the potatoes and carrots

and stir-fry for 4–5 minutes. Then add the vegetable stock, cover the pan and simmer for 30 minutes until the vegetables are tender.

Puree the vegetables in a blender. Return them to the saucepan and add the sugar, nutmeg, salt and pepper. Stir well. Add a little extra vegetable stock or water if you want a thinner soup.

Serve the soup hot by bringing it back to a simmer when required. Alternatively, chill in the refrigerator.

50 minutes to make
Good source of vitamin A, B group vitamins, vitamin C, potassium

Gazpacho

A simple, quick and delicious cold soup, this is my version of the traditional Spanish soup which is best eaten with fresh, crusty bread. Add more garlic if you can take it!

1lb ripe tomatoes
1 green pepper
1 cucumber
1 medium onion
1 clove garlic, crushed
1 egg
2 tablespoons wine vinegar or lemon juice
4 tablespoons olive oil
1 cup tomato juice
salt and freshly ground black pepper to taste

Skin the tomatoes by plunging them into boiling water, leave them for 1–2 minutes, then plunge them into cold water and peel off the skins. Then place them in a blender.

Remove the seeds from the pepper, chop it coarsely and add to the tomatoes.

Peel and chop the cucumber and onion, and add, with the garlic and egg, to the ingredients in the blender.

Measure the remaining ingredients into the blender. Cover and liquidize thoroughly. Add a little cold water to thin the mixture if necessary. Pour the soup into a chilled bowl and serve immediately.

20 minutes to make
Good source of vitamin A, vitamin C

Lentil Soup

A gorgeous, nourishing soup for the thick of winter, makes enough for 4–6 people.

1 medium onion, chopped
2 tablespoons vegetable oil
1 clove garlic, crushed
1 cup carrots, chopped
2 sticks celery, chopped
½ cup lentils
1 bay leaf
1 tablespoon freshly chopped parsley
salt and freshly ground black pepper to taste
2¼ cups vegetable stock or water

Heat the oil in a very large saucepan and gently sauté the garlic and onion. Add the carrots and celery and cook, stirring frequently, for 10 minutes.

Wash the lentils twice in cold water. Drain them and add to the pan. Add the bay leaf, parsley, salt and pepper and stir well.

Pour in the vegetable stock, cover the pan and simmer the soup for 1½ hours, until the lentils are very soft. Add a little extra stock or water if necessary.

1 hour 45 minutes to make
Good source of vitamin A, vitamin C

Minestrone

Another all-time favourite, this soup takes a little time to prepare, but it's well worth it. Served with a green salad and crusty bread, it makes a meal on its own.

½ cup dried flageolet, haricot or white kidney beans, soaked overnight
1 tablespoon olive oil
2 medium onions, chopped
2 cloves garlic, crushed
1 teaspoon dried parsley
1 teaspoon dried basil
2 zucchini, chopped
1 cup hard white cabbage, chopped
1 medium turnip, chopped
2 carrots, chopped
2 medium potatoes, chopped
3 sticks celery, chopped
4 tomatoes
1 tablespoon tomato paste
2 cups water
½ cup macaroni
salt and freshly ground black pepper to taste
½ cup Parmesan cheese, grated

Drain the beans and rinse. Boil fast for 10 minutes, then turn down the heat and simmer gently for 50–60 minutes.

Heat the oil in a very large saucepan and sauté the onion and garlic. Add the herbs and continue to sauté.

Add the prepared vegetables to the saucepan and stir over a medium heat for about 5 minutes. Peel the tomatoes (plunge them into boiling water for 1–2 minutes, then into cold water, and remove the skins). Chop the tomatoes finely, removing the larger seeds. Add the tomatoes and the tomato paste to the vegetable mix and cover all with the water. Put a lid on the pan and simmer slowly for 45–60 minutes, until the vegetables are tender.

Add the macaroni and the cooked beans to the soup, with a little extra water if necessary, and cook for another 15 minutes, stirring well. Season with salt and pepper. Ladle into soup bowls and sprinkle with a little Parmesan cheese.

1 hour 30 minutes to make
Good source of vitamin A, B group vitamins, vitamin C, potassium

Parsley, Celery and Green Pea Soup

A beautiful and substantial soup. If you like a really thick texture, remove half of the soup halfway through cooking and puree in a blender, then return it to the pot.

> 1 cup split green peas
> 2 tablespoons butter or margarine
> 1 medium onion, chopped
> 4 sticks celery, chopped
> 2 carrots, chopped
> 3 tablespoons chopped fresh parsley plus extra for garnish
> 1 bay leaf
> 2¼ cups vegetable stock or water
> salt and freshly ground black pepper to taste

Wash the peas and soak them either overnight in cold water or in hot water for 1 hour. Drain them and set to one side.

In a large saucepan, melt the butter and sauté the onion for 3–4 minutes, then add the celery and carrots and cook over a medium heat until lightly browned.

Add the drained peas, parsley and bay leaves. Mix well. Add the vegetable stock and stir well.

Cover the pan, bring to the boil, and simmer for 1 1½ hours until the peas are really tender. Stir the soup occasionally, and add more water or stock if desired. Season to taste and serve immediately, with a little chopped parsley sprinkled on top.

1 hour 45 minutes to make
Good source of protein, vitamin A, B group vitamins, vitamin C

Pasta Flageolet Soup

> ½ cup dried white beans (flageolet, haricot, or soy) soaked for several hours or ready cooked
> 2 cups vegetable stock or water
> 3 sticks celery, chopped
> 1 medium onion, chopped
> 1 carrot, chopped
> 1 16oz can chopped tomatoes
> salt and freshly ground black pepper to taste
> 1 teaspoon chopped fresh herbs (optional)
> ½ cup macaroni or broken spaghetti

Drain the beans, cover them with fresh water and bring to the boil. Boil rapidly for 10 minutes, then cover the pan and simmer for 45–55 minutes or until tender. Drain the beans and reserve the stock.

Put the celery, onion and carrot in a large pan together with the tomatoes, beans and 1 cup of the stock and stir well. Add the salt and pepper and cook the mixture, covered, for a further 45 minutes.

Remove half of the mixture and puree in a blender, then return it to the pan, stir well and leave it on the heat. At this point add the fresh herbs and a little extra stock or water if desired.

In a separate pan cook the pasta in plenty of boiling, salted water until tender, then drain and set aside.

Place a small serving of the cooked pasta in each of the serving bowls, pour the hot soup over it and serve immediately.

2 hours 30 minutes to make
Good source of vitamin A, B group vitamins, vitamin C, potassium

Potato and Carrot Bortsch

This variation on classic Bortsch may be served hot or cold.

> 1½ cups beets, diced
> 1 medium potato, diced
> ½ cup carrots, diced
> 1 cup water
> 1 tablespoon butter or margarine
> 1 medium onion, finely chopped
> 1 stick celery, chopped
> 1 cup cabbage, shredded
> 1 16oz can chopped tomatoes
> 1 teaspoon dill weed to taste
> salt and freshly ground black pepper to taste
> ½ cup light cream
> 1 cup sour cream

Peel and finely dice the beets, potatoes and carrots and place them in a saucepan with the water. Bring to the boil and simmer, covered, until the vegetables are tender.

Melt the butter in a frying pan and sauté the onions, celery and cabbage.

Add the sauté to the vegetables in the saucepan. Add the tomatoes and dill weed and simmer the mixture for a further 15 minutes. Season to taste.

Just before serving, gradually add the light cream to the soup, stirring constantly. Place a dollop of sour cream in each serving bowl and ladle the soup on top.

45 minutes to make – unchilled
Good source of vitamin A, vitamin C, potassium

Sweet Corn Noodle Soup

Simple to make, delicious to eat, this hot soup is warming and filling on a winter's night.

1 quart vegetable stock or water
½ cup noodles (ribbon or flat, broken)
2 cups fresh sweet corn kernels
½ cup celery, chopped
2 hard-boiled eggs, chopped
½ teaspoon turmeric
salt and freshly ground black pepper to taste

Bring the vegetable stock to the boil. Add the noodles and the sweet corn and boil for 5 minutes. Add the celery, chopped eggs and turmeric, stir well, reduce the heat and cook for a further 10 minutes. Season to taste. Serve immediately.

25 minutes to make
Good source of vitamin A

Turnip, Carrot and Split-Pea Soup

A real country soup, best eaten with lashings of hot buttered brown bread.

¾ cup split dried peas
2 tablespoons butter or margarine
1 medium onion, chopped
1 cup carrots, chopped
1 cup turnip, chopped
2–3 cups vegetable stock or water
salt and freshly ground black pepper to taste

Wash the peas and soak them overnight in cold water, or in hot water for 1 hour. Drain them and set to one side.

Heat the butter in a saucepan and sauté the onion until light brown. Add the carrots and turnip and continue cooking for 5 minutes. Add the peas and the vegetable stock, and stir well.

Cover the pan, bring to the boil and simmer for 1–1½ hours until the peas are really tender. Stir the soup occasionally and add a little water if necessary. Season to taste, and serve.

2 hours to make
Good source of vitamin A, vitamin C

Vegetable Soup

Everyone has their own favourite vegetable soup, and this is mine – try it and it could become yours too! Serves plenty.

2 tablespoons vegetable oil
1 large onion, chopped
2 leeks, sliced
3 sticks celery, chopped
1 clove garlic, crushed
4 medium carrots, sliced
1 cup cabbage, shredded
2 medium potatoes, chopped
1 teaspoon chopped fresh thyme
1 teaspoon chopped fresh rosemary
2 tablespoons chopped fresh parsley
2½ cups vegetable stock or water (2 cups if using canned tomatoes)
8 medium tomatoes or 1 16oz can chopped tomatoes
salt and freshly ground black pepper to taste

Heat the oil in a large saucepan and sauté the onion, leeks, celery and garlic for 5 minutes.

Add the carrots, cabbage and potatoes and stir well. Add the herbs. Cover with vegetable stock and simmer, with the lid on, for about 1 hour. Stir occasionally, and add more liquid if necessary.

If you are using fresh tomatoes, sit them on top of the vegetables for a minute or two, until their skins peel away easily. Then stir the skinned tomatoes into the soup. If you are using canned tomatoes, add to the soup and stir well.

Season the soup with salt and pepper and serve piping hot.

1 hour 15 minutes to make
Good source of protein, vitamin A, B group vitamins, vitamin C

Omelette (p 65)

Vichyssoise

An elegantly simple cold soup, stunning at dinner parties where I usually serve it garnished with chopped chives. In the winter you can serve it hot.

4 tablespoons vegetable oil
1 medium onion, chopped
4 leeks, thinly sliced
2 medium potatoes, chopped
2½ cups vegetable stock
1 cup cream
½ cup milk
2 tablespoons soy sauce (optional)
salt and freshly ground black pepper to taste

for the garnish:
chopped chives

Heat the oil in a large saucepan and sauté the onion, leeks and potatoes for 5 minutes, until the onions are translucent.

Cover the vegetables with stock, and simmer them for about 15–20 minutes until the potatoes are tender.

Transfer the cooked vegetables and liquid to a blender and puree, slowly adding the cream, milk, soy sauce, salt and pepper.

Pour the soup into a serving tureen and chill for 1 hour. Serve with a garnish of chopped chives.

1 hour 30 minutes to make – including chilling
Good source of vitamin A, vitamin C

Wine and Vegetable Soup

An unusual and sophisticated soup, perfect for late evening parties or celebrations.

4 large potatoes
2½ cups vegetable stock or water
2 tablespoons butter or margarine
1 clove garlic, crushed
1 large onion, chopped
2 sticks celery, chopped
2 carrots, chopped
2 teaspoons chopped fresh thyme and/or basil
1 tablespoon olive oil
½ cup white wine
1–2 tablespoons soy sauce, to taste

Peel and cube the potatoes and boil them in the stock for 15 minutes, until they are tender.

In a large saucepan, melt the butter and sauté the garlic and onion. Add the celery, carrots and herbs.

Add the olive oil, potatoes and stock. Stir well, cover and simmer for 20 minutes.

Pour in the wine and the soy sauce, stir again, cover and simmer for a further 20 minutes, adding extra vegetable stock or water if necessary. Serve piping hot.

1 hour to make
Good source of vitamin A, B group vitamins, vitamin C

SNACKS, APPETIZERS AND LIGHT DISHES

Most of these recipes are extremely quick to prepare, and are suitable for use either as appetizers before the main course or as fast meals in themselves. Since they're so easy to make, most of them can be made by any member of the family.

Cheddar Cheese Balls

Makes 8 small balls, enough to serve as an appetizer for 4 people.

4 tablespoons plain flour
1 cup Cheddar cheese, grated
salt and freshly ground black pepper to taste
1 egg white
oil for frying

Mix the flour, cheese, salt and pepper in a bowl. In another bowl, beat the egg white until firm. Fold the flour and cheese mixture into the beaten egg white.

Shape this mixture into little balls and drop into very hot oil. Fry until golden brown, then serve immediately.

15 minutes to make
Good source of calcium

Cheese and Caper Dip

Try slivers of carrot, small stems of cauliflower, spring onions or other raw vegetables with this dip, or use with potato crisps or corn chips as a party dip.

4oz cottage cheese
2 tablespoons chopped capers
1 teaspoon caraway seeds
½ cup sour cream
1 tablespoon diced onion or spring onion
freshly ground black pepper to taste

In a mixing bowl combine all the ingredients and mix with a fork until everything is very well distributed. If the mixture is too thick for dipping, add a little milk.

Transfer into a pretty bowl and serve.

5 minutes to make

Corn Bread

This tasty bread can be served hot or cold, and is great with soups and salads.

½ cup self-rising flour
2 cups corn meal
½ teaspoon salt
½ teaspoon sugar
¾ teaspoon baking powder
3 eggs
1 cup + 2 tablespoons milk
6 tablespoons butter or margarine

Pre-heat the oven to 400°F and grease an 8 inch square baking tin. Mix the dry ingredients together in a mixing bowl.

Beat the eggs and milk together, pour into the dry mix and stir thoroughly.

Melt the butter and pour it over the mixture. Stir well.

Pour into the prepared tin and bake for 20 minutes.

30 minutes to make
Good source of vitamin A, B group vitamins, calcium

Corn Bread Mexican Style

Serve warm with butter or margarine.

2 eggs
4 tablespoons vegetable oil
2 4oz cans green chilies in brine
4 medium ears sweet corn or 1 12oz can sweet corn, drained
½ cup sour cream
1 cup corn meal
2 ½ teaspoons baking powder
1 cup Cheddar cheese, grated

Pre-heat the oven to 350°F and lightly grease and flour an 8 inch round baking pan. Beat the eggs and oil together in a large bowl until they are well blended.

Drain and chop the chilies and trim the corn away from the cob. Add the chilies, sweet corn and sour cream to the egg and oil mixture. Stir well.

Mix the corn meal and baking powder together and add to the batter. Add most of the cheese to the batter, but save enough to sprinkle on top.

Give the batter a very good stir and pour it into the baking pan. Sprinkle the remainder of the cheese on top and bake for 35–40 minutes, until a knife or piece of raw spaghetti inserted into it comes out clean.

1 hour 15 minutes to make
Good source of protein, vitamin A,. B group vitamins, calcium

Devilled Eggs

I learned to make these as a kid, and was always asked to make them whenever my parents had a dinner party.

6 eggs
5 tablespoons mayonnaise
1 tablespoon pickle relish
1 tablespoon mild mustard

for the garnish:
paprika or chopped gherkin
lettuce leaves (optional)

Hard-boil the eggs (about 10–12 minutes), then shell them and slice them in half lengthways.

Scoop out the yolks, mash, and combine them in a mixing bowl with all the other ingredients.

When blended thoroughly, spoon the mixture into the egg white halves. Garnish, and serve on a bed of lettuce.

20 minutes to make
Good source of protein, B group vitamins

Egg Salad Sandwich Spread

Use this spread in sandwiches, on crackers, as a filling for baked potatoes, in a salad or to fill an avocado.

3 eggs
2 sticks celery
1 tablespoon pickle relish
4 tablespoons mayonnaise
1 tablespoon mild mustard

Hard-boil the eggs (for about 10–12 minutes). Allow them to cool, then peel and chop them finely.

Chop the celery finely. Combine the eggs and celery in a mixing bowl.

Add the pickle relish, mayonnaise and mustard and mix well.

15 minutes to make
Good source of B group vitamins

Garlic Bread

1 long stick French bread
6 tablespoons butter or margarine
2 cloves garlic, crushed (or more to taste)
1 teaspoon chopped fresh parsley (optional)

Pre-heat the oven to 350°F. Make diagonal cuts all along the French stick at about 1 inch intervals: cut well into the bread but don't slice it all the way through.

Melt the butter in a small pan and stir in the garlic and parsley. Brush the garlic butter on each side of each cut in the bread until it is all used up.

Wrap the whole French stick in baking foil and heat it through for 10 minutes. Unwrap and serve immediately.

15 minutes to make
Good source of vitamin A

Guacamole (p 64), Refried Bean Dip (p 67) and Corn Fritters (p 96)

Guacamole

This addictive Mexican dip/spread should be served with corn chips or toast – enough for 6–8 people.

2–3 large ripe avocados
3–4 tablespoons fresh lemon juice or lime juice (or more to taste)
1–2 4oz cans green chilies in brine
½ clove garlic, crushed (optional)
salt to taste

Slice the avocados in half lengthways and remove the stones. Scoop out the avocado pulp and mash it in a mixing bowl. Pour the lemon juice over the mashed avocado.

Drain and finely chop the chilies and garlic, if desired. Add them, with the salt, to the avocado. Stir the mixture very well to make a smooth paste.

15 minutes to make
Good source of vitamin A, vitamin C

Herb Bread

1 long stick French bread
6 tablespoons butter or margarine
4 teaspoons chopped fresh parsley
3 teaspoons chopped fresh basil or oregano or other fresh herbs

Pre-heat the oven to 350°F. Slice the French stick along its length, but don't cut all the way through.

Melt the butter in a small pan and stir in the herbs. Brush this mixture all along the inside of each cut in the bread until it is all used up.

Wrap the whole French stick in foil and bake for 10 minutes. Serve immediately.

15 minutes to make

Hummus

3 cups cooked chick peas
¼ cup water
¼ cup lemon juice
4 cloves garlic, finely chopped
½ teaspoon salt
3 tablespoons tahini
2 tablespoons fresh parsley, chopped
3 tablespoons olive oil

Place all ingredients in a blender or food processor and puree to a fine consistency, adding a little more liquid as necessary to make a smooth, light paste. Serve immediately with salad and pita bread.

5 minutes to make
Good source of iron

Irish Brown Bread

4 cups wholewheat flour
2 cups all-purpose white flour
½ cup rolled oats
1 teaspoon salt
1½ teaspoons baking soda
1½ cups buttermilk

Pre-heat the oven to 425°F and lightly grease a baking tray. Mix all the dry ingredients together in a large mixing bowl.

Make a well in the centre of this mixture and add enough buttermilk to make a soft dough. Mix the dough using a wooden spoon at first, then your hands.

Form the dough into one large or four small balls and flatten to 2 inches thick on the baking tray. Slice a cross in the top of each flattened loaf to a depth of ¾ inch. The cross should mark nearly the whole surface of the loaf.

Bake for 25 minutes, then reduce the oven temperature to 350°F and bake for a further 10 minutes. Place on a wire rack until cool.

50 minutes to make
Good source of protein, B group vitamins, calcium

Mexican Corn Bread

1½ cups yellow corn meal
1 cup wholewheat pastry flour
1 tablespoon baking powder
1 teaspoon salt
1 egg
1 cup milk
¾ cup canned creamed sweet corn
¼ cup honey or fructose
1 4oz can green chilies in brine
4 tablespoons butter or margarine
½ cup onion, chopped
1 cup mild Cheddar or Edam cheese, grated

Pre-heat the oven to 350°F and grease an 8 × 8 inch tin. Mix all the dry ingredients together in a large bowl.

Beat the egg and milk together in a jug and add the creamed corn and the honey. Set this mixture aside.

Drain and chop the chilies. Melt the butter in a frying pan and sauté the onion and chilies in it until the onion is transparent.

Pour the egg and milk mixture then the sauté into the dry ingredients in the large bowl. Add the cheese and stir the whole mixture until it is just mixed. Pour the batter into the greased pan and bake for 35–40 minutes. Allow to cool before serving.

50 minutes to make
Good source of protein, vitamin A, B group vitamins, vitamin C

Omelette

This simple recipe is the basis for countless variations according to your individual taste. Serves 1 person.

> *2 eggs*
> *salt and freshly ground black pepper to taste*
> *1 tablespoon butter or margarine*
> *filling of your choice (grated cheese, hot chopped fried onion, hot cooked spinach etc)*

Beat the eggs together in a mixing bowl until they froth. Season to taste.

Melt the butter in a 6 inch frying pan and keep it over a medium to high heat. Pour the eggs into the hot pan and leave it undisturbed while it cooks.

When the upper surface begins to bubble, lift the cooked edges and allow the uncooked egg to run underneath. When lightly browned underneath, flip it over like a pancake and lightly brown it on the other side.

Remove the omelette from the pan with the help of a spatula, and turn it on to a hot dish. Fold it in half if it is to be eaten plain; otherwise place the filling (cheese, onion, spinach, fried chopped mushrooms, etc) on one half and fold the other half of the omelette over it. Serve immediately.

5 minutes to make

Turnovers

A meal in themselves, especially with a nice green salad.

> *2 medium potatoes*
> *12oz shortcrust pastry (enough for 2 9" pie pans)*
> *2 medium onions*
> *2 tablespoons butter or margarine*
> *half a 4½oz packet TVP mince or 4 vegetable burgers, crumbled*
> *salt and freshly ground black pepper to taste*

Pre-heat the oven to 350°F. Cut the potatoes into cubes and parboil for 5 minutes, until slightly tender but not soft.

Roll out the pastry into a number of 9 inch rounds and set aside.

Chop the onions and sauté them in the butter in a frying pan until light brown. Add the potatoes and the crumbled vegetable burgers to the sauté and cook for 5 minutes, stirring frequently.

Spoon the mixture into the centre of one half of each round of pastry. Sprinkle a little salt and pepper over the stuffing, then fold the pastry over the filling and press the edges together using a fork.

Cut one or two small slashes in each turnover and bake on a greased baking sheet for 45 minutes until lightly golden in colour.

1 hour to make
Good source of protein

Pizza Bread

A quick and tasty snack that young people love to make for themselves.

> *4 slices wholewheat bread*
> *1–2 teaspoons oregano*
> *1–2 cloves garlic, crushed*
> *4 teaspoons olive oil*
> *2 tablespoons tomato paste*
> *1 cup Cheddar cheese, grated*

Toast the bread lightly. Sprinkle with the oregano, garlic and oil. Spread the toast with the tomato paste, then add the cheese.

Place the pizzas under a hot grill until the cheese is bubbly and lightly golden. Serve immediately with a little extra oregano sprinkled on top if desired.

10 minutes to make
Good source of protein, B group vitamins, calcium

Pressed Egg and Tomato

8 eggs
2 tablespoons mayonnaise
1 iceberg lettuce
4 fresh tomatoes
¼ to ½ cup salad dressing

Place the eggs in boiling water for 10 minutes until they are hard-boiled. Peel them and mash them well together with the mayonnaise, then press the mashed eggs into a greased, tall, straight glass (1 cup size) and chill in the refrigerator for at least 30 minutes.

Shred the lettuce and arrange it on serving plates. Place the sliced tomatoes over the lettuce.

Take the chilled egg from the refrigerator and run a knife round the inside of the glass to loosen the egg. Tip it out carefully and cut ¾–1 inch slices from it.

Place the egg slices over the tomatoes and cover the salad with the dressing of your choice.

40 minutes to make
Good source of protein, vitamin A, vitamin C, iron

Refried Bean Dip

Serve with corn chips or toast.

1 4oz can green chilies in brine
¼ cup Cheddar cheese, grated
1 small onion, chopped
4 teaspoons ready bought taco sauce
1 16oz can refried beans (or make your own: see page 141)

Drain and chop the chilies. Mix all the ingredients together in a saucepan and cook over a low heat until the cheese starts to melt. Serve immediately.

10 minutes to make
Good source of protein, vitamin C, calcium

Sauerkraut and Veggy Dogs

Great with mashed potatoes, boiled potatoes or potato pancakes, and a touch of apple sauce.

2 tablespoons vegetable oil
1 medium onion, sliced
salt and freshly ground black pepper to taste
4 cups sauerkraut (see page 41)
6 vegetable sausages
1 teaspoon caraway seeds
½ cup water

Heat the oil and sauté the onion until tender. Stir in the salt and pepper and add this mixture to the sauerkraut in a large saucepan.

Add the uncooked sausages and the caraway seeds and stir gently. Add the water, cover the pan and simmer for 15–20 minutes.

Alternatively, pre-heat the oven to 350°F and pour the mixture into a greased casserole dish. Bake, covered, for 30 minutes, adding extra water if necessary towards the end of the cooking time.

40 minutes to make
Good source of vitamin C, iron

Sausage Rolls

A great quick lunch, served with a salad.

6oz puff pastry
8 vegetable sausages (about 3 inches long), cooked
1 egg, beaten

Pre-heat the oven to 425°F. Roll the puff pastry into a thin rectangle 24 × 5 inches and cut into 8 long, thin strips, 3 × 5 inches. This can be varied according to the size of the sausage.

Place a sausage across the centre of each strip of pastry and wrap the pastry round the sausage, pinching the ends of the pastry together with a moist fork.

Cut the prepared sausage rolls in half and brush the pastry with the beaten egg.

Bake for 15–20 minutes on a greased baking tray. Cool on a wire rack, or serve immediately.

40 minutes to make

Scrambled Eggs

Serves 1 person.

2 eggs
salt and freshly ground black pepper to taste
2 tablespoons butter or margarine

Beat the eggs in a bowl and add the seasoning. In a frying pan, heat the butter over a medium high heat until it browns slightly.

Pour the beaten eggs into the frying pan. Scramble with a fork for a few seconds until cooked but still soft, and serve immediately.

5 minutes to make
Good source of protein, vitamin A, B group vitamins

Shirred Eggs

Serve with toast. Serves 1.

1 teaspoon butter or margarine
2 eggs

Pre-heat the oven to 350°F.

Melt the butter in a small, individual size heat-proof dish. Crack the eggs into the dish and bake for 10–15 minutes. The whites of the eggs should be cooked through, but not hard. Serve immediately.

15 minutes to make
Good source of protein, B group vitamins

Sloppy Joes

Serve hot over muffins, in toasted soft rolls (like hamburger buns) or over rice with green salad. Serves 2.

1 medium onion, chopped
2 tablespoons butter or margarine
4 vegetable burgers
1 small red or green or yellow pepper, sliced (optional)
½ cup mushrooms, sliced
4 tablespoons tomato ketchup
salt and freshly ground black pepper to taste

Sauté the onion in the butter until light brown. Crumble the burgers and add them to the sauté, stirring often.

Add the sliced pepper and mushrooms and continue stirring.

Add the ketchup, salt and pepper and cook the mixture, uncovered, for 5 minutes, stirring occasionally.

20 minutes to make
Good source of protein, vitamin C

Stilton Pâté

Serve with raw vegetables, crackers or toast.

4oz Stilton cheese
2 tablespoons lemon juice
3oz cream cheese
2 teaspoons chopped fresh chives
½ teaspoon paprika

Blend the Stilton, lemon juice and cream cheese together in a bowl.

Add the chives and the paprika. Blend well.
Keep chilled until ready to serve.

10 minutes to make

Stuffed Curried Eggs

Serve cold with salads.

10 eggs
½ cup mayonnaise
1 tablespoon curry powder
2 teaspoons soy sauce
1 tablespoon relish
1 tablespoon chopped fresh parsley
salt and freshly ground black pepper to taste

Hard-boil the eggs for about 10 minutes in boiling water. Peel the eggs and slice them in half lengthways. Remove the yolks and put them in a mixing bowl.

Mix the remaining ingredients in with the egg yolks and beat the mixture well to make a smooth paste.

Stuff the egg whites generously with the mixture, so that the filling stands up in a little mound on top.

25 minutes to make
Good source of vitamin A, B group vitamins, iron

Tomato and Potato Mousse

This makes a delicious savoury starter for a dinner party or a late night snack. You can be as elaborate as you like with the decoration (try small slivers of tomato and sprigs of dill, parsley, mint or basil), or serve with a small quantity of béchamel sauce (see page 143).

2lb tomatoes
1 tablespoons sugar
salt and freshly ground black pepper to taste
1 tablespoon lemon juice
3 teaspoons agar-agar flakes (vegetable gelatine)
½ cup hot water
1 cup cold potato puree
1 cup heavy cream

Skin the tomatoes and remove the seeds. Press the tomatoes in a saucepan to squeeze out a little of their juice and begin to cook them to a puree.

Add the sugar, salt, pepper and lemon juice to the tomatoes and continue cooking. Meanwhile, dissolve the agar-agar in the hot water and then add it to the tomatoes. Simmer for 2–3 minutes.

Add the potato puree to the tomato and gently fold together. Remove the mixture from the heat and allow it to cool. Taste it at this point, and add more seasoning if desired.

Lightly whip the cream and, when the puree is cool, blend the cream in with it. Pour the mixture into a lightly buttered 2 cup mould and allow to chill until firm (1–1½ hours). To serve, carefully turn the mousse onto a colourful serving plate and serve immediately.

2 hours to make
Good source of vitamin A, vitamin C

Welsh Rarebit

Serve poured over toast, mashed potatoes, baked potatoes or rice and green vegetables.

2 cups Cheddar cheese
3 tablespoons cream
salt and freshly ground black pepper to taste
½ teaspoon mild mustard
Worcestershire sauce to taste

Melt the cheese in the top of a double boiler. Gradually add the cream, stirring the mixture constantly. Add the salt, pepper, mustard and Worcestershire sauce and continue to stir until the mixture is very smooth and very hot. Serve immediately.

15 minutes to make
Good source of protein, calcium

Yorkshire Pudding

1 egg
1 cup milk and water mixed
½ cup plain flour
pinch of salt
2 tablespoons vegetable suet

Pre-heat the oven to 425°F. Beat the egg and milk together in a mixing bowl until light and frothy.

Sift the flour and salt into a bowl, make a well in the centre and pour in a little of the milk. Beat them together, gradually adding the rest of the milk to make a smooth batter.

Heat the vegetable suet in the oven in an 11 × 7 inch deep tin, or in 12 individual tartlet tins, for 2–3 minutes. Then pour the batter into the hot fat and bake for 20–25 minutes if you are making a single large pudding, 15–20 minutes if individual size.

35 minutes to make

SALADS

Being an American, I'm big on salads. We have them all the year round, almost every day – and with tempting recipes like these, you'll see why!

Beet and Celery Salad

1 egg
2 medium beets
3 sticks celery
4 tablespoons olive oil
2 tablespoons vinegar or lemon juice
salt and freshly ground black pepper to taste

garnish:
lettuce leaves
chopped chives (optional)

Hard-boil the egg, then peel and slice it. Wash the beets but leave the 'tail' attached. Boil rapidly for 45 minutes, until tender, then peel and chop into small cubes. Chop the celery.

Combine the vegetables in a wooden bowl, then mix the oil, vinegar, salt and pepper and pour the dressing over the salad.

Toss gently and serve on a bed of lettuce, topped with slices of hard-boiled egg and chopped chives.

50 minutes to make
Good source of B group vitamins, vitamin C

Beet and Onion Salad

Serve with cottage cheese and lettuce.

6 medium beets
3–4 bunches scallions
½ cup sour cream
1 teaspoon mild mustard
1 tablespoon lemon juice
1 tablespoon freshly chopped parsley or dill
salt and freshly ground black pepper to taste

Wash the beets but leave the 'tail' attached. Boil rapidly for 45 minutes, until tender, then peel and cut into long, thin strips. Place the strips in a mixing bowl.

Trim and thinly slice the scallions and add them to the beets. Stir well.

Mix together the sour cream, mustard, lemon juice and seasoning in a cup, and pour it over the onion and beet mixture. Stir well and serve immediately or allow to chill.

50 minutes to make
Good source of vitamin A, vitamin C

Cabbage and Caraway Seed Salad

It helps to have a food processor for this recipe to make sure the cabbage is very finely shredded.

1 small white cabbage (12oz–1lb), shredded
½ small onion, finely chopped
2 tablespoons lemon juice
½ cup mayonnaise
1 tablespoon caraway seeds
salt to taste

Mix all the ingredients together in a large salad bowl. Sprinkle with the salt and serve immediately.

10 minutes to make
Good source of vitamin C

Caesar Salad

1 clove garlic, crushed
1 teaspoon mild mustard
1 tablespoon lemon juice
1 tablespoon vinegar
4 tablespoons olive oil
1 egg
2 tablespoons grated Parmesan cheese
salt and freshly ground black pepper to taste
1 crisp lettuce
2 tomatoes, quartered (optional)
1 teaspoon capers (optional)

Rub the garlic around the inside of a large wooden bowl for flavour. Then mix the garlic with the mustard, lemon juice, vinegar, oil and egg in a jug. Whisk together. Add the cheese, salt and pepper, and whisk again.

Break the lettuce into the bowl, and add the tomatoes and capers if desired. Pour the dressing over the salad and mix well.

15 minutes to make
Good source of vitamin A, B group vitamins, vitamin C

Celeriac Salad

A simple but classic salad for that gourmet touch, great as a side dish at dinner parties. Do make sure that the celeriac is tossed in the dressing as soon as possible, or it will discolour.

1lb celeriac roots
½ cup mayonnaise
1 tablespoon lemon juice
1 teaspoon mild mustard

Peel and wash the celeriac roots. Cut into very thin, almost transparent, strips or shred the roots coarsely. Mix the mayonnaise, lemon juice and mustard together in a serving bowl. Add the shredded celeriac and stir very well. Serve immediately or chill.

10 minutes to make

Celery and Rice Salad

Serve as a stuffing for avocados or tomatoes, or on a bed of lettuce with a sprinkling of sesame seeds. The mayonnaise needs to be quite thin – if it isn't, mix in 1–2 tablespoons of natural yoghurt or sunflower oil.

3 scallions, chopped
6 sticks celery, chopped
½ cup mayonnaise
1½ cups cooked rice
1 tablespoon chopped pickle or relish
1 tablespoon lemon juice
salt and freshly ground black pepper to taste

Mix all the ingredients together in a large bowl and serve.

10 minutes to make
Good source of vitamin A, vitamin C

Chef's Salad

A meal in itself – great when friends come round for lunch!

2 large crisp lettuces
8oz Cheddar cheese, sliced or cubed
4 medium tomatoes, quartered
6 slices vegetable luncheon 'meat' in long strips

for the dressing:
1 tablespoon vinegar
1 tablespoon lemon juice
6 tablespoons vegetable oil or olive oil
salt to taste
1 teaspoon mild mustard
1 clove garlic, crushed
1 tablespoon chopped chives
1 tablespoon chopped parsley

Wash and thoroughly dry the lettuces and break them into small pieces. Place in a large wooden bowl. Add the cheese, tomatoes and luncheon 'meat' to the lettuce. Mix the dressing ingredients together in a jug. Beat well and pour over the salad. Toss, and serve immediately.

10 minutes to make
Good source of vitamin A, vitamin C, calcium

Chick Pea Salad

Chick peas are amongst the most delicious of legumes, with a distinct nutty flavour. If cooking them yourself, do make sure that they are very soft before using them – you should be able to squash them onto the roof of your mouth with your tongue.

3 cups cooked or canned chick peas
6 sticks celery, trimmed and chopped
½ cup mayonnaise
2 tablespoons lemon juice
1 clove garlic, crushed
2 tablespoons chopped fresh parsley
1 tablespoon chopped onion or chives or scallion
salt and freshly ground black pepper to taste
1 lettuce

Mix the chick peas and celery together. In a small bowl combine the mayonnaise with the lemon juice, garlic, parsley and onion. Season to taste. Stir the dressing into the chick peas and celery.

Wash the lettuce and line a salad bowl with the leaves. Pile the chick pea salad into the centre and serve immediately.

10 minutes to make
Good source of protein, vitamin A, B group vitamins, vitamin C

Coleslaw

½ head red or green or white cabbage, shredded
1 carrot, shredded
4 tablespoons lemon juice
½ cup vegetable oil
salt and freshly ground black pepper to taste

Mix the cabbage and carrot together in a large bowl.

Stir the remaining ingredients together in a jug and pour the dressing over the salad. Stir very well and serve immediately or chill for 30–60 minutes.

10 minutes to make – unchilled
Good source of vitamin A, vitamin C

Cucumber Salad

1 large cucumber
1 tablespoon cooking salt
1 cup sour cream
1 tablespoon chopped chives or chopped onion
1 tablespoon lemon juice
3–6 sprigs fresh dill weed, chopped
1 tablespoon freshly chopped parsley
salt and freshly ground black pepper to taste

Peel and cube the cucumber. Place in a colander, cover it with the salt and leave for 30 minutes. The cucumber will 'sweat' off some of its excess juice.

Mix all the ingredients together in a large salad bowl and serve immediately, or chill for about 1 hour.

35 minutes to make – unchilled

Egg and Cheese Salad

This is a creative variation on an old favourite, and it tastes quite unlike any ordinary egg and cheese salad you've ever had before!

6 eggs
8oz Swiss cheese
1 cup sour cream
1 tablespoon lemon juice
1½ teaspoons mild mustard
1 teaspoon horseradish sauce
pinch cumin seed
salt and freshly ground black pepper to taste

to serve:
1 lettuce
1 bunch watercress
4 tomatoes, sliced

Hard-boil the eggs for 10–12 minutes. Allow them to cool, then peel and chop them and place in a salad bowl.

Cut the cheese into small cubes and add to the eggs in the salad bowl.

Mix all the remaining ingredients together except for the garnish, and then mix them with the egg and cheese. Season to taste.

Chill the mixture, or serve immediately on a bed of lettuce, surrounded by watercress and tomatoes.

25 minutes to make – unchilled
Good source of protein, vitamin A, B group vitamins, calcium

Egg and Potato Salad

2 eggs
1½lb potatoes
2 tablespoons chopped onion or chopped chives or
*   chopped scallion*
1 teaspoon mild mustard
1 tablespoon lemon juice or vinegar
½ cup mayonnaise
salt and freshly ground black pepper to taste

Hard-boil the eggs for 10–12 minutes. Allow them to cool, then peel and chop them.

Peel the potatoes and boil or steam them until tender. Allow them to cool, then cut them into small chunks.

Mix the chopped scallion with the eggs and potato in a large bowl. Stir the remaining ingredients together in a small bowl, then gently mix into the salad. Serve immediately, or chill briefly first.

30 minutes to make – unchilled
Good source of vitamin C, potassium

Four Seasons Salad

1 cup carrots, shredded
1 cup cucumber, chopped or sliced
6 sticks celery, finely chopped
1 bunch scallions, finely chopped

to serve:
1 lettuce
½ cup mayonnaise or French dressing

Mix all the vegetables together in a large salad bowl. Serve with mayonnaise or French dressing on a bed of lettuce.

10 minutes to make
Good source of vitamin A, B group vitamins, vitamin C

German Potato Salad

Serve with a selection of other salads, or chill and serve in small portions for packed lunches or picnics.

4 large potatoes, cubed
1 teaspoon mild mustard
½ cup sour cream

1 tablespoon white wine vinegar
2 tablespoons mayonnaise
salt and freshly ground black pepper to taste

Boil or steam the potatoes until they are just tender but don't fall apart. Allow them to cool, then place in a large salad bowl.

Mix the remaining ingredients together in a jug. Pour this sauce over the cooled potatoes, and stir gently until the potatoes are well coated. Serve immediately.

30 minutes to make

Lemon Coleslaw

2 cups white cabbage, shredded
juice of ½ lemon
4–5 tablespoons oil
salt to taste

Shred the cabbage and place it in a large salad bowl.

Mix the remaining ingredients together and pour them over the cabbage. Let the cabbage absorb the dressing for at least 30 minutes before serving.

40 minutes to make
Good source of vitamin C

Lemon Rice Salad

2 tablespoons chopped fresh parsley
1 tablespoon chopped onion
1½ cups cooked rice
2 tablespoons lemon juice
4 tablespoons olive oil

to serve:
lettuce

Mix all the ingredients together and serve on a bed of lettuce.

5 minutes to make

Chef's Salad (p 72)

Moroccan Carrot Salad

½ cup currants
4 seedless oranges, peeled and sliced
3 cups carrots, grated
1 medium onion, finely chopped
3 tablespoons walnuts, finely chopped
¼ teaspoon dried red pepper or paprika or cayenne
3 tablespoons olive oil
juice of 1 lemon
salt and freshly ground black pepper to taste

Measure the currants into a small bowl and cover them with warm water. Leave them to soak for 10 minutes.

Peel and thinly slice the oranges. Mix these and all the remaining ingredients together in a large salad bowl and toss gently together.

Drain the currants and add them to the salad. Stir well and chill the salad for at least 30 minutes before serving.

45 minutes to make
Good source of vitamin A, B group vitamins, vitamin C, potassium

New Potato Salad

1lb new potatoes
4 heaped tablespoons mayonnaise
1 tablespoon finely chopped celery
1 tablespoon chopped pickle or relish
1–2 tablespoons natural yoghurt or sunflower oil
salt and freshly ground black pepper to taste

for the garnish:
2 tablespoons chopped fresh parsley

Scrub the new potatoes (do not peel) and boil or steam them for about 15 minutes until tender. Drain, allow to cool then cut into quarters. Place the cooled potatoes in a large salad bowl.

In a separate bowl, mix the mayonnaise, celery, pickle and yoghurt or sunflower oil. Season to taste. Add this to the potatoes and stir gently until the potatoes are well coated.

Top the salad with the chopped parsley and serve immediately, or chill and serve with other salads.

25 minutes to make – unchilled
Good source of vitamin C

Noodle Salad

½lb noodles, uncooked
1 cup red cabbage, shredded
1 cup mushrooms, sliced
½ large cucumber or 1 small cucumber, sliced
6 tablespoons olive oil
6 tablespoons red wine vinegar
salt and freshly ground black pepper to taste

Cook the noodles and divide them into three portions. Place one portion in a large salad bowl.

Spread the shredded cabbage over these noodles. Place another portion of the cooked noodles over the cabbage.

Spread the sliced mushrooms over the noodles. Place the third portion of cooked noodles over the mushrooms. Top the salad with the cucumber.

Mix the oil, vinegar, salt and pepper together and pour over the salad. Do not toss. Serve after it has stood for 30 minutes.

50 minutes to make
Good source of B group vitamins, vitamin C

Potato Salad and Mayonnaise

Serve with a selection of salads, a quiche, or a barbecue.

1½lb potatoes
1 tablespoon chopped onion
6 sticks celery, chopped
salt and freshly ground black pepper to taste
½ cup mayonnaise
1 tablespoon lemon juice

Peel and chop the potatoes, then steam or boil them until just tender. Drain and allow to cool.

Mix the onion and celery together in a large salad bowl. Stir the remaining ingredients together in a small bowl. Add the cooled potatoes and the dressing to the salad bowl and stir gently. Serve immediately.

30 minutes to make
Good source of vitamin C

Potato Salad Vinaigrette

8 medium potatoes
4 tablespoons vinegar
6 tablespoons olive oil
1 tablespoon chopped chives
2 tablespoons chopped fresh parsley
1 sprig tarragon, chopped
salt and freshly ground black pepper to taste

Peel the potatoes and cube them. Boil, covered, for about 15 minutes until they are tender but not crumbling. Place them, still hot, in a large salad bowl.

Mix the remaining ingredients together in a jug, season to taste and pour over the potatoes. Stir gently and serve warm.

20 minutes to make
Good source of B group vitamins, vitamin C, potassium

Spinach Salad

If you grew up hating the taste of spinach, this salad is a real eye-opener! Do make sure that the spinach is new and fresh (i.e. the leaves are not too deep green in colour, and don't feel tough or leathery).

½lb fresh spinach
2 eggs
2 large tomatoes, chopped
1 mild onion, chopped
2 cloves garlic, crushed
3 tablespoons crumbled cooked vegetable 'bacon'
  (optional)
2 tablespoons lemon juice
1 tablespoon vinegar
6 tablespoons olive oil
salt and freshly ground black pepper to taste

Trim and wash the spinach, then dry it using a clean tea towel. Tear or slice the spinach leaves and put them on one side.

Hard-boil the eggs in boiling water for 10 minutes, then peel and chop them.

Mix the eggs together with the remaining ingredients in a large salad bowl, and stir gently.

Add the torn spinach to the salad, toss it well and serve immediately.

20 minutes to make
Good source of vitamin A, B group vitamins, vitamin C, potassium

Tabouli Salad

1½ cups cracked wheat (bulgur wheat)
2 cups boiling water
½ cup scallions
2–3 whole tomatoes
4 tablespoons chopped fresh parsley
2 tablespoons chopped fresh mint
juice of 1½ lemons
½ to ¾ cup olive oil
pinch of ground allspice
salt and freshly ground black pepper to taste
3 tablespoons pine nuts (optional)

Measure the cracked wheat into a large bowl and pour the boiling water over it. Stir well, and leave to sit for 15–20 minutes while you prepare the vegetables.

Chop the scallions and finely chop the tomatoes. Add them with the parsley and mint to the cracked wheat, and stir well.

Pour the lemon juice and oil over the salad, sprinkle with the spice, seasoning and pine nuts and gently toss the salad.

Chill the tabouli for 1 hour before serving, to allow the flavours to blend.

1 hour 30 minutes to make – including chilling
Good source of vitamin A, vitamin C

Tomatoes Stuffed with Cottage Cheese and Basil

4 large tomatoes
1 cup cottage cheese
2 tablespoons chopped fresh basil
3 tablespoons mayonnaise
freshly ground pepper to taste

for the garnish:
lettuce leaves

to serve:
French dressing

Slice the tops off the tomatoes and scoop out their insides. Sieve the pulp to remove the seeds.

Add the remaining ingredients to the pulp, and mix them all together.

Spoon this mixture back into the tomato shells, and serve on a bed of lettuce with French dressing.

10 minutes to make
Good source of vitamin A, vitamin C, calcium, iron

Watercress and Lettuce Salad

1 bunch watercress
1 large lettuce
4 tablespoons olive oil
2 tablespoons vinegar or lemon juice
salt and freshly ground black pepper to taste
1 tablespoon chopped onion
1 clove garlic, crushed
1 teaspoon mild mustard

Wash and trim the watercress and lettuce, and leave to drain.

Mix the remaining ingredients together in a jug. Coarsely chop the drained watercress and lettuce and place in a large salad bowl. Add the dressing, toss well and serve.

15 minutes to make

Spinach Salad (*p 77*)

MAIN COURSES

In this section you'll find most of the main course recipes I like best, ranging from quick and easy lunches to hearty casseroles, stews and stroganoffs. I've included a great variety, so you can really choose according to your mood. These have all stood the test of time, and all of them have become firm favourites not just with me, but with my family and friends too. I hope you enjoy them as much as we do.

Asparagus and Egg Casserole

This is a luxurious casserole dish which is best accompanied by a light salad or vegetable dish such as New Orleans Broad Beans (see page 138).

4 eggs
1½lb asparagus spears
4 tablespoons butter or margarine
2 tablespoons plain flour
1¾ cups vegetable stock or water
¼ cup cream
¼ teaspoon ground nutmeg (optional)
1 teaspoon chopped tarragon
salt and freshly ground black pepper to taste
½ cup Cheddar cheese, grated

Pre-heat the oven to 400°F and lightly grease a casserole dish. Place the eggs in boiling water for 10 minutes, until they are hard-boiled.

Wash and trim the asparagus. Simmer or steam it, in batches if necessary, for 4–5 minutes, depending on the thickness of the spears. Drain the asparagus when cooked.

Melt the butter in a saucepan and sprinkle the flour into it, stirring constantly to make a thick paste. In another saucepan, mix the vegetable stock and cream together and heat to a low boil.

Gradually add the stock and cream mixture to the flour paste, stirring constantly to make a creamy sauce. Add the nutmeg, tarragon, salt and pepper and continue to stir. Peel and chop the hard-boiled eggs and add them to the sauce. Stir gently and remove from the heat.

Arrange the asparagus spears in the bottom of the casserole dish and pour the sauce over them. Sprinkle the grated cheese over the sauce and bake for 15 minutes until the cheese is bubbly.

50 minutes to make
Good source of vitamin A, B group vitamins, vitamin C

Asparagus Casserole with Sour Cream

When you feel like a change, try adding the juice of one lemon to the sour cream before pouring it over the asparagus. Serve with a salad or any vegetable.

1½lb asparagus spears
salt and freshly ground black pepper to taste
1 clove garlic, crushed
2 teaspoons cornstarch
1 cup sour cream
½ cup fresh breadcrumbs
2 teaspoons chopped fresh tarragon (optional)
2 tablespoons butter or margarine

Pre-heat the oven to 375°F and lightly grease a casserole dish. Wash, trim and simmer or steam the asparagus spears, in batches if necessary, for 4–5 minutes depending on the thickness of the spears. Drain well and arrange in the casserole dish.

Sprinkle the salt, pepper and garlic over the asparagus, then stir the cornstarch into the sour cream, pour it over the asparagus and spread to the edges of the dish.

Sprinkle the breadcrumbs and tarragon over the sour cream and place small pieces of butter over the breadcrumbs. Bake for 15–20 minutes.

45 minutes to make
Good source of vitamin A, B group vitamins, vitamin C

Asparagus in Divine Sauce

1½lb asparagus spears
1 onion, chopped
4 tablespoons butter or margarine
4 tablespoons plain flour
pinch of ground nutmeg (optional)
1¾ cups vegetable stock or water
2 egg yolks
1 tablespoon lemon juice

to serve:
rice or toast (optional)

Wash and trim the asparagus, then simmer or steam, in batches if necessary, for 4–5 minutes, depending on the thickness of the spears. Drain and cover to keep hot.

Meanwhile, heat the butter in a saucepan and sauté the onion for 4–5 minutes until lightly browned. Sprinkle the flour over the sauté and stir into a thick, smooth paste. Add the nutmeg. Gradually add the vegetable stock and stir continuously to make a smooth sauce. Bring this sauce to the boil, reduce the heat and simmer for 2–3 minutes.

Remove the sauce from the heat. Beat the egg yolks and lemon juice together then gradually add to the sauce, stirring very well after each addition. Place the sauce back on the heat and gently warm through until the sauce begins to thicken again.

Arrange the hot asparagus on a platter (or on a plate of rice, or even on toast) and pour the hot sauce over the spears. Serve immediately.

20 minutes to make

Asparagus with Cheese

Serve with rice or potatoes, and a salad.

1½lb asparagus spears
2 tablespoons butter or margarine
2 tablespoons lemon juice
4 cups Gruyère or Emmenthal cheese, grated
freshly ground black pepper to taste

Pre-heat the oven to 350°F and lightly grease a casserole dish. Wash and trim the asparagus, then simmer or steam it, in batches if necessary, for 4–5 minutes depending on the thickness of the spears. Drain well, and arrange it in the casserole dish.

Place small pieces of butter on top of the asparagus and pour the lemon juice over it. Sprinkle the grated cheese over the asparagus and bake for 10 minutes. Season with pepper and serve hot.

25 minutes to make
Good source of protein, vitamin A, B group vitamins, calcium

Aubergine Caponata

This dish is best chilled for 24 hours before serving. Serve with pasta or rice, and a salad.

1 large aubergine
1 small onion
1 stick celery
1oz olives
1oz capers
2½ tablespoons olive oil
1 tablespoon chopped fresh parsley
1 tablespoon wine vinegar
2 teaspoons sugar
1 cup chopped tomatoes
1 tablespoon tomato puree

Dice the aubergine into small cubes and sprinkle generously with salt. Leave on a plate for about 20 minutes to draw out the bitterness.

While the aubergine is standing, prepare the rest of the ingredients. Chop the onion, celery, olives and capers into small pieces.

Heat the olive oil in a deep frying pan and sauté the onion and celery for about 5 minutes, until lightly browned. Now wash the salted aubergine thoroughly, drain, and add to the sauté, a few cubes at a time so the pieces do not absorb too much oil. However, add more oil if necessary.

Add the remaining ingredients, cover the pan and simmer, over a medium heat, for 30 minutes.

55 minutes to make
Good source of vitamin C

Aubergine Casserole

Serve with a green vegetable or salad.

1 large aubergine
4 tablespoons butter or margarine
1 large or 2 medium onions
2 cloves garlic, crushed
1lb mushrooms, sliced
6 zucchini, sliced
1 16oz can chopped tomatoes
salt and freshly ground black pepper to taste
1 teaspoon chopped fresh oregano
1 tablespoon breadcrumbs
4 tablespoons Parmesan cheese, grated

Pre-heat the oven to 350°F and lightly oil a casserole dish. Peel and cube the aubergine, then cover it with boiling water and simmer for 10 minutes. Drain well.

Melt the butter in a frying pan and sauté the onion and garlic for 4–5 minutes until soft. Add the mushrooms, zucchini and aubergine and continue to cook for 10 minutes, stirring often.

Mix the tomatoes, salt, pepper and oregano together in a small saucepan and simmer gently for 10 minutes.

Spoon some of the tomato sauce into the casserole dish. Then place on top a layer of aubergine and mushroom mixture, followed by another layer of tomato sauce, and so on until both mixtures are used up. Sprinkle the top with Parmesan and breadcrumbs, cover and bake for 40 minutes, removing the lid for the last 10 minutes to brown the top lightly.

1 hour 15 minutes to make
Good source of vitamin A, B group vitamins, vitamin C, potassium

Aubergine Fritters

This recipe should produce about 10 fritters. Serve hot with a selection of steamed vegetables or salads.

1 aubergine
½ cup plain flour
1 teaspoon baking powder
1–2 tablespoons chopped fresh herbs
salt and freshly ground black pepper to taste
2 tablespoons milk
1 egg
oil for frying

Cover the aubergine with boiling water and cook for 15 minutes. Slice the hot aubergine in half, scoop out the seeds and discard. Spoon the flesh into a bowl and mash with a fork.

Mix the flour, baking powder, herbs, salt and pepper together in a bowl. Stir well.

Whisk the milk and egg together in a jug. Make a well in the dry ingredients and gradually add this liquid, stirring well after each addition. Finally, add the mashed aubergine and work into a thick paste.

Drop spoonsful of the paste into hot oil and fry until light brown, drain and serve immediately.

40 minutes to make

Aubergine Parmigiano

Serve with pasta or rice, and green vegetables or a salad.

2 aubergines
8–10 tablespoons olive oil
1 medium onion, chopped
2 16oz cans chopped tomatoes
1 small can tomato paste
1 tablespoon chopped fresh oregano
1 teaspoon chopped fresh basil
3 tablespoons plain flour
8oz Mozzarella cheese, sliced (more to taste)

Pre-heat the oven to 350°F and lightly grease a baking dish. Wash the aubergines and slice length-ways into thin strips.

Heat 1 tablespoon of the olive oil in a saucepan and sauté the onion. Add the canned tomatoes to the sauté, then the tomato puree and the herbs. Stir well and bring this sauce to a simmer. Cover the pan and cook over a low heat for 30 minutes.

Meanwhile, place the flour in a small bowl and dip the aubergine strips into it so that each piece is well coated. Heat the remaining olive oil in a frying pan and sauté the floured aubergine until lightly browned. Add more oil if necessary.

Pour some tomato sauce into the baking dish and place a layer of sautéd aubergine over it. Add another layer of sauce, another of aubergine, and continue in this way until both ingredients are used up. Arrange the cheese slices over the top layer. Bake for 30–40 minutes until the topping is golden brown. Serve immediately.

1 hour 15 minutes to make
Good source of protein, vitamin A, vitamin C, calcium

Aubergine Parmigiano *(p 83)*

Aubergine and Pasta

Depending on the size of aubergine you use, this dish should serve 4 very hungry people, or 6 quite hungry ones! Serve with salad or a green vegetable.

3 aubergines
6 tablespoons olive oil
1lb macaroni
1 16oz can chopped tomatoes
2 tablespoons tomato paste
1 teaspoon dried oregano or 1 tablespoon fresh
1 clove garlic, crushed (optional)
salt and freshly ground black pepper to taste
a little water or vegetable stock
8oz Mozzarella cheese, sliced
2 tablespoons butter or margarine
½ cup Parmesan cheese, grated

Pre-heat the oven to 350°F, and lightly grease a casserole dish. Peel the aubergines and slice them lengthways into strips. Heat the oil in a frying pan and brown the aubergine slices on both sides, a few pieces at a time. Use a little more oil if necessary. Remove the slices and place to one side.

Cook the macaroni, following the instructions on the packet, in a large pan of salted water. When cooked, drain thoroughly and return to the large pan.

Add the tomatoes, tomato puree, oregano, garlic and oil from the frying pan to the cooked macaroni. Mix well and season to taste. Add a little water or stock if necessary to make the mixture moist.

Place the aubergine, Mozzarella and macaroni mixture in alternate layers in the casserole dish. Continue until all the ingredients are used.

Place a few dabs of butter over the top layer, sprinkle with Parmesan cheese, and bake uncovered for about 30 minutes, until the top is a bubbling, golden brown.

1 hour to make
Good source of protein, vitamin A, calcium

Baked Macaroni Cheese

Serve with green vegetables or a salad. Delicious any time of year.

¾lb macaroni, uncooked
1 egg
2 cups milk
2 tablespoons butter or margarine
2½ cups Cheddar cheese, grated
salt and freshly ground black pepper to taste

Pre-heat the oven to 350°F. Lightly boil the macaroni, for about 5 minutes until half cooked.

Whisk the egg and milk together in a large cup. Melt the butter and add it, with the grated cheese, to the egg and milk. Stir well.

Place the lightly cooked macaroni in a greased baking dish. Pour the egg and cheese liquid over the macaroni, sprinkle with salt and pepper and stir well. Press the mixture evenly around the baking dish. Bake, uncovered, for 30–40 minutes, until the top is brown.

55 minutes to make
Good source of protein, vitamin A, B group vitamins, calcium

Baked Steaklets

The 'steaklets' I'm talking about here are made from TVP – see page 12 for more information about them. In fact you can use any similar TVP product, such as vegetable burgers, sausages or frankfurters. While you can make them up from packet mixes, it is probably easier to buy them ready made – either from the freezer department in supermarkets, or in cans from health food shops. Serve with rice or potatoes, and green vegetables or a salad.

3 tablespoons butter or margarine
1 large onion, chopped
1lb mushrooms, sliced
6 vegetable burgers or steaklets
2 cloves garlic, crushed or 1 teaspoon garlic powder
1 cup tomato ketchup

Pre-heat the oven to 400°F and lightly grease a casserole dish.

Melt half the butter in a frying pan. Sauté the onion until lightly browned, then remove and place to one side. Sauté the mushrooms in the same butter until light brown, then remove, keeping separate from the onions.

Heat the remaining butter in the frying pan and brown the burgers – about 5 minutes in total. Remove from the heat and sprinkle both sides with garlic. Place the burgers in the casserole dish.

Cover the burgers with the onions, spreading them to the edges of the dish. Now pour the ketchup over the onions and spread it evenly also. Finally, top the dish with the sautéed mushrooms. Cover the dish and bake for 30 minutes. Serve immediately.

45 minutes to make
Good source of protein, B group vitamins, potassium

Baked Sweet Corn

You can't always get fresh ears of sweet corn, so do substitute canned sweet corn if necessary – it tastes almost as good. Serve with green vegetables or a salad.

3 tablespoons butter or margarine
3 tablespoons plain flour
1½ cups cream
2 cups sweet corn kernels (cut from 9–10 ears corn)
3 eggs, beaten
½ cup breadcrumbs
salt and freshly ground black pepper to taste

Pre-heat the oven to 350°F and lightly grease a casserole dish. Melt 2 tablespoons of the butter in a saucepan and sprinkle the flour over it. Stir constantly over the heat to make a thick paste.

Heat the cream in another saucepan, then add it very gradually to the paste, stirring after each addition to make a smooth sauce. Remove from the heat.

Add the corn and eggs to the sauce and stir well.

Melt the remaining butter in a deep saucepan and stir in the breadcrumbs, salt and pepper. Pour the corn mixture into the casserole, cover with the breadcrumbs and place the casserole in a baking tray filled with hot water. Bake, uncovered, for 25–30 minutes. Serve immediately.

45 minutes to make
Good source of protein, vitamin A

Bean Tacos

You can find taco shells in most supermarkets these days – Mexican food is increasingly popular, because it's both tasty and quick to make.

for the taco sauce:
2 medium onions
1 4oz can green chilies in brine
4 large tomatoes
juice of ½ lemon

to serve:
2 tablespoons olive oil
1 16oz can refried beans (or use recipe on page 141)
¾ cup Cheddar cheese, grated
6 taco shells
1 iceberg, shredded

Pre-heat the oven to 325°F.

To make the sauce – finely chop the onions, drain and finely chop the chilies. Peel and chop the tomatoes, then mix the onions, chilies and tomatoes

with the lemon juice in a mixing bowl.

Heat the oil in a pan, add the beans and cook gently for 4–5 minutes, then mash roughly with a fork. Place the taco shells in the oven until they are warm – approximately 3 minutes.

Spoon the beans into the hot taco shells. Top with the lettuce, grated cheese, and a spoonful of sauce. Serve immediately.

20 minutes to make
Good source of protein, vitamin A, B group vitamins, vitamin C

Beefless Pie

It may be called 'Beefless', but it really does have all the flavour and texture of beef, particularly if you buy beef-flavoured TVP chunks (see page 11). Vegetable shortening is easy to buy in any supermarket. Serve this pie with vegetables or a salad.

¼ cup vegetable shortening
1 large onion
1 4½oz packet TVP chunks, or 4 vegetable burgers, cubed
1 clove garlic, crushed
1½ cups vegetable stock or water (1 cup if using vegetable burgers)
1 tablespoon soy sauce
1 bay leaf
1 teaspoon mixed herbs
salt and freshly ground black pepper to taste
2 tablespoons plain flour
6oz shortcrust pastry (enough for one 9 inch pie pan)

Pre-heat the oven to 425°F. Melt the vegetable shortening in a large saucepan. Chop the onion and place it in the hot fat with the TVP chunks and garlic. Sauté until the onion and garlic are lightly browned, stirring often.

Stir in the vegetable stock, soy sauce, bay leaf and mixed herbs. Cover the mixture and simmer for 20 minutes, until the chunks are tender.

Mix the flour with a little vegetable stock to make a smooth solution, and stir this into the dish after it has simmered for 15 minutes, to thicken the sauce.

Roll out the pastry to fit the top of a casserole dish.

Transfer the TVP mixture into the casserole dish and cover with the pastry. Prick the pastry lid in several places with a fork, and place the pie in the hot oven.

After 10 minutes, reduce the heat of the oven to 350°F and bake for a further 20 minutes.

55 minutes to make
Good source of protein

Beefless Rice Casserole

As with all dishes including TVP, this is both easier and quicker to make than a beef casserole that uses butcher's meat. Choose beef-flavoured TVP chunks if you want to keep a beef-type taste. If you use vegetable burgers instead, do remember to reduce the amount of liquid you use.

3 tablespoons vegetable oil
1 stick celery, chopped
1 large onion, chopped
1 cup white rice
1 4½oz packet TVP chunks, or 4 vegetable burgers, cubed
1 cup vegetable stock or water (½ cup if using vegetable burgers)
2 16oz cans chopped tomatoes
1 tablespoon soy sauce
salt and freshly ground black pepper to taste
1 teaspoon chili powder (optional)
1 teaspoon mixed herbs (optional)

Pre-heat the oven to 325°F and lightly grease a casserole dish. Heat the oil in a saucepan and sauté the celery and onion until just tender.

Add the rice and TVP chunks, and stir for a few minutes until the chunks are slightly browned. Now add the vegetable stock, tomatoes, soy sauce, salt pepper and optional seasonings if desired. Stir well and bring to the boil.

Remove the mixture from the heat and pour into the casserole dish. Bake, covered, for 30 minutes.

40 minutes to make
Good source of protein, vitamin A, vitamin C

Beefless Stew

Serve with mashed potatoes or rice, and green vegetables or a salad.

1 large onion, chopped
4 medium carrots, chopped
4 medium potatoes, cubed
2 cloves garlic, crushed
2 sticks celery, chopped
½ red pepper, chopped and seeded
4 tablespoons butter or margarine
1 4½oz packet TVP chunks or 4 vegetable burgers, cubed
1 16oz can chopped tomatoes

2 cups vegetable stock or water (1 cup if using vegetable burgers)
2 tablespoons soy sauce
salt and freshly ground black pepper to taste

Prepare the vegetables, then melt the butter in a large saucepan and lightly brown the onion. Add the other vegetables and sauté for a few minutes. Then add the TVP chunks and brown for 3 minutes over a gentle heat. Add the tomatoes and enough vegetable stock just to cover the mixture.

Season with soy sauce, salt and pepper, cover the stew and simmer for 30–40 minutes or until thick and well cooked. Take care to add extra vegetable stock or water if the mixture seems dry.

55 minutes to make
Good source of vitamin A, B group vitamins, calcium, potassium

Beefless Stroganoff

Serve with rice and green vegetables or a salad. As a variation to this warming dish, put the whole vegetable burgers in the bottom of a casserole and warm through. Cover with the sauce.

4 tablespoons butter or margarine
1 large onion, chopped
6 cups mushrooms, sliced
1 teaspoon paprika
¼ cup plain flour
6 vegetable burgers, cubed
1 cup white wine
a little vegetable stock or water
6 tablespoons sour cream
½ teaspoon mild mustard

Melt the butter in a pan, and fry the onions and mushrooms, with the paprika, for 10 minutes. Add the flour and the cubed vegetable burgers, stir well and brown for 2 minutes.

Pour in the wine and and simmer very gently for 10–15 minutes. Stir often and add a little vegetable stock if the mixture seems dry.

Finally, add the sour cream and mustard, then heat through but do not boil or simmer. Serve immediately.

25 minutes to make
Good source of vitamin A, B group vitamins

Bean Tacos (p 85)

Beer Fondue

Serve with sautéd mushrooms and greens, or new potatoes and a salad.

8 slices bread
2–4 tablespoons butter or margarine
4oz Swiss or Cheddar cheese, sliced
3 eggs
1 teaspoon soy sauce
½ teaspoon mild mustard
1 cup beer
salt and freshly ground black pepper to taste

Pre-heat the oven to 350°F and lightly oil a large casserole dish. Remove the crusts from the slices of bread and lightly butter them on both sides.

Arrange the bread and cheese slices in alternate layers in the casserole dish.

Beat the remaining ingredients together in a jug. Pour this mixture over the bread and cheese layers, pressing the bread down well with a wooden spoon.

Bake the casserole, uncovered, for 30 minutes. Serve immediately.

40 minutes to make
Good source of protein, B group vitamins, calcium

Beer Rarebit

This is very good accompanied with a salad or a vegetable specialty such as Green Bean Savoury (see page 137).

4 tablespoons butter or margarine
1 cup Cheddar cheese, grated
4 tablespoons beer
1 tablespoon mild mustard
½ teaspoon paprika
salt and freshly ground black pepper to taste
1 teaspoon Worcestershire sauce

to serve:
rice or toast

Melt the butter in a deep saucepan, then add the remaining ingredients. Stir well, over a gentle heat, until the cheese has melted. Pour over rice or toast, and serve immediately.

15 minutes to make
Good source of protein, vitamin A, calcium

Burger Goulash

Serve with rice or mashed potatoes, and green vegetables or a salad.

2 tablespoons butter or margarine
1 large onion, chopped
1 clove garlic, crushed
6 vegetable burgers, cubed
¼ cup plain flour
1 tablespoon paprika
1 16oz can chopped tomatoes
1 cup red wine
8 small new potatoes or 2 large baking potatoes, cubed
salt and freshly ground black pepper to taste
½ cup sour cream (optional)

Melt the butter in a pan and fry the onion and garlic for 4–5 minutes. Coat the burger chunks in flour, then add them to the pan and brown gently. Add the paprika, tomatoes, wine and potatoes. Season to taste.

Cover the goulash and simmer gently for about 25 minutes.

Just before serving, stir in the sour cream and sprinkle a little extra paprika over the dish to garnish.

45 minutes to make
Good source of vitamin A, B group vitamins, vitamin C, potassium

Burgers à la King

Serve hot over rice or crispy noodles, or as a vol-au-vent filling. Great with green vegetables or salads.

for the white sauce:
4 tablespoons butter or margarine
4 tablespoons plain flour
2 cups milk

for the rest of the recipe:
2 tablespoons butter or margarine
1 medium onion, chopped
4 vegetable burgers, cubed
3 cups button mushrooms, chopped
½ green pepper, chopped
2 teaspoons paprika
1 cup vegetable stock or water
4 tablespoons sherry
2 egg yolks, beaten
salt and freshly ground black pepper to taste

Prepare the white sauce with the butter, flour and milk (see recipe on page 150) and keep it warm over a very low heat.

Melt the butter in a small saucepan and sauté the onion in it for 4–5 minutes until lightly browned.

Add the burger chunks to the pan and lightly brown – about 5 minutes in total.

Add the mushrooms, green pepper and paprika, then pour in the white sauce, vegetable stock and sherry. Simmer, covered, for 15 minutes. Stir in the egg yolks, salt and pepper and cook for a further 2 minutes. Serve immediately.

30 minutes to make
Good source of protein, vitamin A, B group vitamins, vitamin C

Burgers Bourguignonne

Serve with potatoes and green vegetables or a salad. Remember to reduce the liquid if using vegetable burgers rather than TVP chunks.

> *4 tablespoons butter or margarine*
> *10 small onions, peeled*
> *5 medium carrots, chopped*
> *6 large mushrooms, chopped*
> *1 stick celery, chopped*
> *1 4½oz packet TVP chunks or 6 vegetable burgers, cubed*
> *2 teaspoons plain flour*
> *1½ cups vegetable stock or water (¾ cup if using vegetable burgers)*
> *1 tablespoon tomato paste*
> *1 teaspoon vegetable extract or soy sauce*
> *½ cup red wine*
> *1 bay leaf*
> *2 cloves garlic, crushed*
> *3 tablespoons chopped fresh parsley*
> *1 teaspoon chopped fresh thyme*
> *salt and freshly ground black pepper to taste*

Melt the butter in a large saucepan, add the onions and sauté for 2–3 minutes. Add the remaining vegetables and sauté them for 5–6 minutes, stirring often. Add the TVP chunks to the sauté and brown for 3 minutes over a low heat.

Mix the flour into a paste using a little of the vegetable stock. Add this paste, the tomato paste and the yeast extract to the sauté.

Stir in the remaining vegetable stock and the wine, bay leaf, garlic and herbs. Reduce the heat, cover, and simmer for 30–40 minutes until the chunks are tender and the flavours well developed. Season to taste with the salt and pepper.

55 minutes to make
Good source of vitamin A, B group vitamins, calcium, iron

Burgers Chop Suey

Serve with rice or noodles and any vegetable.

> *3 tablespoons vegetable oil*
> *6 vegetable burgers*
> *1 clove garlic, crushed*
> *2 medium onions, chopped*
> *½lb mushrooms, sliced*
> *4 sticks celery, chopped*
> *½ cup water chestnuts, thinly sliced*
> *4oz beansprouts*
> *2 tablespoons cornstarch*
> *1 tablespoon sherry*
> *2 tablespoons soy sauce*
> *up to 1 cup vegetable stock*

Pre-heat the oven to 350°F. Heat 1 tablespoon of the oil in a frying pan and brown the burgers on both sides, about 5 minutes in total. Remove them from the pan and place to one side.

Sauté the garlic and onions in the remaining oil until they just begin to soften. Add the mushrooms, celery and water chestnuts and sauté for 10 minutes. Add the beansprouts and cook for a further 5 minutes.

Mix the cornstarch, sherry, soy sauce and stock together in a large jug. Add this liquid to the sauté and stir gently until it thickens into a sauce. Cook for a further 10 minutes.

Put the burgers in the bottom of a large casserole, cover with the sauce and bake, uncovered, for 20 minutes. Stir gently before serving.

55 minutes to make
Good source of B group vitamins, vitamin C

Burgers with Fried Onion

Serve with pasta, and green vegetables or a salad.

4 cloves garlic, crushed or 2 teaspoons garlic powder
6 vegetable burgers
2 tablespoons butter or margarine
2 medium onions, chopped

Press the garlic into both sides of the burgers. Melt the butter in a saucepan and sauté the onions until lightly browned. Add the burgers to the pan and fry 5 minutes each side, until well browned. Serve immediately.

15 minutes to make

Burgers with Parsley Butter

Serve with potatoes, rice or pasta, and green vegetables or a salad.

6 tablespoons butter or margarine
2 tablespoons chopped fresh parsley
6 vegetable burgers
1 clove garlic, crushed or ½ teaspoon garlic powder

In a mixing bowl, mix two-thirds of the butter with the chopped parsley. Chill until firm.

Place the burgers in a frying pan with the remaining butter and fry on both sides until brown, for about 5 minutes. Remove the burgers from the pan and rub the garlic over both sides.

Put the burgers on a serving plate and scoop a little ball of parsley butter on to each burger. Serve immediately.

15 minutes to make
Good source of vitamin A

Burgers in Sour Cream and Red Wine

Serve with rice, pasta, and green vegetables or a salad.

6 tablespoons butter or margarine
1 clove garlic, crushed
6 vegetable burgers
2 medium onions, chopped
½ cup carrots, chopped

4 sticks celery, chopped
½ cup red wine
½ cup vegetable stock or water
2 bay leaves
3 tablespoons chopped fresh parsley
salt and freshly ground black pepper to taste
1 tablespoon chopped fresh thyme or 1 teaspoon dried thyme
1½ cups sour cream
1 teaspoon paprika
1 tablespoon soy sauce

Pre-heat the oven to 350°F and lightly grease a casserole dish. Melt the butter in a saucepan and sauté the garlic. Then add the burgers and brown them on both sides, for about 5 minutes. Put the burgers in the casserole dish.

Add the onions to the hot fat and sauté until tender, then add the chopped carrot and celery and sauté for a further 5 minutes.

Add the remaining ingredients – except the sour cream, paprika and soy sauce – and stir gently for 5 minutes. Pour this mixture over the burgers in the casserole. Cover, and bake for 1 hour.

Just before serving, stir in the sour cream, paprika and soy sauce.

1 hour 30 minutes to make
Good source of vitamin A, vitamin C, calcium

Cauliflower Gratin

1 large cauliflower
1 tablespoon olive oil
1 large onion, chopped
½ cup raisins
¼ cup pine nuts
¼ cup Parmesan cheese, grated

Cut the cauliflower into florets and steam for about 10 minutes, until it is just tender.

Heat the oil in a large frying pan and sauté the onion. Add the raisins and pine nuts, and continue the sauté. Add the steamed cauliflower and mix well.

Spoon the mixture into a wide casserole dish and top with the grated Parmesan. Put under a medium broiler for 5 minutes, until the cheese has browned. Serve hot.

20 minutes to make
Good source of protein, B group vitamins, vitamin C, calcium

91

Burgers Bourguignonne (p 89)

Cauliflower Mexican Style

Serve with a selection of steamed vegetables. For a spicier variation, substitute the capers, cloves and cinnamon with 1 4oz can green chilies, drained and finely chopped.

1 large cauliflower
2 cups Home-made Tomato Sauce (see recipe on page 147)
1 tablespoon capers
2 tablespoons chopped onion
3 tablespoons chopped fresh parsley
large pinch of ground cloves
large pinch of ground cinnamon
salt and freshly ground black pepper to taste
½ cup breadcrumbs
1 cup Cheddar cheese, grated

Pre-heat the oven to 400°F and lightly grease a casserole dish. Cut the cauliflower into florets and steam or simmer until tender, then drain.

Place the cauliflower florets in a large mixing bowl, add the tomato sauce, capers, onion, parsley, cloves, cinnamon, salt and pepper and mix well. Pour the mixture into the casserole dish.

Mix the breadcrumbs and cheese together in a separate bowl, then sprinkle them over the casserole.

Bake, uncovered, for 30 minutes, until the topping is golden brown. Serve immediately.

1 hour to make
Good source of protein, vitamin A, vitamin C, calcium

Cheddar Cheese Bake

Serve hot with spinach or green vegetables and salad.

1 tablespoon olive oil
2 cloves garlic, crushed
8oz Cheddar cheese, sliced thinly
3 eggs, beaten
¼ cup plain flour
1¼ cups milk
½ cup light cream
salt and freshly ground black pepper to taste

Pre-heat the oven to 375°F. Heat the oil in a small frying pan and sauté the garlic. Pour the sauté into a casserole dish.

Place half the cheese in the baking dish and spread to cover the bottom. Combine the remaining ingredients and pour over the cheese in the casserole dish.

Top the dish with the remaining Cheddar slices and bake, uncovered, for 30 minutes. Serve immediately.

40 minutes to make
Good source of protein, vitamin A, B group vitamins, calcium

Cheddar Cheese Pie

This is as tasty cold as it is hot. Serve with greens, carrots or a salad.

6oz shortcrust pastry (enough to line a 9 inch pie pan)
3 eggs, beaten
1 medium onion, chopped
2 tablespoons butter or margarine
1 cup heavy cream
2 cups Cheddar cheese, grated
salt and freshly ground black pepper to taste

Pre-heat the oven to 400°F. Grease a 9 inch pie dish, then line it with the pastry and flute the edges. Brush a little beaten egg on the pastry and bake it blind for about 10 minutes. Remove from the oven, and reduce the oven heat to 375°F.

Sauté the onion in the butter for 4–5 minutes or until golden brown, and spread the mixture on to the cooked pastry. Mix the cream, grated cheese and seasoning in with the remaining beaten egg. Pour this mixture into the pie crust.

Bake for 30 minutes until the crust is nicely browned and the filling firmly set.

50 minutes to make
Good source of vitamin A, B group vitamins, calcium

Cheese and Green Chili Corn Bread

This delicious bread can be served hot or cold, and makes a satisfactory addition to any Mexican meal or can be served with a bowl of soup.

⅔ cup self-rising flour
2 tablespoons sugar
2 cups yellow corn meal
1 teaspoon baking soda
1 egg
1 cup sour cream
⅔ cup milk
1 4oz can green chilies in brine
½ cup Cheddar cheese, grated

Pre-heat the oven to 350°F and lightly grease and flour an 8 inch square baking pan. Mix the flour, sugar, corn meal and baking soda together in a mixing bowl.

Beat the egg with the sour cream and milk, then stir this liquid into the dry ingredients. Drain the chilies, chop finely and add, with the cheese, to the batter mixture.

Transfer the batter to the baking pan and bake for 35 minutes. Leave to cool in the tin for 10 minutes, then remove and cool on a wire rack.

45 minutes to make
Good source of protein, vitamin A, vitamin C, calcium

Cheese with Herbs and Pasta

2 tablespoons butter or margarine
1 large onion, chopped
3 cloves garlic, crushed
1lb small pasta (e.g. macaroni or pasta shells)
1 cup sour cream
2 cups ricotta or cottage cheese
2 tablespoons chopped fresh parsley or 1 tablespoon dried
4 tablespoons chopped fresh basil or 1 tablespoon dried
2 tablespoons chopped fresh oregano or 1 tablespoon dried
salt and freshly ground black pepper to taste
1 tablespoon grated Parmesan cheese

Melt the butter in a large frying pan and gently sauté the onion and garlic until tender, about 5 minutes. Set the pasta to cook in boiling water.

Mix the sour cream and ricotta cheese to a smooth consistency. Add the parsley, basil and oregano and stir well. Season with the salt and pepper. Add this mixture to the sauté and place over a very low heat, stirring frequently.

When the pasta has cooked, drain and rinse it well. Turn it into a serving dish and stir in the hot cheese sauce. Serve immediately, sprinkled with a little grated Parmesan.

35 minutes to make
Good source of protein, vitamin A, B group vitamins, vitamin C

Cheese and Noodle Casserole

1lb noodles
1 cup sour cream
12oz cream cheese (or soft cheese)
1 cup cottage cheese
8 tablespoons milk
2 tablespoons chopped chives
salt and freshly ground black pepper to taste
up to 1 tablespoon chopped fresh herbs (e.g. marjoram) or 1 teaspoon caraway seeds
2 tablespoons butter or margarine
1 tablespoon chopped fresh parsley
½ cup Parmesan cheese, grated

Pre-heat the oven to 350°F and lightly grease a baking dish. Boil the noodles, rinse under cold water, drain and put to one side.

In a large mixing bowl combine the sour cream, cream cheese, cottage cheese and milk. Add the noodles and toss gently. Add the chives, salt, pepper and herbs or caraway seeds, and stir well. Then tip the mixture into the baking dish and dab pieces of butter over the top.

Sprinkle the parsley and Parmesan over the dish and bake, uncovered, for 30 minutes. Serve hot.

45 minutes to make
Good source of protein, vitamin A, B group vitamins, calcium

Cheese and Tomato Casserole

8 tomatoes
4 tablespoons butter or margarine
1 small onion, chopped
1/3 cup plain flour
2 cups milk
salt and freshly ground black pepper to taste
1/2 teaspoon paprika
2 egg yolks, beaten
2 tablespoons heavy cream
1 cup Swiss cheese, grated

for the garnish:
1 tablespoon freshly chopped parsley or tarragon

Pre-heat the oven to 350°F and lightly grease a casserole dish. Quickly plunge the tomatoes into boiling water, then into cold water, then skin them. Cut them into thick slices and arrange them in the casserole dish.

Melt the butter in a large saucepan and sauté the onions until tender. Reduce the heat, and sprinkle the flour over the onions, stirring to make a thick paste.

Heat the milk in a separate pan and add it gradually to the paste, stirring constantly to make a smooth sauce. Add the salt, pepper and paprika. Stir well then allow the sauce to cool for a couple of minutes.

Mix the egg yolks with the cream. Add these to the sauce, stirring over a very low heat. Add the cheese, and stir as it melts.

Pour the sauce over the tomatoes and bake, uncovered, for 15–20 minutes. Sprinkle the fresh herbs over the cooked dish and serve immediately.

35 minutes to make
Good source of protein, vitamin A, B group vitamins, vitamin C

Cheese Soufflé

It helps to have an electric blender for this recipe, because it will save you a lot of effort! Don't be intimidated by soufflés – once you've got the hang of them they're easy to make, and always go down well. My kids make great soufflés! For a tasty variation on this recipe, finely chop some fresh tarragon into the soufflé mixture.

2 tablespoons butter or margarine
2 tablespoons plain flour
1 cup milk
salt and freshly ground black pepper to taste
1 cup Cheddar cheese, grated
4 eggs, separated

Pre-heat the oven to 375°F. Grease a 1 pint soufflé dish. Melt the butter in a saucepan then add the flour, whisking to a smooth paste. Cook for 1 minute over a low heat.

Heat the milk in a separate pan and add it gradually to the flour paste, stirring constantly. When all the milk is added, simmer the sauce for 2–3 minutes, stirring occasionally. Season to taste. Remove from the heat and allow to cool for 2 minutes.

Now add the grated cheese, and stir the mixture, off the heat, until the cheese has melted. Beat the egg yolks, add to the cheese mixture and stir until well blended.

In another bowl, whisk the egg whites until they are stiff but not dry. Then fold them carefully into the cheese mixture. Turn the whole mixture into the soufflé dish and bake for 30–35 minutes. Serve immediately.

50 minutes to make
Good source of protein, vitamin A, B group vitamins, calcium

Chili non Carne

The best chili you'll get this side of Tijuana! Serve with rice, mashed potatoes or avocado salad.

2 tablespoons vegetable oil
1 medium onion, chopped
1½ level teaspoons chili powder (or more according to taste)
2 4½oz packets TVP chunks or 4 vegetable burgers, crumbled
1½ cups vegetable stock or water (¾ cup if using vegetable burgers)
1 16oz can chopped tomatoes
1 16oz can red kidney beans
2 Mexican green chilies in brine, drained and chopped (optional)
salt and freshly ground black pepper to taste

Heat the oil in a large saucepan and sauté the onion until golden brown. Add the chili powder and TVP chunks and brown for 5 minutes.

Add the vegetable stock and tomatoes, together with their juice. Cover the mixture and simmer for 20 minutes.

94

Cauliflower Mexican Style (p 92)

Add the kidney beans – and the chilies if you are using them – and simmer for about 15 minutes, adding a little extra stock or water if necessary. Season to taste and serve hot.

45 minutes to make
Good source of protein, vitamin A, vitamin C

Corn Fritters

Great with a green salad.

> *1 cup sweet corn or 2 medium ears sweet corn, trimmed*
> *1 egg*
> *1¼ cup milk*
> *1 cup plain flour*
> *½ teaspoon salt*
> *freshly ground black pepper to taste*
> *vegetable oil for frying*

Cook the corn until it is tender, and drain well.

To make the batter, beat the egg and milk together. Then add the flour, salt and pepper and blend until smooth.

Stir the corn into the batter. Drop spoonsful into very hot oil, and fry on both sides until lightly browned.

Drain on paper towels to remove excess oil, and serve immediately.

25 minutes to make
Good source of B group vitamins

Corn Soufflé

Serve with a selection of vegetables or a salad.

> *2 tablespoons butter or margarine*
> *1 teaspoon salt*
> *¼ teaspoon freshly ground black pepper*
> *¼ cup plain flour*
> *1 cup milk*
> *1 cup sweet corn kernels, cooked and drained*
> *4 eggs, separated*

Pre-heat the oven to 375°F and lightly grease a 2 cups soufflé dish. Melt the butter in a saucepan. Stir the salt and pepper into the flour, then sprinkle the flour over the hot butter. Stir well to make a thick paste.

Gradually add the milk to the paste, stirring after each addition, to make a smooth white sauce. Simmer for 2 minutes, then remove the saucepan from the heat.

Add the sweet corn to the white sauce and stir well. Remove the sauce from the heat and allow to cool briefly. Then stir the egg yolks into the sauce.

Beat the egg whites until they are very stiff, then fold them gently into the corn and white sauce mixture. Turn the mixture into the soufflé dish and bake, undisturbed, for 30 minutes. Serve immediately.

45 minutes to make
Good source of protein, B group vitamins

Cottage Cheese Pie

Serve with a salad, steamed vegetables or grilled tomatoes and a sauce or relish.

> *6oz shortcrust pastry (enough to line a 9 inch pie dish)*
> *1¼lb potatoes*
> *1 cup cottage cheese*
> *½ cup sour cream*
> *2 tablespoons chopped chives*
> *1 tablespoon chopped tarragon*
> *salt and freshly ground black pepper to taste*
> *1 tablespoon butter or margarine*

Pre-heat the oven to 400°F. Grease the pie dish, then roll out the pastry to line it. Flute the edges and bake blind for 10 minutes. When you remove the pie dish from the oven reduce the oven temperature to 350°F.

Boil the potatoes and mash them, while still hot, with the cottage cheese, sour cream and herbs. Season to taste.

Spoon this mixture into the pie shell, spread it evenly and dot with small pieces of the butter. Bake for 20–25 minutes or until the filling is nicely browned on top and the pastry has finished cooking. If the top becomes too brown, cover with foil. Serve immediately.

1 hour to make
Good source of protein, vitamin A, B group vitamins, vitamin C

Curried Eggs

You can try some variations by adding 1 tablespoon chopped tarragon, or 1 clove garlic, or 1 tablespoon capers, or 2 tablespoons basil.

6 eggs
½ teaspoon curry powder
1 teaspoon pickle relish
1 teaspoon mild mustard
2 tablespoons mayonnaise
salt and freshly ground black pepper to taste

to serve:
lettuce

Hard-boil the eggs, then peel them and slice them in half lengthways.

Scoop out the the yolks and place in a mixing bowl with the remaining ingredients. Blend thoroughly, then spoon this mixture back into the egg white halves. Serve on a bed of lettuce.

15 minutes to make
Good source of B group vitamins

Curried Lentils

2 tablespoons olive oil
2 medium onions, chopped
2 cloves garlic, crushed
1–2 tablespoons curry powder (or to taste)
1 teaspoon ground cumin
1 cup lentils
2 cups vegetable stock or water
2 tablespoons lemon juice
½ tablespoon grated lemon rind
salt and freshly ground black pepper to taste

Heat the oil in a deep saucepan and sauté the onions for 4–5 minutes. Add the garlic and spices and cook for 2 minutes. Wash, rinse and drain the lentils and add them to the sauté. Cook for a further 2 minutes.

Pour the stock into the pan, and add the lemon juice and rind. Bring to the boil, then season to taste. Cover, reduce the heat and simmer for 20–25 minutes, stirring occasionally. Add a little extra stock if necessary. The lentils should be quite soft when cooked. Serve hot.

45 minutes to make
Good source of protein, vitamin C, iron

Eggs Florentine

1½lb spinach
4 tablespoons butter or margarine
¼ cup plain flour
¼ teaspoon ground nutmeg
salt and freshly ground black pepper to taste
6 eggs
1 cup milk
1 cup cream
½ cup Cheddar cheese

Pre-heat the oven to 400°F and lightly grease an oven dish. Wash and trim the spinach then place it in a deep saucepan over a high heat. Do not add any water. Cover the pan and leave to cook for 2 minutes, then reduce the heat and cook for a further 5 minutes. Remove the pan from the heat, allow the spinach to cool slightly, and then puree it in a blender.

Melt half of the butter in a saucepan, sprinkle half of the flour over it and stir well. Add the spinach puree and cook for 2–3 minutes, then season well with nutmeg, salt and pepper. Spoon the puree into a shallow oven dish. Poach the eggs and place them over the puree.

Melt the remaining butter, and stir the remaining flour into it, then gradually add the milk and cream and bring to simmering point. Cook for 3 minutes. Then remove from the heat, stir in the grated cheese and pour the sauce over the poached eggs. Bake for 10–15 minutes, until the cheese topping is a golden brown.

45 minutes to make
Good source of protein, vitamin A, B group vitamins, vitamin C

Eggs au Gratin

2 cups medium White Sauce (see page 150)
6 eggs
1 tablespoon chopped chives
1 cup Cheddar cheese, grated
½ cup breadcrumbs

Pre-heat the oven to 350°F and lightly grease a casserole dish.

Prepare the white sauce and keep warm over a low heat. Hard-boil the eggs and, when cool enough to handle, peel and slice them.

Line the casserole dish with the hard-boiled eggs. Sprinkle the chopped chives over the eggs and spread half the grated cheese over the chives.

Pour the white sauce over the eggs and cheese and sprinkle the remaining grated cheese over the sauce. Top the casserole with the breadcrumbs and bake for about 15–20 minutes, until golden brown. Serve immediately.

30 minutes to make
Good source of protein, B group vitamins, calcium

Festive or Sunday Roast with Savoury Stuffing

'But what do you eat for Christmas dinner?' is the usual question friends ask us when they hear we don't eat meat. Well, here it is! It may take a little time to prepare, but even so, it's still much less hassle than wrestling with a dead turkey on Christmas day! And it's *so* much tastier too. Decorate the table with holly, Christmas bowls, and crackers, and you can really enjoy a traditional Christmas dinner – in fact the only thing missing is the cruelty! Like us, you'll probably find that you will want to use this recipe for other occasions, such as birthdays, New Year's Eve, Easter, Thanksgiving, and dinner parties.

2 garlic cloves, minced
12oz vegetable sausage mix
1 egg
4 vegetable schnitzels or 5 vegetable burgers
1 4½oz packet TVP mince, unflavoured
4 tablespoons soy sauce or vegetable extract
3 tablespoons vegetable oil

Start preparing the roast the day before it is needed. Pre-heat the oven to 350°F. Grease and flour a large casserole dish or mould. Sprinkle one half of the garlic all over the inside of this dish.

Measure the sausage mix, egg, and 1 pint water into a large mixing bowl. Stir well and leave for 5 minutes for the liquid to be absorbed.

Measure ¼ pint water into a food blender. Add the vegetable burgers and blend to an even consistency.

Mix the TVP mince and 1 pint of water in a bowl. Stir well and leave to stand for 5 minutes.

Combine the sausage mix, pureed burgers and the soaked TVP mince together in a large bowl. Add the remaining garlic and the soy sauce. Mix well. Coat the casserole dish with the vegetable oil, and pour the mixture into the dish, pressing it firmly on to the sides and bottom. Leave a large cavity in the middle for the stuffing. Firm the mixture with the back of a spoon or your knuckles.

Bake for 1½ hours in the hot oven. Allow to cool, then cover and place overnight in the refrigerator. The next day, make the savoury stuffing.

Savoury Stuffing

1 loaf brown bread, cubed
6 tablespoons margarine
5 stalks celery, chopped
1 large onion, chopped
4 fresh sage leaves, finely chopped
1 tablespoon mixed dried herbs

Pre-heat the oven to 350°F.

Place the cubes of brown bread in a large mixing bowl. Melt the margarine in a large frying pan. Add the celery and onion and, stirring frequently with a wooden spoon, sauté for 5 minutes, until lightly brown.

Pour the sauté into the mixing bowl with the bread cubes. Add ¼ cup water, the sage and the mixed herbs. Mix very well and use.

10 minutes to make

Fill the roast cavity with this stuffing. Any remainder may be placed in a baking dish and baked separately later.

Turn the casserole dish upside down on to a baking tray or roasting pan without removing the dish, place in the oven and bake for 45 minutes. Remove the casserole dish and continue to bake for 1 more hour. After half an hour, place the extra stuffing in the oven and bake for the remaining 30 minutes.

Serve the stuffed roast hot with gravy, the extra stuffing, and side dishes of baked sweet potatoes, cranberry sauce, mashed and roast potatoes, onions and parsnips, steamed Brussels sprouts and green peas.

1 hour 50 minutes, plus 2 hours to make
Good source of protein, calcium, potassium, iron, zinc.

French Baked Eggs

Serve on a bed of rice or with a green salad.

6 large tomatoes
2 cloves garlic, crushed
2 tablespoons chopped fresh parsley
salt and freshly ground black pepper to taste
6 eggs
4 tablespoons grated Parmesan cheese

Pre-heat the oven to 350°F and lightly grease a baking dish. Slice the tops off the tomatoes, scoop out their centres and discard the pulp. Arrange the tomato shells in the baking dish.

Mix the garlic and parsley together in a small bowl. Season to taste. Spoon equal amounts into the tomato shells. Bake for 5–6 minutes.

Remove the tomatoes from the oven and break one egg into the centre of each. Return to the oven and bake for a further 10 minutes, until the eggs are well cooked.

Sprinkle the eggs with a little Parmesan and brown under a hot grill if desired. Serve immediately.

20 minutes to make
Good source of protein, vitamin A, B group vitamins, vitamin C

Fried Mozzarella

Serve hot with a tomato sauce.

1lb Mozzarella cheese
1 egg
½ cup plain flour
¼ cup breadcrumbs
oil for frying

Cut the cheese into 2¾ inch squares, approximately 1 inch thick.

Break the egg into a small bowl and beat it well. Measure the flour into a second bowl and the breadcrumbs into a third bowl.

Dredge the cheese squares in flour, then dip them into the beaten egg. Immediately dip them in breadcrumbs, then the egg again, then the breadcrumbs again.

Fry the cheese squares in the oil until they are golden. Drain before serving.

15 minutes to make
Good source of protein, vitamin A, calcium

Fried Rice

This is a little bit different from the usual recipes for fried rice. I find that it makes a great dish all by itself, and is extremely adaptable – you can serve it with a selection of vegetables, such as French Fried Vegetables (see page 136), Green Beans and Mushrooms in Sour Cream (page 137) or New Orleans Okra (page 138).

1½ cups long grain rice
2 tablespoons vegetable oil
1 medium onion, chopped
2 sticks celery, chopped
4 cups mushrooms, chopped
2–3 tablespoons soy sauce
2 eggs, beaten
2 scallions, chopped
1 tomato, chopped

Cover the rice with twice its volume of water (i.e. 1 cup of rice to 2 cups water) in a medium-sized saucepan. Bring to a boil, then cover the pan, reduce the heat and leave the rice to simmer for about 20 minutes or until all the water is absorbed.

Heat the oil in a large pan and sauté the onion, celery and mushrooms for about 5 minutes. Add the cooked rice and the soy sauce, then stir for about 3 minutes.

Add the eggs to the rice mixture, stirring as it cooks, about 5 minutes.

Add the scallions and tomatoes and cook for a final 5 minutes.

50 minutes to make
Good source of vitamin A, vitamin C

Ghivetch Casserole

A friend gave me this recipe. It should be served with rice or pasta.

3 tablespoons olive oil
2 onions, chopped
2 cloves garlic, crushed
5oz acorn squash, cubed
2 medium carrots, sliced
1½ cups mushrooms, halved if large
1 cup zucchini, sliced
½ medium cauliflower, or 1 small cauliflower, broken into florets
1 small aubergine, cubed
1 green pepper, seeded and roughly chopped
2 sticks celery, chopped
2 potatoes, diced
1 cup broad beans or sweet corn
1 cup peas or green beans
juice of ½ lemon
1 cup vegetable stock
1 16oz can tomatoes
2 tablespoons tomato puree (optional)
1 teaspoon chopped dill
salt and freshly ground black pepper to taste

Pre-heat the oven to 350°F. Heat the oil in a very large pan and sauté the onion and garlic for 3–4 minutes. Then add the remaining vegetables and mix well. Cook, covered tightly, for 5 minutes to bring out the flavour.

Add the remaining ingredients to the vegetables and pour the mixture into a large casserole dish. Bake for 1 hour, stirring the casserole twice during that time. Season to taste.

1 hour 25 minutes to make
Good source of vitamin A, B group vitamins, vitamin C, potassium

Gnocchi

Unlike most of the other recipes, this is a dish that requires a fair amount of skill – but persevere and you'll get it right!

1lb potatoes
2 egg yolks
salt and freshly ground black pepper to taste
1 cup plain flour, plus a little sprinkling flour
1¼ cups Home-made Tomato Sauce (see page 147)
3–4 tablespoons grated Parmesan cheese

Scrub the potatoes and boil them in their jackets. When tender, peel them and mash in a mixing bowl.

Add the egg yolks and seasoning and beat the mixture until it is light and fluffy. Add the flour and mix well. Turn out on to a floured board and knead lightly, adding more flour if necessary to make a very smooth dough.

Divide the dough into 6 parts. Use your hands to roll each part on a lightly-floured board to make a long sausage shape, about 1¼ inches in diameter. Cut each roll into 1 inch lengths, indent them with a fork and sprinkle lightly with flour.

Bring a large saucepan of water to the boil and drop the gnocchi pieces into it. Boil about 12–15 at a time for 2–3 minutes or until they float to the surface. Remove and drain.

In a separate saucepan, heat the tomato sauce. Place the gnocchi on a serving plate, cover with the hot tomato sauce and sprinkle with Parmesan cheese.

1 hour to make
Good source of vitamin A, B Group vitamins, vitamin C, potassium

Greek Beefless Stew

4 tablespoons butter or margarine
6 vegetable burgers, cubed
12 small onions or 4 medium onions, chopped
2 tablespoons tomato paste
2 cups vegetable stock or water
4 carrots, chopped
2 medium potatoes, chopped
1 teaspoon ground cinnamon
salt and freshly ground black pepper to taste

Melt the butter in a frying pan, brown the burger chunks for about 5 minutes, then place them in a deep stew pot or saucepan. Arrange the onions on top.

Add the tomato paste to the remaining hot fat in the frying pan and stir well. Gradually add the vegetable stock, stir well and bring this mixture to the boil. Pour the sauce over the onions and burger chunks, add the carrots, potatoes, cinnamon, salt and pepper and stir well. Add a little more liquid if necessary.

Cover the pot and cook for 40–45 minutes over a low heat. Serve immediately in bowls. Have plenty of fresh bread on hand.

1 hour to make
Good source of vitamin A, vitamin C

Green Chili and Rice

1 cup long grain rice
1 4oz can green chilies in brine
2 cups Cheddar cheese, grated
1 cup sour cream
1 tablespoon cornstarch
salt and freshly ground black pepper to taste
2 tablespoons butter or margarine

Pre-heat the oven to 350°F and lightly grease a baking dish. If necessary, wash the rice in cold water once or twice, then drain. Cover the rice with twice its volume of water (i.e. 1 cup rice to 2 cups water) in a medium-sized saucepan. Bring to a boil, then cover the pan, reduce the heat and leave the rice to simmer for about 20 minutes or until all the water is absorbed.

Drain and chop the chilies. When the rice has finished cooking, stir in the chopped chilies and half the grated cheese. Mix the sour cream with the cornstarch and add to the rice. Season to taste.

Transfer the rice mixture into a greased baking dish and dab small pieces of butter on top. Sprinkle the remaining Cheddar over the dish and bake for 15 minutes, uncovered, until the cheese is brown and bubbly.

45 minutes to make
Good source of vitamin A, vitamin C, calcium

Hearts of Artichoke with Mushroom Sauce

Serve hot with rice, vegetables and a side salad.

4 large artichokes
2 tablespoons butter or margarine
2 cups mushrooms, finely diced
salt and freshly ground black pepper to taste
1 tablespoon chopped fresh tarragon
1 egg yolk
½ cup cream
2 tablespoons lemon juice

Bring a large pot of water to the boil. Remove the stems, outer leaves and the top quarter of each artichoke and place them in the boiling water so that the hearts are covered. Simmer for 30 minutes or until tender.

Heat the butter in a frying pan and add the chopped mushrooms. Cook for 3–4 minutes, stirring constantly. Add the salt, pepper and tarragon and continue stirring.

Whisk the egg yolk in a small bowl. Add the cream and mix well. Then add the lemon juice and whisk together. Add this sauce to the mushrooms and stir constantly over a low heat. Do not allow the sauce to boil.

When the artichokes are tender, remove their remaining leaves and the prickly 'choke' from the centre. Discard the chokes and place the hot hearts on a warm serving dish. Spoon the mushroom sauce over them and serve immediately.

45 minutes to make
Good source of vitamin A, B group vitamins, vitamin C, iron

Herby Cheese and Rice Bowl

1 cup white rice
2 tablespoons olive oil
3 tablespoons chopped fresh basil or parsley or a mixture of the two or 1 tablespoon dried herbs
1½ cups Mozzarella cheese, chopped
2–3 tablespoons grated Parmesan cheese

If necessary, wash the rice in cold water once or twice, then drain. Cover the rice with twice its volume of water (1 cup rice to 2 cups water) in a medium-sized saucepan. Bring to a boil, then cover the pan, reduce the heat and leave the rice to simmer for about 20 minutes or until all the water is absorbed.

Empty the rice into a large bowl and stir in the olive oil and herbs. Stir the Mozzarella into the hot rice – the Mozzarella must melt. Sprinkle the Parmesan over the top of the dish and serve immediately.

30 minutes to make
Good source of protein, vitamin A, calcium, iron

Hot Dogs and Tomatoes

This German dish is great accompanied with Sauerkraut (see page 141) and mashed or boiled potatoes, or potato pancakes.

2 tablespoons vegetable oil
2 cloves garlic, crushed
2 large onions, chopped
1 green pepper, seeded and chopped
1 tablespoon caraway seeds
2 16oz cans chopped tomatoes
1 tablespoon paprika
8–12 (depending on size) vegetable frankfurters or sausages
salt and freshly ground black pepper to taste

Heat the oil in a large saucepan and sauté the garlic and onions over a medium heat.

Add the chopped green pepper, cover the saucepan, reduce the heat and cook for 10 minutes, stirring occasionally.

Stir in the caraway seeds, tomatoes and paprika. Cover again, and simmer for a further 20 minutes.

Add the vegetable frankfurters and allow to cook for 3–5 minutes. Add the seasoning, stir well and cook for 10 minutes.

50 minutes to make
Good source of vitamin A, vitamin C

Hot Mozzarella Sandwich

Serve hot with a salad.

8 slices whole wheat bread
8 thin slices Mozzarella cheese
2 eggs, beaten
½ cup milk
¼ cup plain flour
enough olive oil or vegetable oil to cover the bottom of a frying pan

Trim the crusts from the slices of bread. Make 4 closed sandwiches, using two slices of cheese per sandwich. Heat the oil in the frying pan until it is hot but not smoking.

Mix the beaten eggs with the milk. Measure the flour onto a plate.

Brush a little of the egg mixture around the edges of each sandwich so that it holds together. Then dip each sandwich completely, but quickly, into the egg-and-milk mixture. Lift the sandwich out of the egg, on to the plate and lightly coat both sides with flour.

Fry the sandwiches in the hot oil for 3–4 minutes each side, or until lightly browned. When the cheese starts to melt, remove the sandwich from the pan. Place in a warm oven or under a grill until all 4 sandwiches are ready, then serve immediately.

25 minutes to make
Good source of protein, B group vitamins, calcium

Italian Burgers

Serve hot with rice, pasta or potatoes and a green salad.

2 tablespoons olive oil
6 vegetable burgers
1 large onion, chopped
2 cloves garlic, crushed
2 16oz cans chopped tomatoes
1 tablespoon freshly chopped oregano or basil or 1 tablespoon dried
salt and freshly ground black pepper to taste
16 black olives, pitted and chopped (optional)
1 cup Mozzarella cheese, sliced

Pre-heat the oven to 350°F. Heat the oil in a frying pan and brown the burgers on both sides, about 5 minutes in total. Then remove them from the pan and put to one side.

Sauté the onion and garlic in the hot oil until tender, then add the tomatoes, oregano and seasoning. Simmer for 15 minutes to thicken.

Put the burgers in a casserole dish. Place the olives on top and pour the sauce over them. Cover with slices of Mozzarella and bake for 30 minutes.

55 minutes to make
Good source of protein, vitamin A, vitamin C, calcium

Cheese Soufflé (p 94)

Lasagna Italiano

Serve with a salad or green vegetables. Serves 6.

4 tablespoons olive oil
2 cloves garlic, crushed
1 medium onion, chopped
2 sticks celery, chopped
2 16oz cans chopped tomatoes
1 small can tomato paste
8 tablespoons tomato juice
¼ teaspoon sugar
salt and freshly ground black pepper to taste
12–15 sheets lasagna
2 cups Mozzarella cheese, finely chopped

Pre-heat the oven to 350°F and lightly grease a deep casserole dish. Heat the oil in a saucepan and sauté the garlic and onion until soft and golden. Add the celery, tomatoes, tomato paste, tomato juice, sugar, salt and pepper. Stir well, cover the pan and simmer gently for 45 minutes.

Cook the lasagna in boiling water following the manufacturer's instructions, until it just begins to soften. Drain, and cover with cold water until needed.

Arrange the lasagna layers in the casserole dish: pasta, sauce, Mozzarella. Repeat these layers until all the ingredients are used.

Top the dish with a layer of cheese and bake for 30 minutes. Cut into portions and serve immediately.

1 hour 30 minutes to make
Good source of protein, vitamin A, vitamin C, calcium

Lentil Cheese Loaf

Serve with a vegetarian gravy, tomato sauce or cheese sauce and a green salad.

¾ cup lentils
1 cup Cheddar cheese, grated
1 onion, chopped
salt and freshly ground black pepper to taste
1 teaspoon dried herb (rosemary or sage or thyme)
1 cup fresh breadcrumbs
1 egg, beaten
3 tablespoons butter or margarine

Pre-heat the oven to 350°F and lightly grease a 1lb loaf tin. Wash the lentils twice in cold water and drain them well. Cover them with twice their volume of cold water in a large saucepan, cover and bring to a boil. Reduce the heat and simmer the lentils for 20 minutes, until they are quite soft.

Mix the cheese, onion, salt, pepper and herbs in with the cooked lentils.

Add the breadcrumbs, egg and butter to the lentil mixture and stir well. Add more breadcrumbs if the mixture is sloppy.

Press the mixture into the loaf tin and bake for 40–45 minutes. Turn out on to a platter and serve hot.

1 hour 15 minutes to make
Good source of protein, calcium

Lentil and Steaklets Stew

Serves 6–8.

1 large onion, chopped
2 sticks celery, chopped
1 clove garlic, crushed
1 bay leaf
6 cups vegetable stock or water (3 cups if using vegetable burgers)
1 16oz can chopped tomatoes
1 4½oz packet TVP chunks or 4 vegetable burgers, cubed
1 cup lentils
½ cup macaroni
1 teaspoon dried thyme
1 teaspoon dried oregano
salt and freshly ground black pepper to taste

In a large saucepan combine the onion, celery, garlic, bay leaf, vegetable stock, tomatoes and TVP chunks. Cover tightly and simmer for 30 minutes over a medium heat.

Wash the lentils twice in cold water. Drain them well.

Stir the lentils, macaroni, thyme, oregano, salt and pepper into the stew. Cover, and cook for 25 minutes. Serve hot.

1 hour 10 minutes to make
Good source of protein, vitamin A, vitamin C, iron

Linda's Lasagna

This is rather more filling than the Lasagna Italiano recipe above, and a little more special. Avoid using a thick, heavy pasta or you'll find the whole dish becomes stodgy. It will keep well in the fridge or freezer – just cover it when reheating to avoid drying the pasta. This makes enough for 6 people – serve hot with a side salad.

12–15 strips lasagna
4 tablespoons olive oil
1 large onion, chopped
2 cloves garlic, crushed
half a 4½oz packet TVP mince
3 16oz cans chopped tomatoes
1 teaspoon dried oregano
salt and freshly ground black pepper to taste
a little vegetable stock or water
1 cup cottage cheese
1 cup Cheddar cheese, grated

Pre-heat the oven to 350°F. Place the lasagna strips in a saucepan, cover with water and boil for a few minutes until they are just starting to soften (most brands advise you to do this, but check the instructions on the packet).

Heat the oil in a large saucepan and sauté the onion and garlic. Then add the TVP mince, chopped tomatoes with their juice, oregano, salt and pepper. Simmer for 20–30 minutes, adding a little stock or water if necessary to make a moist sauce. Remove from the heat.

Pour a layer of tomato sauce into a large, deep baking dish. Spoon a layer of cottage cheese over the sauce, then arrange a layer of lasagna over that, followed by a layer of grated Cheddar. Repeat this layering process until you're about 1½ inches away from the top of the baking dish. Finish with a layer of tomato sauce topped by a final layer of Cheddar cheese.

Bake the lasagna for 30 minutes, until the cheese is brown and bubbly.

1 hour 10 minutes to make
Good source of protein, B group vitamins, calcium, iron

Madras Onion Curry

Serve with rice and condiments such as nuts, grated coconut and chutneys.

3 tablespoons vegetable oil
1 large onion, chopped
1 clove garlic, crushed
1 tablespoon curry powder
1 4½oz packet TVP chunks or 4 vegetable burgers, cubed
1 small apple

3 cups vegetable stock or water (2 cups if using vegetable burgers)
1 tablespoon soy sauce
1 teaspoon grated lemon rind
1 tablespoon brown sugar
salt and freshly ground black pepper to taste
¼ teaspoon ground ginger
2 tablespoons cornstarch
2 tablespoons cold water

Heat the vegetable oil in a large saucepan and sauté the onion, garlic and curry powder until lightly browned.

Add the TVP chunks or cubed vegetable burgers to the mixture and stir for 5 minutes over a low heat.

Peel, core and chop the apple and add it to the sauté. Now add the remaining ingredients (except the cornstarch and cold water). Stir well, cover the pan, and simmer for 10 minutes.

Mix the cornstarch and cold water together in a small bowl. Add this mixture to the curry and simmer, stirring often, until the sauce thickens. Leave to cook, uncovered, for a further 5 minutes.

30 minutes to make

Maine Sauerkraut

Serve with veggy hot dogs and noodles.

2lb fresh Sauerkraut (see recipe on page 141)
1 apple
2 tablespoons vegetable oil
1 medium onion, chopped
half a 4½oz packet TVP chunks (or 2 vegetable burgers, cubed)
1 large potato, grated
1 tablespoon caraway seeds
2 cups water

Prepare the sauerkraut. Peel, core and slice the apple.

Heat the oil in a deep saucepan and sauté the onion until it is lightly browned. Add the TVP chunks and sauté for a further 5 minutes, stirring often.

Add the potato and caraway to the pan and cover with the water. Bring to the boil, then simmer, covered, for 1 hour over a low heat. Stir occasionally, adding extra water if necessary.

1 hour 10 minutes to make
Good source of vitamin C, iron

Meatless Balls

Serve with vegetables or as part of another recipe.

1lb vegetable burgers
¼ cup breadcrumbs
salt and freshly ground black pepper to taste
2 tablespoons butter or margarine
1 large onion, chopped
1 cup milk
1 egg, beaten
1 tablespoon chopped fresh parsley
1 tablespoon soy sauce
vegetable oil for frying

Crumble the burgers into a mixing bowl and use your fingers to work in the breadcrumbs, salt and pepper. Set to one side.

Melt the butter in a frying pan and sauté the onion until transparent.

Mix the milk and egg together and add, with the parsley and soy sauce, to the dry mix. Stir well, then add the onion sauté also. Stir this mixture thoroughly, and shape into 24 small balls.

Fry the meatless balls until well browned all over. Serve immediately.

1 hour to make
Good source of protein

Meatless Loaf

This recipe is an all-time favourite with me and with just about everyone who tries it (usually the main complaint is that there's never enough). I serve it with any green vegetable (such as gently steamed broccoli, spinach or French beans), and a helping of mashed potatoes, boiled rice or pasta. A green salad is a good starter or accompaniment.

2 tablespoons sunflower oil
2 medium onions, chopped
1 4½oz packet TVP mince
2 cups hot water or vegetable stock
1½ cups breadcrumbs
½ tablespoon mixed herbs
1 tablespoon freshly chopped parsley
2 cloves garlic, crushed
1 egg, beaten
1 cup sour cream
2 tablespoons soy sauce
salt and freshly ground black pepper to taste

for the sauce:
2 16oz cans chopped tomatoes

1 small can tomato paste
salt and freshly ground black pepper to taste

Pre-heat the oven to 350°F. Heat the oil in a large saucepan and sauté the onions until lightly browned. Add the TVP mince, stir and cook for 2 minutes. Pour the hot water or stock over the sauté and simmer for 4 minutes.

In a separate bowl, mix the breadcrumbs, herbs and garlic together with 1 cup cold water. Stir in the egg and leave to one side for 10 minutes.

Combine the cooked TVP mince with the breadcrumb mixture, then add the sour cream and soy sauce. Stir well and season to taste.

Using your hands, shape the mixture into an oval mound and place it in the centre of a large baking dish, leaving plenty of space all round for the tomato sauce to run.

Heat the tomatoes, tomato paste and seasoning in a small saucepan, and pour over the loaf, then bake for 1 hour.

1 hour 20 minutes to make
Good source of protein, vitamin A, vitamin C, potassium

Meatless Loaf with Herbs

¾ cup fresh breadcrumbs
6oz vegetable sausage mix
salt and freshly ground black pepper to taste
1 teaspoon sweet dried herb mixture (sage, rosemary, thyme)
1 tablespoon chopped fresh parsley
2 eggs, beaten
1 cup cold water
1 tablespoon butter or margarine
1 medium onion, chopped
1 4½oz packet TVP mince
2¼ cups tomato juice

Pre-heat the oven to 325°F. Mix the breadcrumbs, sausage mix, salt, pepper, dried herbs, parsley, eggs and water together in a mixing bowl. Stir very well and leave the mixture to one side.

Melt the butter in a frying pan. Sauté the onion for about 5 minutes until lightly browned. Add the TVP mince and continue to sauté for 1–2 minutes, then add the tomato juice, stir and simmer for 10 minutes.

Stir the contents of the frying pan into the sausage mixture in the bowl.

Press into a greased and lined 2lb loaf pan and bake for 1 hour.

1 hour 20 minutes to make
Good source of vitamin A, vitamin C

Festive, or Sunday, Roast with Savoury Stuffing (*p 98*)

Mexican Corn Pudding

You can substitute carrots, potatoes, onions or any other vegetable (or combination) for corn in this recipe – experiment for yourself!

6 ears sweet corn or 3 cups canned sweet corn, drained
2 cups milk
2 eggs, beaten
1 4oz can green chilies in brine
salt and freshly ground black pepper to taste
2 tablespoons butter or margarine

Pre-heat the oven to 350°F. Slice all the corn kernels away from the raw cob.

Warm the milk and stir the corn and eggs into it. Drain, rinse and chop the chilies. Add them, with the salt and pepper, to the corn mixture.

Dab a baking dish with the butter and pour the pudding mixture into it. Place this inside a larger dish filled with water, then put them both into the hot oven.

Bake for 30–40 minutes, until a single piece of uncooked spaghetti inserted into the pudding comes out clean.

50 minutes to make
Good source of vitamin A, B group vitamins, vitamin C, calcium

Mexican Loaf

This recipe fills two 2lb loaf pans, and should serve 6–8 people. To make 2 cups tomato sauce, sauté 1 onion in 1 tablespoon olive oil. Add 1 16oz can of tomatoes, chopped, 1 tablespoon tomato paste and 1 teaspoon dried basil and 1 clove crushed garlic. Simmer for 15–20 minutes.

2 tablespoons butter or margarine
1 clove garlic, crushed
4 vegetable burgers, crumbled or 1 4½oz packet TVP chunks
1 cup fresh sweet corn or 1 cup canned sweet corn
1 4oz can green chilies in brine, drained and chopped
½ teaspoon chili powder
salt and freshly ground black pepper to taste
1 cup cold tomato sauce (double this if using TVP chunks instead of burgers)
1¼ cups corn meal
2 eggs

Pre-heat the oven to 350°F and lightly grease two 2lb loaf pans. Melt the butter in a large frying pan and sauté the garlic. Crumble the burgers into the sauté and stir well.

Slice the corn off the raw cob. Add the corn, chilies, chili powder, salt and pepper to the sauté and stir well.

In a separate bowl, whisk the tomato sauce, corn meal and eggs to a smooth consistency. Add this to the mixture in the pan and remove from the heat.

Stir the mixture well, then spoon into the prepared pans. Place the tins in a large tray of water and bake for 1 hour.

1 hour 15 minutes to make
Good source of protein, vitamin A, vitamin C

Mexican Omelette

2 large eggs
1 4oz can green chilies in brine, drained and chopped
1 teaspoon butter or margarine
salt and freshly ground black pepper to taste

Drain and chop the chilies. Whisk the egg in a mixing bowl and add the chopped green chilies.

Heat the butter in the frying pan, pour in the egg mixture, season with salt and pepper and cook for 1–2 minutes over a high heat.

Keeping the omelette over the heat, use a spatula to fold it over. Slide it out of the pan on to a warm plate. Serve piping hot.

10 minutes to make
Good source of vitamin A, vitamin C

Mexican Rarebit

Serve over toast, rice or baked potato.

3 tablespoons butter or margarine
1 small onion, chopped
1 4oz can green chilies in brine, drained and chopped
2 tablespoons plain flour
1 cup milk
1 cup Cheddar cheese, grated
1 16oz can chopped tomatoes, drained
salt and freshly ground black pepper to taste

Melt the butter in a saucepan and sauté the onion. Add the chilies and stir well.

Sprinkle the flour over the sauté and stir well to make a thick paste. Gradually add the milk, stirring constantly, to make a smooth sauce.

Add the cheese, tomatoes, salt and pepper and stir well. Serve immediately.

15 minutes to make
Good source of protein, vitamin A, B group vitamins, vitamin C

Mince and Aubergine Casserole

3 medium aubergines
4 tablespoons butter or margarine
1 large onion, chopped
1 medium green pepper, chopped (optional)
half a 4½oz packet TVP mince (or 2 vegetable burgers, crumbled)
1 tablespoon plain flour
2 16oz cans chopped tomatoes
1 small can tomato paste
1 teaspoon dried oregano
salt and freshly ground black pepper to taste
1 cup vegetable stock (optional)
1½ cups Cheddar cheese, grated

Pre-heat the oven to 350°F and lightly grease a casserole dish. Peel the aubergine using a potato peeler and cut into strips.

Cook the aubergine strips for 5 minutes in boiling water until they are tender, then drain them. Melt the butter in a large saucepan and sauté the onion and green pepper for 2–3 minutes. Add the TVP mince and stir over a low heat for about 3 minutes. Add the flour and cook for 2 minutes longer.

Stir in the tomatoes, tomato paste, oregano and

seasoning. Allow to simmer for 5 minutes, stirring occasionally. Add a little vegetable stock or water if a moist sauce is desired.

Spread a layer of aubergine on the bottom of the casserole dish. Add a layer of the mince/tomato mixture, and then a layer of grated cheese. Alternate these layers until all the ingredients are used. End with a layer of cheese. Bake, uncovered, for 30 minutes, until the cheese makes a golden crust.

55 minutes to make
Good source of protein, vitamin A, vitamin C, calcium

Moussaka

This famous Greek dish is, in my opinion, even better for using TVP mince. You can eat it straight from the oven, with greens such as broccoli or spinach, but I really prefer the flavour when it's been allowed to cool for at least 6 hours and then reheated. It keeps very well in the fridge or freezer.

3 medium aubergines
6–8 tablespoons olive oil
2 onions, chopped
half a 4½oz packet TVP mince or 2 vegetable burgers, cubed
1 cup red wine
1 cup vegetable stock (½ cup if using vegetable burgers)
4 tablespoons chopped fresh parsley
¼ teaspoon ground cinnamon
¼ teaspoon ground nutmeg
salt and freshly ground black pepper to taste
3 tablespoons tomato puree

for the sauce:
3 tablespoons butter or margarine
3 tablespoons plain flour
1½ cups milk
2 eggs, beaten
1 cup cottage cheese
1 cup breadcrumbs
1 cup Parmesan cheese

Pre-heat the oven to 375°F and grease a large (12 × 18 inches) baking tray. Peel the aubergines and slice into ½ inch strips. Heat 4–6 tablespoons of the oil in a frying pan and brown the aubergine strips on both sides, then remove them from the pan and set them aside. Add more oil if necessary and sauté the onions.

Add the TVP mince to the frying pan and sauté for 5 minutes. Add the red wine, stock, parsley, cinnamon, nutmeg, salt, pepper and tomato puree.

Simmer this mixture over a low heat, uncovered, for about 15 minutes until most of the liquid has been absorbed. Remove from the heat and set aside.

Make a white sauce – melt the butter and sprinkle the flour over it. Stir into a smooth, thick paste. Heat the milk and slowly add it to the paste, stirring well after each addition to make a smooth sauce. Remove the sauce from the heat, leave to cool, then stir in the eggs and cottage cheese.

Sprinkle some breadcrumbs evenly over the baking tray. Place a layer of aubergine over the breadcrumbs, cover them with a layer of the TVP mince in sauce, then sprinkle with a thin layer of Parmesan cheese. Repeat the layering process, starting with the breadcrumbs, until the aubergine strips have been used up. Pour the cheese sauce over the dish and top with more Parmesan cheese. Bake for 40–50 minutes, until the cheese turns golden brown.

1 hour 35 minutes to make
Good source of protein, vitamin A, B group vitamins, calcium

Mozzarella Croquettes

Serve with a selection of green vegetables, and top with Home-made Tomato Sauce (see page 147).

3 cups plain flour
salt and freshly ground black pepper to taste
2 eggs
1lb Mozzarella cheese, grated
1 cup fresh breadcrumbs
vegetable oil for frying

for the garnish:
1 tablespoon chopped fresh parsley

Mix the flour, salt and pepper together in a mixing bowl.

Break the eggs into the centre of the flour mixture and stir in ever-increasing circles. When a doughy consistency is reached, add the grated Mozzarella and keep stirring.

Shape this mixture into balls or croquettes and roll them in the breadcrumbs until they are well coated.

Deep-fry until the croquettes are a golden brown. Serve hot with a sprinkling of parsley.

15 minutes to make
Good source of protein, vitamin A, B group vitamins, calcium

Mozzarella French Loaf

1 medium stick French bread
1lb Mozzarella cheese, sliced
2 tablespoons butter or margarine, melted
2 cloves garlic, chopped
1 teaspoon chopped fresh oregano

Pre-heat the oven to 425°F. Make diagonal cuts into the French loaf all the way along its length, at ½ inch intervals, but without slicing it all the way through. Place the loaf on a baking tray.

Push a slice of Mozzarella into each cut. Brush the melted butter over the loaf, and sprinkle the garlic and oregano over all.

Bake for 10–15 minutes until the crust is lightly browned and the cheese is bubbly.

20 minutes to make
Good source of protein, vitamin A, calcium

Ratatouille (p 117)

Mushroom Loaf

Serve with a fresh green salad or green vegetables or pasta.

1 cup breadcrumbs
1 cup milk
1 medium onion, chopped
1 cup mushrooms, chopped
2 tablespoons butter or margarine
1 tablespoon soy sauce
1 4½oz packet TVP mince or 4 vegetable burgers, crumbled
1¼ cups tomato juice (¾ cup if using vegetable burgers)
2 eggs, beaten
1 cup mashed potatoes
salt and freshly ground black pepper to taste
2 tablespoons chopped fresh herbs, to taste

Pre-heat the oven to 350°F. Lightly grease a 2lb loaf pan and line it with greaseproof paper. Soak the breadcrumbs in the milk and put on one side for 10 minutes.

Sauté the onion and mushrooms in the butter until light brown, then add the soy sauce and the TVP mince. Pour in the tomato juice and simmer for 4–5 minutes. In a separate bowl, mix all the other ingredients.

Add the soaked breadcrumbs and the sauté to the mixture in the bowl. Mix very well and press into the loaf pan.

Bake for 1 hour. Leave in the pan for 5 minutes before turning out on to a serving dish.

1 hour 30 minutes to make
Good source of protein, vitamin A, B group vitamins, vitamin C

Mushroom Pie

12oz shortcrust pastry (enough for a 9 inch two-crust pie)
4 tablespoons butter or margarine
1 medium onion, chopped
2 tablespoons plain flour
1 cup cream or milk
1 tablespoon brandy or sherry
1 tablespoon chopped fresh tarragon
salt and freshly ground black pepper to taste
1lb mushrooms, chopped

Pre-heat the oven to 400°F. Line a greased pie dish with half of the pastry, so that it overhangs the edges by approximately ½ inch.

Melt the butter in a saucepan and sauté the onion until tender. Sprinkle the flour over the onion and stir well as it thickens. Keep the pan over a low heat and gradually add the cream, stirring constantly to create a thick, smooth sauce.

Add the brandy, tarragon, salt and pepper and mix well, still over a low heat. Stir the mushrooms into the sauce and cook for 2 minutes, then remove from the heat and pour this mixture into the prepared pie dish.

Roll out the other half of the pastry, cut into strips and weave together to make a pretty lattice top for the pie. (Alternatively, you can just roll the crust in the ordinary manner and place it over the pie filling, decorating it with long cuts to let the steam out.) Crimp and trim the edges of the pastry and bake for 25–30 minutes, until the crust is golden brown.

50 minutes to make
Good source of protein, B group vitamins, potassium

Mushroom and Rice

4 tablespoons vegetable oil
1 cup mushrooms, finely chopped
1 cup long grain rice
2 cups vegetable stock or water
sprig of tarragon or other herb for flavouring

Heat the oil in a saucepan and brown the mushrooms over a medium heat for about 5 minutes.

Add the rice and vegetable stock, and flavour with the herb. Cover the pan, reduce the heat and simmer for about 20 minutes, until the water has been absorbed. Serve immediately.

25 minutes to make
Good source of vitamin A, B group vitamins

Mushroom Risotto

4 tablespoons butter or margarine
2 medium onions, chopped
1 cup mushrooms, chopped
1 cup white rice
2 cups boiling vegetable stock or water
salt and freshly ground black pepper to taste
1/4 cup Parmesan cheese
2 tablespoons butter or margarine, melted

Melt the butter in a deep saucepan, and sauté the onions for 5 minutes, until tender. Then add the mushrooms, and cook gently for 10 minutes.

Add the rice to the pan and cook for about 5 minutes, until it begins to go clear.

Add the vegetable stock, salt and pepper and bring the mixture to a simmer, stirring all the while. Then reduce the heat, cover the pan and leave it to cook for 15–20 minutes, until the liquid is absorbed.

Remove the lid, sprinkle the cheese over the top and pour the melted butter over that. Serve immediately.

35 minutes to make
Good source of vitamin A, B group vitamins

Mushrooms and Onions in Sherry

Serve over rice or mashed potatoes.

4 tablespoons butter or margarine
1 medium onion, chopped
1lb mushrooms, sliced
2 tablespoons plain flour
4 tablespoons chopped fresh parsley
1/2 cup vegetable stock or water
1/4 cup sherry or brandy
salt and freshly ground black pepper to taste

Melt the butter in a saucepan and sauté the onions until soft. Add the mushrooms and cook them until they begin to release their juices. Sprinkle the flour over the sauté and cook for 1 minute, stirring constantly.

Add the parsley and stock, and stir over a low heat until the mushrooms are tender and the sauce has thickened.

Add the sherry or brandy, increase the heat and cook for a further 5 minutes. Season to taste. Serve immediately.

20 minutes to make
Good source of B group vitamins

Noodles and Garlic

1 cup noodles
6 tablespoons olive oil
3 cloves garlic, finely chopped

to serve:
1/2 cup Parmesan cheese, grated

Cook the noodles in a large saucepan of boiling, salted water until tender. Rinse under cold water, drain and return them to the saucepan.

Heat the oil in a small saucepan and sauté the garlic very gently for 2–3 minutes until slightly crisp. Toss the oil and garlic in with the cooked pasta and sprinkle with Parmesan cheese. Serve immediately.

20 minutes to make
Good source of calcium

Noodles German Style

1 cup noodles
4 tablespoons butter or margarine
1lb mushrooms, sliced
4 tablespoons chopped fresh parsley
1/2 cup breadcrumbs

Cook the noodles in a large saucepan of boiling, salted water until just tender. Rinse under cold water and drain.

Melt the butter in a frying pan and sauté the mushrooms until lightly browned.

Add the cooked noodles, parsley and breadcrumbs, mix thoroughly and serve immediately.

25 minutes to make
Good source of vitamin A, B group vitamins

Olive and Steaklet Bake

To prevent curdling, make sure you don't put the casserole back in the oven after adding the sour cream. Covering the casserole at the last stage of the recipe will ensure that the cream is warmed through.

2 tablespoons vegetable oil
6 vegetable burgers
4 cloves garlic, crushed
1 12oz bottle pimento-stuffed olives, chopped
1 teaspoon mild mustard
1 tablespoon chopped scallion
1 tablespoon pickle
½ cup vegetable stock or water
1 cup sour cream

Pre-heat the oven to 350°F and lightly grease a casserole dish. Heat the oil in a frying pan over a medium heat. Put in the burgers and brown them on both sides, about 5 minutes in total, then place them on a plate.

Press the garlic on to both sides of the burgers, and place them in the casserole dish.

Add the olives and the rest of the ingredients, apart from the sour cream, to the frying pan. Stir over a medium heat for 3–5 minutes.

Pour .this sauce over the burgers and bake, uncovered, for 45 minutes. Remove from the oven. Pour the sour cream over the burgers. Cover the casserole and leave for 5 minutes. Serve immediately.

1 hour 10 minutes to make
Good source of vitamin A

Oriental Beefless Casserole

2 tablespoons butter or margarine
1 large onion, chopped
4 sticks celery, chopped
2 cloves garlic, crushed
2 teaspoons grated fresh ginger root
half a 4½oz packet TVP mince
½ cup long grain rice
2½ cups tomato juice
4 tablespoons soy sauce

Pre-heat the oven to 350°F and lightly grease a casserole dish. Melt the butter in a saucepan and sauté the onions, celery, garlic and ginger until light brown.

Add the TVP mince and stir together for 3–4 minutes. Spoon half of this mixture into the casserole dish and cover with the uncooked rice.

Place the remaining onion and celery mixture over the rice. Blend the tomato juice and soy sauce together and pour over the casserole.

Bake, covered, for 30 minutes.

45 minutes to make
Good source of vitamin A, calcium

Pasta with Herbs

1lb noodles (spaghetti or macaroni)
3 tablespoons chopped fresh parsley
3 tablespoons chopped fresh basil
1 tablespoon chopped fresh oregano
1 clove garlic, crushed
½ cup olive oil
1 cup cottage cheese

Cook the pasta until tender, rinse under cold water and drain.

Mix the herbs, garlic, oil and cheese in a blender, and liquidize to make a sauce.

Add the sauce to the cooked pasta and gently heat, while stirring. Serve immediately.

25 minutes to make
Good source of protein, vitamin A, calcium, iron

Greek Beefless Stew (*p 100*)

Penne with Vodka

A friend and fellow pasta-lover passed this on to me – serve with a green salad.

1 tablespoon olive oil
1 small onion, finely chopped
2–3 chilies, finely chopped
1 teaspoon dried basil or 2 fresh leaves
4 tablespoons vodka
1 16oz can tomatoes
1 tablespoon tomato paste
2 cups pasta (Penne)
1 cup light cream
1 cup Parmesan cheese
freshly ground black pepper to taste

Heat the oil in a saucepan and lightly sauté the onions, then add the chilies and fry for 2–3 minutes.

Add the basil and half the vodka to the saucepan, then increase the heat and add the tomatoes and tomato paste, breaking up the tomatoes with a wooden spoon. Bring to the boil, then reduce the heat and simmer, uncovered, for about 30 minutes, until you have a thick sauce.

Cook the pasta until it's tender (al dente). While it's cooking, add the remaining 2 tablespoons of vodka to the sauce.

When the pasta has cooked, drain it and turn it into the sauce. Take the saucepan off the heat and slowly add the cream, tossing it all together in the pan. Add the Parmesan and black pepper, and serve immediately.

50 minutes to make
Good source of protein, vitamin A, vitamin C, calcium

Pepper Steaklets

6 vegetable burgers
2 tablespoons olive oil
3 tablespoons whole peppercorns, crushed
1 tablespoon butter or margarine
½ cup red wine
2 tablespoons brandy
salt and freshly ground black pepper to taste
1 clove garlic, crushed

Brush the burgers with a little oil, and pat the peppercorns on to both sides.

Heat the remaining oil in a frying pan and brown the burgers on both sides (about 5 minutes in total). Reduce the heat and cook, covered, for 8 minutes.

Remove the burgers from the pan and keep them warm. Add the butter, wine, brandy, salt, pepper and garlic to the pan. Heat it well, stirring until it starts to bubble, then reduce the heat for 3–4 minutes.

Pour the hot sauce over the burgers and serve immediately with vegetables.

20 minutes to make

Peruvian Burgers

Serve with rice or potatoes and a green vegetable such as broccoli.

2 tablespoons butter or margarine
6 vegetable burgers, cubed
2 medium onions, chopped
2 teaspoons ground cumin
1 16oz can chopped tomatoes
2 tablespoons tomato ketchup
½ cup white wine
salt and freshly ground black pepper to taste
12 stuffed olives
¼ cup sliced almonds
⅓ cup raisins

Melt the butter in a frying pan and brown the burger chunks (about 5 minutes in total). Remove them from the pan and place on one side.

Sauté the onions in the butter until lightly browned. Add the cumin and cook for 1 minute to draw out the flavour.

Add the remaining ingredients to the sauté and stir well. Bring the mixture to a gentle boil, then add the burger chunks. Cover the pan, reduce the heat and simmer for 30 minutes.

45 minutes to make
Good source of vitamin A, vitamin C

Potato Torte à la Faranto

This is based on a fabulous Spanish/Mexican dish (torte means 'cake') which must be served piping hot.

for the sauce:
3 tablespoons olive oil
1 small onion, chopped
½ stick celery, chopped
2 cloves garlic, crushed
1 16oz can chopped tomatoes
1 tablespoon tomato paste
1 bay leaf
½ teaspoon dried basil
½ teaspoon dried oregano
1 teaspoon chopped fresh parsley

for the potatoes:
3 cups potatoes, peeled and cubed
1 tablespoon butter or margarine
2 tablespoons milk
1 egg, beaten
¼ teaspoon salt
¼ cup plain flour
1 tablespoon olive oil
1 cup Mozzarella cheese, grated
3 tablespoons grated Parmesan cheese

Pre-heat the oven to 350°F and grease an ovenproof dish. Make the sauce first – the longer ahead you make it, the better it tastes. Heat the oil in a saucepan and sauté the onions, celery, and garlic together until lightly browned. Then add the tomatoes, the tomato paste and the bay leaf, and simmer over a very low heat for 45 minutes. Add the basil, oregano and parsley for the last 10 minutes of simmering time.

Boil the potatoes until soft (about 25 minutes). Put them in a mixing bowl and mash them together with the butter, milk and egg. Add the salt and flour and work the mash together very well.

Press the potato mixture into the bottom and sides of the gratin dish to a thickness of ½ inch. Sprinkle with the olive oil and bake this potato shell for 15 minutes.

Pour the sauce into the baked potato shell to a depth of ¾ inch and sprinkle the Mozzarella and Parmesan over the sauce. Bake for 10–20 minutes, until the cheeses are bubbly and the edges of the potato are lightly browned.

1 hour 30 minutes to make
Good source of protein, vitamin A, vitamin C, calcium

Quiche

6oz shortcrust pastry (enough for 1 9 inch pie crust)
2 tablespoons butter or margarine
1 large onion, chopped
4 eggs, beaten
1½ cups milk
1 cup cream
2⅔ cups Cheddar or Swiss cheese, grated
salt and freshly ground black pepper to taste

Pre-heat the oven to 400°F. Grease your quiche dish, roll out the pastry and press it round the bottom and sides of the dish. Place some greaseproof paper filled with baking beans or dry rice on the pastry, and bake it blind for about 10 minutes, until the pastry turns a pale brown colour. Heat the butter in a frying pan and sauté the onion until lightly browned. Allow to cool.

Whisk the eggs in a mixing bowl and gradually add the milk and cream, beating after each addition. Add the cheese, salt, pepper and, last of all, the cool onions to the egg mixture. Pour this mixture into the pastry shell. Bake for 25–30 minutes.

55 minutes to make
Good source of protein, vitamin A, B group vitamins, calcium

Ratatouille

Use good-quality olive oil in this recipe, and be careful not to stir the dish too vigorously because it will break up the vegetables. Instead, use a wooden spatula and lift, like tossing a salad, to preserve the texture of each vegetable.

2lb whole tomatoes
1 medium (8oz) aubergine
4 tablespoons olive oil
1 large zucchini, sliced
2 medium onions, chopped
1 large green pepper, seeded and sliced
1 cup mushrooms, sliced
2–3 cloves garlic, crushed
1 tablespoon chopped fresh parsley
salt and freshly ground black pepper to taste

for the garnish:
2 tablespoons capers
1 lemon, cut into wedges

Plunge the tomatoes into boiling water for 1 minute. Remove them, then cut out the cores and peel them. Slice them in half and remove the pulp and seeds.

Then turn the tomato shells on to a paper towel and leave to drain.

Peel and slice the aubergine. Pour the olive oil into a large, deep pan and place over a medium flame. Sauté the aubergine and zucchini slices for 1–2 minutes until they are lightly browned. Remove them from the oil and drain on paper towels.

Use the same oil to sauté the onions, green pepper, mushrooms and garlic for about 10 minutes over a low heat, stirring frequently.

Place the aubergine and zucchini slices over this sauté and sprinkle with the parsley. Top with the tomato shells, cover the pan and cook over a low heat for 15 minutes. Remove the lid and continue cooking for 1 hour, until the mixture is thick and most of the liquid is gone. Season to taste.

Serve hot or cold with a garnish of capers and lemon wedges.

1 hour 45 minutes to make
Good source of vitamin A, B group vitamins, vitamin C

Rice with Asparagus

1½lb asparagus spears
6 tablespoons butter or margarine
1 cup long grain rice (part wild rice, if desired)
2 cups vegetable stock or water
salt and freshly ground black pepper to taste
½ cup Parmesan cheese, grated

Trim any woody stems from the asparagus. Melt the butter in a saucepan, add the asparagus tips and sauté for 2–3 minutes.

Add the rice, vegetable stock and seasoning, cover and simmer on a low heat for 15–20 minutes, until the rice is dry and fluffy.

Sprinkle with cheese and serve hot.

30 minutes to make
Good source of protein, vitamin A, B group vitamins, vitamin C

Rice and Beans

1 cup dried navy beans or similar beans
2 tablespoons butter or margarine
1 medium onion, chopped
1 stick celery, chopped
1 16oz can chopped tomatoes
1¼ cups water
1 cup long grain rice
salt and freshly ground black pepper to taste

Wash then soak the beans overnight. Bring to the boil in plenty of fresh water and boil rapidly for 10 minutes. Simmer for 40–45 minutes or until soft.

Melt the butter in a saucepan and lightly brown the onions and celery.

Add the beans, tomatoes, water and rice. Stir well, cover and cook for about 20 minutes until all the water has been absorbed. Season to taste and serve immediately.

1 hour 20 minutes to make
Good source of vitamin A, B group vitamins, vitamin C

Rice in Tasty Vegetable Stock

4 tablespoons vegetable oil
1 large onion, chopped
1½lb mushrooms, chopped
1 clove garlic, crushed
1 cup long grain rice
2 tablespoons wild rice (optional)
2 cups vegetable stock or water
2 tablespoons dried mixed herbs
salt and freshly ground black pepper to taste

Heat the oil in a large saucepan and sauté the onion, mushrooms and garlic over a low flame.

Add the rice and stir for 1–2 minutes to soak up the flavour.

Cover the rice with the vegetable stock and add the herbs and seasoning. Put a lid on the pan and gently simmer for about 20 minutes, until the liquid has been absorbed and the rice is tender and fluffy.

35 minutes to make
Good source of vitamin A, B group vitamins, vitamin C, potassium

Rice and Vegetables in Wine

2 tablespoons vegetable oil
1 onion, chopped
1 medium zucchini, chopped
1 medium carrot, chopped
1 stick celery, chopped
1 cup long grain rice
1¼ cups vegetable stock or water
1 cup white wine

Heat the oil in a saucepan and sauté the onion. Add the rest of the vegetables and stir them over a medium heat until lightly browned.

Add the rice, vegetable stock and white wine, cover and cook for about 15–20 minutes until all the liquid has been absorbed.

30 minutes to make
Good source of vitamin A

Sauté Schnitzel

2 tablespoons butter or margarine
6 vegetable schnitzels or vegetable burgers
8 tablespoons white wine
1 teaspoon lemon juice
1 clove garlic, crushed

for the garnish:
1 tablespoon chopped fresh parsley

Melt the butter in a frying pan and brown the burgers on both sides (about 5 minutes in total), then remove them from the pan.

Add the white wine, lemon juice and garlic to the saucepan and cook for 1 minute. Bring to a slow boil and let the wine reduce slightly.

Place the burgers back in the pan and heat them thoroughly for another 3 minutes. Serve immediately, over rice or toast, with a garnish of fresh parsley.

10 minutes to make

Savoury Rice

Serve with steamed vegetables or salad.

1 tablespoon vegetable oil
1 medium onion, chopped
1 cup long grain rice (part wild rice if desired)
2 cups vegetable stock or water
1 tablespoon soy sauce

Heat the oil in a deep saucepan and sauté the onion.

Add the rice to the sauté and stir over a medium heat until the rice begins to go clear.

Add the vegetable stock and soy sauce and cook, covered, for about 15–20 minutes, or until the liquid has been absorbed. Stir and serve hot.

30 minutes to make
Good source of vitamin A

Savoury Turnovers

Serve hot with a selection of vegetables.

1 tablespoon butter or margarine
1 medium onion, chopped
1 clove garlic, crushed (optional)
4 vegetable burgers, crumbled
2 tablespoons chopped fresh parsley
2 tablespoons chopped fresh chives
½ cup sour cream
1 teaspoon cornstarch
salt and freshly ground black pepper to taste
12oz shortcrust pastry (enough for 2 9 inch pie crusts)

Pre-heat the oven to 400°F and lightly grease a baking tray. Melt the butter in a large frying pan and sauté the onion and garlic until lightly browned.

Crumble the burgers into the sauté with the parsley and chives. Stir for 5 minutes, until the burgers begin to brown.

Mix the sour cream with the cornstarch and add enough to the burger mixture to make it moist but not sloppy. Stir to an even consistency and season to taste. Roll the pastry and cut into 5 inch rounds.

Place a spoonful of the filling on each pastry round and fold the pastry over. Crimp the edges, prick the top with a fork and arrange on the baking tray. Bake for 15 minutes. Serve hot or cold.

35 minutes to make

Schnitzel Scaloppini in White Wine

Serve over noodles or rice with green vegetables.

3 tablespoons butter or margarine
6 vegetable burgers, sliced in half
²⁄₃ cup vegetable stock
1 clove garlic, crushed
4 tablespoons white wine

Melt the butter in a large frying pan and brown the burgers (about 5 minutes in total). Remove them from the pan and place in a hot oven to keep warm.

Add the stock, garlic and wine to the hot oil and bring to the boil.

Pour the hot sauce over the hot burgers, and serve immediately.

15 minutes to make
Good source of protein

Shepherd's Pie

If you like a slightly stronger flavour, try adding 2 large carrots, thinly sliced, to the onion as it sautés.

1½lb potatoes
6 tablespoons butter or margarine
1–2 tablespoons milk
1 large onion, chopped
1 4½oz packet TVP mince or 6 vegetable burgers, crumbled
2 tablespoons soy sauce
1½ cups vegetable stock or water (¾ cup if using vegetable burgers)
salt and freshly ground black pepper to taste

Pre-heat the oven to 400°F. Boil the potatoes and mash them in a bowl with 4 tablespoons of the butter and enough milk to give a good sticky consistency. Put them to one side.

Melt the remaining butter in a frying pan and sauté the onion. Then add the TVP mince, soy sauce and vegetable stock. Simmer for 5–10 minutes. Season to taste.

If you want a thicker mixture, blend a little flour or vegetable gravy mix with some vegetable stock and add to the sauté. Cook until thickened, stirring constantly. Pour the mixture into a baking dish and cover with the mashed potatoes.

Bake for 30 minutes, until the potatoes are nice and brown. For extra browning on top, just place under the grill for a few moments (make sure your baking dish will stand this treatment).

1 hour 15 minutes to make
Good source of vitamin A, B group vitamins, vitamin C, potassium

Simple Beefless Hash

2 cups potatoes
2 tablespoons butter or margarine
1 large onion, chopped
2 teaspoons mixed herbs
1 tablespoon vegetable extract
1 4½oz packet TVP chunks
1¼ cups vegetable stock or water
2 tablespoons tomato paste
salt and freshly ground black pepper to taste

Peel and dice the potatoes, and parboil them for 1 minute, then drain. Melt the butter in a frying pan and sauté the onion and garlic. Then add the herbs.

Add the diced potato and sauté for 2–3 minutes. Now add the vegetable extract and TVP chunks and stir for 2–3 minutes over a low heat.

Stir in the vegetable stock, tomato paste and seasoning. Cover and simmer over a low heat for 15 minutes, adding a little extra stock or water if necessary to make a thick sauce.

25 minutes to make
Good source of vitamin A, vitamin C

Sour Cream, Paprika and Mushrooms

Serve hot over rice, mashed potatoes or toast with broccoli, spinach or any green vegetable.

2 tablespoons butter or margarine
1 medium onion, chopped
1 clove garlic, crushed
1lb mushrooms, sliced
1 teaspoon paprika
1 cup sour cream
salt and freshly ground black pepper to taste

Melt the butter in a frying pan and sauté the onion and garlic until tender. Add the mushrooms and cook gently for a further 3 minutes. Drain off most of the juice, but do not discard.
Add the paprika and cook briefly.
Remove the mixture from the heat and stir in the sour cream. You may return it to the heat, but do not let it boil. Add a little of the drained mushroom juice if the mushrooms need more sauce. Season to taste.

15 minutes to make
Good source of B group vitamins

Sour Cream Soufflé

1 cup plain flour
salt and freshly ground black pepper to taste
½ cup Gruyère cheese, grated
1½ cups sour cream
5 eggs, separated

Pre-heat the oven to 350°F and grease a 2–2½ pints soufflé dish. Mix the flour, salt, pepper and grated cheese together in a mixing bowl. Then stir in the sour cream.
Whisk the egg yolks in a small bowl and add them to the sour cream mixture. Stir well.
In a large mixing bowl, beat the egg whites until they are very stiff. Then fold them gently into the sour cream mixture.
Pour the mixture into the soufflé dish and set this dish in a pan filled with water. Place together in the oven and bake for 40 minutes.

1 hour to make
Good source of vitamin A, B group vitamins, calcium

Sour Cream Steaklet Chunks

Serve with potatoes or rice or pasta and green vegetables.

2 tablespoons vegetable oil
1 large onion, chopped
1 teaspoon thyme
1 bay leaf
salt and freshly ground black pepper to taste
1 4½oz packet TVP chunks or 6 vegetable burgers, cubed
1 cup tomato juice
1 cup water or vegetable stock (if using TVP chunks)
10oz frozen peas
1 cup sour cream
1 teaspoon horseradish sauce

Heat the oil in a large saucepan and sauté the onion. Add the thyme, bay leaf and seasoning. Stir well.
Add the TVP chunks and tomato juice (and vegetable stock too, if using TVP chunks), cover the pan and simmer gently for 30 minutes until the chunks are tender.
Add the peas and a little extra vegetable stock if necessary, and simmer for 5 minutes. Then stir in the sour cream and horseradish sauce. Serve immediately.

45 minutes to make
Good source of vitamin A, B group vitamins, vitamin C

Spaghetti Omelette

Serves 2.

2 cups uncooked spaghetti or 4 cups left-over cooked spaghetti
2 eggs
2 tablespoons butter or margarine
salt and freshly ground black pepper to taste
½ cup Cheddar cheese, grated

If using raw spaghetti, bring a pan of water to a galloping boil and break the spaghetti into it. Leave the pan uncovered and boil the spaghetti for 10–12 minutes. Drain.
Whisk the eggs in a mixing bowl and add the cooked spaghetti.
Heat the butter in a frying pan and pour in the egg and spaghetti mixture. Season, and leave the omelette to cook for 1 minute. Sprinkle the grated cheese over the omelette, then leave to cook for a

further 1 2 minutes. Use a spatula to fold the omelette over. Serve piping hot with toast or a salad.

15 minutes to make
Good source of protein, vitamin A, B group vitamins, calcium, zinc

Spanish Burgers

Serve hot with rice or mashed potatoes.

4 tablespoons butter or margarine
8 vegetable burgers, cubed
1 medium onion, chopped
2 sticks celery, chopped
3 carrots, chopped
1 green pepper, seeded and chopped
1 cup mushrooms, chopped
1 16oz can chopped tomatoes
1 bay leaf
2 teaspoons paprika
salt and freshly ground black pepper to taste
½ cup baby peas
juice of ½ lemon

Melt half of the butter in a large saucepan and brown the burger chunks, about 5 minutes in total. Remove them from the pan and place to one side. Melt the rest of the butter and sauté the onion and celery.

When the onion and celery are tender, return the burger chunks to the pan and stir gently.

Add all the remaining ingredients except the peas and lemon juice. Stir well and cover the pan. Simmer gently for 30 minutes.

Add the peas and simmer for a further 5 minutes, stirring often. Pour in the lemon juice. Serve immediately.

50 minutes to make
Good source of vitamin A, B group vitamins, vitamin C

Spanish Omelette

2 tablespoons butter or margarine
1 medium onion, chopped
3 sticks celery, chopped
½ red or green pepper, seeded and chopped (optional)
2 tomatoes, chopped
2 tablespoons tomato paste
4 eggs, beaten

Melt half the butter in a frying pan and sauté the onion until it is soft.

Add the celery and pepper. Stir well until the onion begins to brown, then add the tomatoes. Cook over a low heat and stir for about 8–10 minutes, adding little more butter if necessary. Stir in the tomato paste.

Put the rest of the butter in a frying pan over a medium heat and add the eggs. Leave the eggs untouched until they begin to cook through, then use a spatula to lift the omelette and turn it over. Place the vegetables on the cooked side, and when the other side is cooked, fold in half and serve immediately.

20 minutes to make
Good source of protein, vitamin A, B group vitamins, vitamin C, iron

Spicy Eggs

3 tablespoons olive oil
1 large onion, chopped
1 clove garlic, crushed
1 green pepper, seeded and sliced
4 large mushrooms, chopped
1 teaspoon chili powder (or more to taste)
½ teaspoon cumin seed
½ teaspoon oregano
salt and freshly ground black pepper to taste
6 eggs
¾ cup Cheddar cheese, grated

Pre-heat the oven to 350°F and lightly oil a baking dish. Heat the oil in a large pan and sauté the onion and garlic for 3–4 minutes, then add the green pepper and mushrooms and cook for approximately 5 minutes.

Add the spices, herb and seasonings. Stir often as the mixture cooks for a further 5 minutes.

Pour the mixture into the baking dish and break the eggs over it. Cover with the grated cheese and bake for 15–20 minutes. Serve hot.

40 minutes to make
Good source of protein, vitamin A, vitamin C, calcium

123

Shepherd's Pie (p 120)

Spinach Cheese Dumplings

A wonderful, tasty winter warmer – serve with a selection of vegatables.

1lb fresh spinach
1 cup cottage or ricotta cheese
2 egg yolks, beaten
½ cup Parmesan cheese, grated
salt and freshly ground black pepper to taste
pinch of nutmeg
½ cup self-rising flour
4 tablespoons butter or margarine

Wash and trim the spinach and cook it, covered, in its own juices. Drain very well, chop finely and allow to cool.

Mix the cottage cheese, egg yolks, half the Parmesan cheese, the salt, pepper and nutmeg in a large mixing bowl. Add the cooled spinach and the flour and mix together.

Take a spoonful of the mixture and using a little flour shape it into a small ball, flouring your hands if necessary. Continue in this way until all the mixture is used.

Drop the dumplings into a pot of boiling water, about 10–12 at a time, and cook for 4–5 minutes. Continue in this way until all the dumplings are cooked.

Melt the butter. Place the dumplings on a hot serving dish and pour the butter over them. Sprinkle with the remaining Parmesan cheese and serve immediately.

35 minutes to make
Good source of protein, vitamin A, vitamin C, calcium, iron

Spinach Pie

6oz shortcrust pastry (enough for 1 9 inch pie crust)
1lb fresh spinach, finely chopped
4 eggs
1 cup sour cream
1 tablespoon butter or margarine
¼ cup Cheddar cheese, grated
1 cup fresh breadcrumbs

Pre-heat the oven to 425°F and grease a 12 inch flan dish. Roll out the pastry to fit the dish, press it in and bake blind for 7 minutes. Remove from the oven and reduce the oven temperature to 350°F.

Press the spinach into the pastry shell.

Beat the eggs and sour cream together and pour them over the spinach.

Melt the butter and mix it with the cheese and breadcrumbs. Spread this mixture over the sour cream. Bake the pie for 30 minutes, until the top is golden. Serve hot.

45 minutes to make
Good source of vitamin A, B group vitamins, vitamin C, calcium

Spinach and Sour Cream Omelette

Serve with steamed carrots and peas or a fresh salad. Serves 2.

½lb fresh spinach
½ clove garlic, crushed
pinch of nutmeg
salt and freshly ground black pepper to taste
⅓ cup sour cream
1 tablespoon butter or margarine
1 large egg
1 tablespoon milk
fresh herbs to taste

Wash and trim the spinach, removing all the stems, and place in a very hot frying pan. Cover, and simmer the spinach in its own juice until it is tender. Then drain off all the liquid and reduce the heat.

Chop the drained spinach while it is still in the pan (use a spatula), then add the garlic, nutmeg, salt, pepper and sour cream. Stir together over a low heat, but don't allow this mixture to boil.

Melt the butter in a frying pan. Beat the egg and milk together in a cup and pour into the hot butter. Cook for 1 minute over a high heat. Use a spatula to lift the omelette and turn it over.

Spoon the spinach mixture on to the centre of the omelette as it finishes cooking. Spread the filling round to the edges of half the omelette, sprinkle with fresh herbs, then use the spatula to fold the omelette over. Lift the omelette out of the pan and slice it in half.

20 minutes to make
Good source of protein, vitamin A, B group vitamins, vitamin C, iron

Steaklets Diane

Serve on a warmed plate with new potatoes, green beans and sautéd mushrooms.

4 tablespoons butter or margarine
4 vegetable burgers
1 tablespoon warmed brandy
1 tablespoon sherry
1 tablespoon finely chopped chives or onion

Pre-heat the oven to 350°F. Melt 3 tablespoons of the butter in a frying pan and brown the burgers on both sides (about 5 minutes in total). Remove the burgers from the pan and put them in the hot oven.

Add the brandy, sherry and the rest of the butter to the frying pan. Sprinkle the chives over it and stir well.

Return the burgers to the frying pan and cook them in the sauce for 1 minute. Serve immediately.

15 minutes to make
Good source of protein

Steaklets Pepper

Serve with wild rice, mashed potatoes or macaroni with any green vegetable and glazed carrots.

3 tablespoons vegetable oil
4 vegetable burgers
1 large onion, chopped
1 clove garlic, crushed
2 green peppers, seeded and chopped
1 cup vegetable stock or water
1 16oz can chopped tomatoes
1½ tablespoons cornstarch
1 tablespoon soy sauce

Pre-heat the oven to 350°F. Heat the oil in a large saucepan and brown the burgers on both sides (about 5 minutes in total). Remove the burgers from the pan and place in a hot oven. Add the onions and garlic to the pan and sauté until they are tender.

Add the peppers and most of the vegetable stock to the sauté, then cover and simmer for 10 minutes.

Add the tomatoes and simmer for a further 10 minutes. Mix the cornstarch and soy sauce with the remaining vegetable stock to make a smooth, lump-free paste. Add this to the sauce and continue to simmer.

When the sauce has thickened, return the burgers

to the pan. Increase the heat for 1 minute. Serve immediately.

30 minutes to make
Good source of protein, vitamin C

Stuffed and Broiled Mushrooms

Try serving with a good-sized salad (such as Chef's Salad, page 72).

9–12 very large mushrooms
2 tablespoons vegetable oil or olive oil
1 medium onion, chopped
1 clove garlic, crushed (optional)
1 4½oz packet TVP mince
1 cup fresh breadcrumbs
2 tablespoons cream
1 teaspoon sherry
1 cup vegetable stock
salt and freshly ground black pepper to taste

Pre-heat the oven to 350°F. Clean the mushrooms and remove their stems. Chop the stems finely and place the mushroom caps bottom-up on a lightly-oiled baking tray. Brush the mushrooms with a little oil, cover the tray and bake for 10–15 minutes.

Heat the oil in a frying pan and sauté the onion and garlic until soft. Add the chopped mushroom stems and the TVP mince. Stir well and continue to sauté the mixture for 4–5 minutes.

Add the rest of the ingredients, stir and cook for a further 4–5 minutes.

Spoon a little of the mixture into each of the mushrooms in the baking tray. Cook under the broiler for about 5 minutes. Serve immediately.

35 minutes to make
Good source of protein

Stuffed Eggs and Tomato

Serve with steamed vegetables.

6 eggs
3 tablespoons butter or margarine
4 tablespoons tomato paste
1 teaspoon mild mustard
salt and freshly ground black pepper to taste
2 cups béchamel sauce (see page 143)

for the garnish:
1 tablespoon chopped fresh parsley

Pre-heat the oven to 350°F and lightly grease a baking dish.

Hard-boil the eggs – about 10 minutes in boiling water. Peel the eggs and slice them in half lengthways. Remove the yolks and place them in a mixing bowl.

Blend the yolks, butter, half the tomato paste and the mustard to make a smooth paste. Fill the egg whites with this mixture and place them in the baking dish.

Combine the remaining tomato puree, salt, pepper and béchamel sauce and pour it over the stuffed eggs.

Bake for 15–20 minutes. Sprinkle the parsley over the hot sauce and serve immediately.

40 minutes to make
Good source of protein, vitamin A

Stuffed Peppers

½ cup long grain rice (can be part wild)
4 medium red or green or yellow peppers, halved
  vertically and seeded
4 tablespoons vegetable oil
1 large onion, chopped
half a 4½oz packet TVP mince
2 tablespoons chopped fresh parsley
2 cups Fresh Tomato Sauce (see page 145)
salt and freshly ground black pepper to taste

Pre-heat the oven to 375°F. Cover the rice with twice its volume of water in a medium-sized saucepan. Bring to the boil, then cover the pan, reduce the heat and leave the rice to simmer for about 20 minutes, or until all the water is absorbed.

Arrange the pepper halves in a large baking dish. Heat the oil in a saucepan and sauté the onion until it is soft. Add the TVP mince and stir well. Add the parsley and cook over a low heat for 5 minutes.

Add the cooked rice and half the tomato sauce. Mix well, season to taste, and spoon the mixture into the pepper halves.

Pour some of the remaining tomato sauce over each stuffed pepper. Cover and bake for 30 minutes. Serve immediately.

1 hour to make
Good source of vitamin A, vitamin C

Sunday Breakfast

This makes a lovely, traditional plate for Sunday breakfast – we all look forward to it!

for the tomato sauce:
1 tablespoon butter or margarine
2 16oz cans chopped tomatoes
salt and freshly ground black pepper to taste

for the sausages:
5oz vegetable sausage mix
½ teaspoon each chopped fresh thyme and chopped
  rosemary, or 1½ teaspoons dried mixed herbs
2 teaspoons chopped fresh parsley
½ teaspoon chopped fresh sage
1 clove garlic, minced
1 egg, beaten
1 teaspoon freshly ground black pepper
1 tablespoon butter or margarine

to serve:
fried eggs
toast

Set the sauce to simmer gently first of all, since it will take the longest to cook. Melt the butter in a saucepan and empty the chopped tomatoes, salt and pepper into it. Simmer, stirring often, until enough water has evaporated for it to take on a thickish consistency.

Make up the vegetable sausage mix according to the directions on the packet, adding the herbs, garlic, beaten egg and seasonings. Mix well. Let the mixture stand for 5–10 minutes, until firm enough to mould into sausage shapes. Melt the butter in the frying pan and brown the sausages, turning often.

Keep the sausages warm while you prepare fried eggs and toast for the family. Serve everything together on warm plates.

25 minutes to make
Good source of vitamin A, vitamin C

Super Curried Eggs Indian Style

Serve with rice.

6 eggs
4 tablespoons butter or margarine
1 medium onion, chopped
1 clove garlic, crushed
2 tablespoons curry powder
2 tablespoons tomato paste
¾ cup water
1 tablespoon lemon juice
salt and freshly ground black pepper to taste
rind of 1 lemon, grated
2 tablespoons fresh parsley, chopped

Hard-boil the eggs for 10 minutes.

Melt the butter in a frying pan and sauté the onion and garlic. Add the curry powder, tomato paste, water, lemon juice, salt and pepper. Stir all these ingredients together. Allow the mixture to cook over a low heat until it is just bubbling.

When the eggs have finished cooking, peel them and slice them in half lengthways. Add these to the curry and stir gently.

Add the lemon rind and the parsley to the curry. Stir once again, and serve hot.

30 minutes to make
Good source of protein, vitamin A, B group vitamins, vitamin C, iron

Swiss Fondue

Perhaps a bit exotic, but it's a great recipe, and will give you something to do with that fondue set you got as a present! Fun for a party.

1½ cups white wine
1 clove garlic, crushed
4 cups Gruyère or other Swiss cheese, grated
1 tablespoon plain flour
salt and freshly ground black pepper to taste

to serve:
French bread

Using a fireproof dish, heat the wine over a low heat until it begins to bubble gently. Add the garlic.

Mix the cheese, flour, salt and pepper together in a bowl.

Gradually add this mixture to the hot wine, stirring constantly to make a very smooth sauce.

Keep the sauce hot over a low heat, stirring from time to time to stop it getting too thick and solid.

Cut the French bread into cubes and give each person a long-handled fork with which to dip the bread cubes into the fondue. Eat immediately!

25 minutes to make
Good source of protein, vitamin A, calcium

Swiss Schnitzel

Serve with salad, hot vegetables or baked potatoes.

4 tablespoons olive oil
6 vegetable schnitzels or vegetable burgers
salt and freshly ground black pepper to taste
4 tablespoons lemon juice
4 eggs
2 tablespoons chopped fresh parsley

Pre-heat the oven to 350°F. Heat 1 tablespoon of the oil in a frying pan and brown the schnitzels (about 5 minutes in total). Place them on an ovenproof plate. Sprinkle the schnitzels with salt, pepper and lemon juice, and put them in the hot oven to keep warm.

Heat the remaining oil and fry the eggs.

Remove the schnitzels from the oven, sprinkle some parsley over each, then top each pair with a fried egg. Pour some of the hot lemon juice over each egg and serve immediately.

20 minutes to make
Good source of protein, B group vitamins, vitamin C

Swiss Steaklets

Serve with rice or green vegetables.

½ cup butter or margarine
1 large onion, chopped
1 clove garlic, crushed
2 cups fresh mushrooms, sliced (optional)
6 vegetable burgers
1 16oz can chopped tomatoes
1 small can tomato paste
1⅓ cup tomato juice or water

Pre-heat the oven to 350°F. Melt the butter in a large frying pan and sauté the onion, garlic and mushrooms until golden brown. Then add as many burgers as will fit into the pan and brown them on both sides (about 5 minutes in total).

Take the burgers out and place them in the warm oven. Add the tomatoes, tomato puree and juice to the pan. Bring to the boil and keep them boiling for 3 minutes, stirring.

Finally turn the heat down to a simmer, put the burgers back into the sauce, cover and cook for 10 minutes. Serve hot.

30 minutes to make
Good source of protein, vitamin A, vitamin C

Tarragon and Herb Eggs

Rice or salad is an excellent accompaniment to this very tasty dish.

1½ cups milk
1½ cups light cream
4 eggs, beaten
2 tablespoons chopped fresh tarragon
1 tablespoon chopped fresh parsley or any fresh herb combination of your choice
salt and freshly ground black pepper to taste

for the garnish:
chopped fresh parsley

Pre-heat the oven to 350°F and lightly grease 4 individual custard cups or ramekins. Place the cups in a baking tray filled with water. Mix the milk and cream together in a saucepan and heat to just below boiling point.

Add the hot milk mixture to the eggs, stirring constantly. As you stir, add the herbs, salt and pepper.

Pour the egg mixture into the ramekins, filling each about three-quarters full. Bake them in the tray

of water for 20 minutes (the water surround ensures they do not cook too fast).

Then insert a piece of raw spaghetti into the contents of one of the ramekins. If the eggs are cooked, the spaghetti will come out clean. Serve hot with a garnish of fresh parsley.

30 minutes to make
Good source of vitamin A, calcium, iron

Teriyaki

Serve the marinated burger chunks over rice or with other vegetables, with a spoonful of the hot sauce to accompany them.

6 vegetable burgers, cubed
1 medium onion, chopped
1 clove garlic, crushed
1 tablespoon fresh grated ginger or 1 teaspoon ground ginger
8 tablespoons soy sauce
8 tablespoons vegetable oil
8 tablespoons orange juice
1 tablespoon lemon juice
3 teaspoons sugar

Place the burger chunks in a deep dish. Mix all the other ingredients together in a large jug or bowl and pour over the burger chunks. Cover, and leave to marinate for 4–6 hours.

At the end of that time, drain the sauce into a saucepan and bring to a simmer. Grill or barbecue the burger chunks until nicely browned.

6 hours 30 minutes to make
Good source of protein

Tomato Pie

6oz shortcrust pastry (enough for 1 9 inch pie crust)
2 tablespoons olive oil
2 onions, chopped
1 clove garlic, crushed
1 small zucchini, chopped
6 large tomatoes, peeled or 1 16oz can chopped tomatoes
4 tablespoons chopped fresh parsley
1 teaspoon dried sage
1 teaspoon chopped tarragon
salt and freshly ground black pepper to taste
2 eggs, beaten
1 cup Cheddar cheese, grated

Preheat the oven to 425°F. Line an 8 inch flan dish with the shortcrust pastry and bake blind for 3–4 minutes. Reduce the heat to 400°F.

Heat the oil in a saucepan and sauté the onions, garlic and zucchini until lightly browned.

Add the tomatoes, herbs and seasoning and simmer this mixture for a further 5 minutes. Pour the sauté into the pie crust.

Pour the beaten eggs over the sauté mixture, top with the grated cheese and bake for 15 minutes. Serve hot.

30 minutes to make
Good source of protein, vitamin A, B group vitamins, vitamin C, calcium

Tomato Rice

For a tasty variation, try adding 1–2 teaspoons of oregano to the tomatoes, or add ½ cup grated cheese at the end of cooking and stir until melted.

4 tablespoons butter or margarine
1 large onion, chopped
1 cup long grain rice
2 16oz cans chopped tomatoes
2 tablespoons tomato paste
1½ cups tomato juice
a little extra boiling vegetable stock or water

Melt the butter in a large saucepan and sauté the onion until tender.

Add the rice and stir well. Add the tomatoes, tomato paste and tomato juice and bring the mixture to a boil. Cover, reduce the heat and simmer for 25–35 minutes or until the rice is tender. Check on the liquid content towards the end of cooking, and add boiling stock if necessary. Serve hot.

45 minutes to make
Good source of vitamin A, vitamin C, potassium

Tomato Soufflé

A wonderful soufflé, easy to make and tasty to eat. Serve with fresh green vegetables or a salad.

6 large tomatoes, peeled
2 tablespoons butter or margarine
3 tablespoons tomato paste
1 tablespoon sugar
1 tablespoon chopped fresh parsley
salt and freshly ground black pepper to taste
1 cup thick White Sauce (see page 150)
3 tablespoons grated Swiss or Parmesan cheese
5 eggs, separated

for the garnish:
sprig of fresh basil

Pre-heat the oven to 400°F and grease an 8 inch soufflé dish. Chop the tomatoes and put them in a frying pan with the butter. Cook over a medium heat for 5–6 minutes, until the liquid reduces.

Add the tomato paste, sugar, parsley, salt and pepper to the frying pan and stir well. Add the white sauce and cheese, stir thoroughly and remove from the heat. Leave to cool slightly.

Beat the egg yolks in a small bowl, then stir them into the tomato mixture. In a separate, larger bowl, beat the egg whites until they are very stiff. Gently fold the beaten egg whites into the tomato mixture and pour the whole mixture into the soufflé dish.

Bake for 35–40 minutes, until well risen and golden. Garnish with the fresh basil and serve immediately.

55 minutes to make
Good source of protein, vitamin A, B group vitamins, vitamin C, iron

Tomatoes Provençal and Mince

Good to eat with fresh vegetables, salad or hot rice. Perfect when accompanied by Chick Pea Salad (see page 73)

6 large tomatoes
6 tablespoons olive oil
2 tablespoons butter or margarine
1 medium onion, chopped
1 clove garlic, crushed
8 vegetable burgers
1½ tablespoons plain flour
1½ cups vegetable stock or water
salt and freshly ground black pepper to taste
2 tablespoons chopped fresh parsley

Pre-heat the oven to 400°F. Halve the tomatoes and place them in a frying pan with the oil, cut side down. Cook for 5 minutes over a medium heat. Pierce the tomato skins with a fork and peel the skins off as they warm. Remove the tomatoes onto a plate.

Melt the butter in the frying pan and sauté the onions and garlic until lightly browned. Crumble the burgers into the sauté and stir well.

Now sprinkle the flour over the sauté and stir to thicken the sauce. Gradually add the vegetable stock, stirring constantly, and cook over a medium heat until this also thickens.

Add the salt, pepper and most of the parsley to the sauté. Stir well and pour the mixture into a casserole dish. Arrange the tomatoes on top, sprinkle the remaining parsley over the tomatoes and bake the casserole, uncovered, for 15 minutes. Serve immediately.

30 minutes to make
Good source of protein, vitamin A, vitamin C

Vegetable Burger Stew with Tomatoes, Peas and Cheese Topping

Serve hot with rice.

3 tablespoons vegetable oil
2 tablespoons chopped shallots or onion
2 tablespoons butter or margarine
6 vegetable burgers, cubed
salt and freshly ground black pepper to taste

1 16oz can chopped tomatoes
1 teaspoon mixed dried herbs
1 bay leaf
2lb fresh peas or 10oz frozen baby peas

for the garnish
½ cup Cheddar cheese, grated

Heat the oil in a frying pan and sauté the onion until lightly browned. Melt the butter in a separate saucepan and brown the burger chunks (about 5 minutes in total).

Mix the onions and burger chunks together and add all the remaining ingredients except the peas and grated cheese. Stir well.

Cover the pan and simmer the mixture for 20 minutes, adding a little vegetable stock or water if necessary to keep the mixture moist.

Add the peas and cook for a further 10 minutes. Serve hot over rice and garnish with grated cheese.

45 minutes to make
Good source of protein, vitamin A, vitamin C, calcium

Vegetable Burger Supreme

Serve with rice, vegetables or noodles.

2 tablespoons olive oil
6 vegetable burgers
2 tablespoons butter or margarine
1 medium onion, chopped
2 cloves garlic, crushed
salt and freshly ground black pepper to taste
4 tablespoons white wine
4 tablespoons sherry
4 tablespoons vegetable stock or water
2 egg yolks
2 tablespoons heavy cream
2 tablespoons chopped fresh parsley

Heat the oil in a frying pan and brown the burgers over a medium heat for about 5 minutes, turning often. Remove from the heat.

Melt the butter in the frying pan and sauté the onion and garlic until lightly browned. Add the seasoning.

Stir in the wine, sherry and stock and simmer for 3–4 minutes. Whisk the egg yolks and heavy cream together in a small bowl.

Pour the cream mixture into the wine sauce and stir well. Add the parsley, then the browned burgers, and bring up to a simmer. Serve hot.

30 minutes to make
Good source of protein, vitamin A

Vegetable Burgers in White Wine

Serve with fresh vegetables, rice or mashed potatoes. As a variation, you could use 1 tablespoon of fresh (or 1 teaspoon dried) rosemary in place of the dill weed.

4 tablespoons butter or margarine
6 vegetable burgers
1½lb mushrooms, sliced
¼ cup plain flour
1¼ cups vegetable stock or water
1¼ cups white wine
½ teaspoon dried dill weed
salt and freshly ground black pepper to taste

Pre-heat the oven to 350°F. Melt half the butter in a large frying pan and brown the burgers (about 5 minutes in total). Remove them on to a plate and keep them warm in the oven.

Sauté the mushrooms in the remaining butter until tender.

Sprinkle the flour over this sauté and stir well to make a thick paste. Gradually add the stock and the wine to make a smooth, thick sauce. Add the dill weed and stir constantly over a low heat for 4–5 minutes. Season well, and pour the sauce over the burgers. Serve hot.

30 minutes to make
Good source of protein, B group vitamins, potassium

Vegetable Curry

3 tablespoons butter or margarine
1 large onion, chopped
6 medium potatoes, chopped
1 apple, peeled and chopped
1 turnip, chopped
3 leeks, thinly sliced
4 medium carrots, thinly sliced
6 sticks celery, thinly sliced
4 tablespoons mild curry powder (or to taste)
1 tablespoon brown sugar
2 tablespoons soy sauce
1 4½oz packet TVP chunks or 4 vegetable burgers, cubed
2 cups water or vegetable stock

Melt the butter in a large soup pan over a medium heat. Add the vegetables and toss them in the butter for a few minutes. Then add the curry powder,

sugar, soy sauce and TVP chunks and stir well. Cover the mixture with water.

Cover the pan and cook over a medium heat until the vegetables are tender. Stir the curry occasionally, but otherwise keep the pan covered. Serve immediately, although this dish will benefit from standing for an hour or so before being either reheated or served cold.

45 minutes to make
Good source of protein, vitamin A, vitamin C, potassium

Vegetables and Baked Schnitzels in White Wine

2 tablespoons butter or margarine
6 vegetable schnitzels or vegetable burgers
2 onions, chopped
1 cup carrots, thinly sliced
2 sticks celery, thinly sliced
salt and freshly ground black pepper to taste
1 cup vegetable stock or water
1 cup white wine

Pre-heat the oven to 375°F.

Melt the butter in a frying pan and brown the schnitzels on both sides (about 5 minutes in total).

Mix the prepared vegetables in an oven-to-table casserole dish, and place the browned schnitzels on top. Sprinkle the salt and pepper over the schnitzels and pour the vegetable stock and white wine over them.

Bake the casserole, uncovered, until most of the liquid has evaporated (about 45–60 minutes). Check it from time to time and baste the schnitzels with the liquid. Serve hot, straight from the casserole dish.

1 hour 15 minutes to make
Good source of protein, vitamin A, B group vitamins, potassium

Wild Rice and Peas

Serve with a side salad.

4 tablespoons butter or margarine
8 scallions, thinly sliced
½ cup wild rice
½ cup white or brown long grain rice
2 cups vegetable stock or water
½ cup baby peas
salt and freshly ground black pepper to taste

Heat the butter in a deep saucepan and sauté the scallions gently over a low heat.

Wash and drain the two measures of rice and stir them into the sauté. Then add the vegetable stock and stir the mixture over a high heat.

Add the peas, salt and pepper when the mixture has come to a simmer. Then stir well, cover the saucepan tightly and leave over a low heat until the liquid has been completely absorbed.

Serve immediately.

40 minutes to make
Good source of vitamin A, vitamin C

VEGETABLE SPECIALTIES

There are so many mouthwatering vegetable dishes you can produce, with a minimum amount of time and fuss, that you'll never want to go back to dull vegetable side-dishes again! A little imagination can enliven even the most mundane vegetable – cabbage, for example, is most schoolchildren's least favourite vegetable, but try serving them Savoury Cabbage and Sour Cream on a lovely bed of rice and watch them change their minds! Most of these recipes are highly adaptable, too. They can be used as fast snacks by themselves, or as accompaniments to an elegant dinner or relaxed Sunday lunch.

Baked and Creamed Sweet Potatoes

For a quick and tasty snack, serve with salad or a green vegetable. Alternatively, serve with other vegetables as an accompaniment to a main course.

4 medium sweet potatoes
2 tablespoons butter or margarine
salt and freshly ground black pepper to taste

Pre-heat the oven to 375°F. Wash the sweet potatoes and bake them for about 45–60 minutes until they are tender.
  Peel the potatoes and mash them in a bowl with the butter, salt and pepper. Whip them to a smooth puree. Serve immediately.

1 hour 10 minutes to make
Good source of vitamin A, vitamin C

Breaded Broccoli

1½lb broccoli
3 tablespoons butter or margarine
1½ cups fresh breadcrumbs
salt and freshly ground black pepper to taste
1 tablespoon lemon juice

Trim the thick stems from the broccoli and steam the heads until tender.
  Melt the butter in a saucepan, add the breadcrumbs and fry until crisp. Sprinkle in the salt and pepper and stir.
  Place the cooked broccoli in a warm serving dish, pour the lemon juice over, then sprinkle with the breadcrumb mixture and serve immediately.

15 minutes to make
Good source of vitamin A, B group vitamins, vitamin C

Carrot and Turnip Puree

Serve hot as a side dish, or as a filling in baked potatoes.

6–8 medium carrots, cubed
1 small white turnip, cubed
3–4 tablespoons butter or margarine
salt and freshly ground black pepper to taste

Place the carrots and turnip in a pan, barely cover with water and boil until tender.
  Put the cooked vegetables in a food processor and puree with the butter, salt and pepper until soft and smooth. Alternatively, mash them by hand. Serve hot.

30 minutes to make
Good source of vitamin A, B group vitamins, vitamin C, potassium

Zucchini with Apples (*p 142*)

Cream of Celery

Serve this over pasta or beside fresh garden peas and baby carrots.

4 tablespoons butter or margarine
8 large sticks celery, sliced
2 tablespoons finely chopped onion or 1 small onion,
* finely chopped*
2 tablespoons plain flour
1¼ cups vegetable stock or water
½ cup heavy cream

Melt the butter in a saucepan over a very low heat. Add the celery and onion and stir well to coat. Cover the pan and leave over the heat, without stirring, for 15 minutes. Shake the pan occasionally if necessary, as the butter must not burn.

Uncover the saucepan and sprinkle the flour over the vegetables. Stir well, then gradually add the vegetable stock and the cream.

Stir constantly until the mixture comes to a boil. Reduce the heat and simmer, uncovered, until the sauce has thickened. Serve hot.

25 minutes to make
Good source of vitamin A

French Fried Vegetables

1lb mixed fresh vegetables
1½ cups plain flour
pinch of salt
1 egg, beaten
1 cup milk
oil for frying

Cut the vegetables into bite-sized pieces and parboil or steam them until they are half-cooked. Drain the vegetables, dry them on a tea towel and put to one side.

Measure the flour into a bowl. Drop the egg into the centre of the flour and begin to stir them together. Gradually add the milk to the egg and flour and stir constantly to make a smooth batter.

Dip the dry vegetable pieces into this batter, drop into very hot oil and fry until golden brown.

Drain the fried vegetables on a paper towel and serve immediately with a light sprinkling of salt.

15 minutes to make

Glazed Carrots

1lb carrots, sliced
2 tablespoons butter or margarine
1–2 tablespoons brown sugar
½ teaspoon ground ginger

Steam or boil the carrots until tender. Drain them.

Melt the butter in a frying pan over a low flame. Stir the sugar and ginger into the melted butter until the sugar is dissolved. This will make a light brown glaze.

Add the sliced carrots to the pan and stir gently but continuously until all the carrots are glazed and hot. Serve immediately.

20 minutes to make
Good source of vitamin A

Greek Squash

1lb summer squash (pattypan or zucchini)
a little salt
½ garlic clove, minced
up to 1 cup sour cream or yogurt
2 teaspoons chopped dill weed
pinch of cayenne

Slice the squash into thick rounds, then slice each round in half. Scoop away the seed pulp and rinse the wedges under cold water.

Sprinkle the surface of each wedge with salt and garlic, then steam the squash until it is tender.

Mix the sour cream, dill and cayenne together in a small bowl. When serving the squash, spoon a generous amount of this sauce over each wedge.

45 minutes to make
Good source of vitamin C

Green Beans and Mushrooms in Sour Cream

Sour cream can sometimes curdle during cooking, which won't spoil the taste but may not be so appealing to look at. To stop this happening, mix a teaspoon of cornstarch into the sour cream before adding it to the vegetables.

½lb string beans
3 tablespoons butter or margarine
1½ cups mushrooms, chopped
½ cup sour cream
salt and freshly ground black pepper to taste

Steam the beans until just tender. Set them aside to drain well.

Melt the butter in a large pan and sauté the mushrooms until they are quite tender. Keep the heat quite high so they do not release their juice.

Stir in the cooked beans and heat them through, then add the sour cream and seasoning.

Cook briefly, without boiling, until the beans are quite hot. Serve immediately.

20 minutes to make
Good source of protein, B group vitamins, potassium

Green Bean Savoury

Serve with rice or quiche (see page 117).

1½lb string beans
2 tablespoons vegetable oil
1 small onion, finely chopped
1 clove garlic, crushed
2 sticks celery, chopped
2 carrots, shredded
1 teaspoon dried basil or 1 tablespoon chopped fresh basil
salt and freshly ground black pepper to taste
4 tablespoons vegetable stock or water
½ cup Parmesan cheese, grated

Steam the beans until just tender. Heat the oil in a frying pan and sauté the chopped onion and garlic, stirring constantly.

Add the celery and carrot and sauté for 3–4 minutes, stirring often.

Add the cooked beans, basil, salt and pepper. Pour in a little stock if necessary if the contents of the pan seem dry. Cover the pan and simmer over a low heat for 5 minutes.

Remove the pan from the heat and stir in half the Parmesan cheese. Pour the savoury into a warmed serving dish, top with the remaining cheese and serve immediately.

25 minutes to make
Good source of vitamin A, vitamin C, calcium, iron

Harvard Beets

2lb beets
2 teaspoons cornstarch
⅓ cup sugar
1 cup cider vinegar
¼ cup water
2 tablespoons butter or margarine

Wash the beets (do not trim the 'tails' yet) and boil until tender. Drain, trim and slice the beets and place to one side.

Combine the cornstarch and sugar in a saucepan. Stir the vinegar and water into it and cook over a low heat until the sauce is thick. Stir constantly.

Add the sliced beets and the butter to the sauce and stir gently until the butter melts. Serve immediately.

30 minutes to make

Jerusalem Artichokes in Lemon Parsley Sauce

1lb Jerusalem artichokes, peeled
4 tablespoons butter or margarine
3 tablespoons chopped fresh parsley or parsley and chives
2 tablespoons lemon juice
salt and freshly ground black pepper to taste

Boil the artichokes for 20–25 minutes, until tender.

Drain the artichokes and puree them in a blender or mash them in the pan. Add the butter, stirring well as it melts, then the parsley, lemon juice, salt and pepper.

Mix very well and serve immediately.

40 minutes to make
Good source of vitamin A, vitamin C

Leeks Vinaigrette

Serve with rice, salad, baked potatoes or as a starter. For an interesting variation, try adding 2 tablespoons pickles or capers.

2lb leeks
1 teaspoon mild mustard
2 cloves garlic, crushed
1 tablespoon lemon juice
1 tablespoon vinegar
4 tablespoons olive oil
salt and freshly ground black pepper to taste
½ cup olives

Wash, trim and steam the leeks until tender. Then slice them in half lengthways and arrange in a serving dish.

Mix the mustard and garlic with the lemon juice, vinegar and olive oil and season to taste.

Chop the olives and stir them into the dressing. Pour over the hot leeks and serve immediately.

15 minutes to make
Good source of vitamin C, B group vitamins, iron

New Orleans Broad Beans

People who were once put off the taste of badly-prepared broad beans will be tempted back again to this southern recipe, which can be served to accompany just about any main course.

1lb broad beans
2 tablespoons olive oil
1 medium onion, chopped
1 small green or red pepper, chopped
2 sticks celery, chopped
1 16oz can chopped tomatoes
1 tablespoon sugar (or to taste)
salt and freshly ground black pepper to taste

Boil the beans until tender (about 7 minutes). Drain them and set aside. Heat the oil in a saucepan and gently sauté the onions, pepper and celery for 5–6 minutes until lightly browned.

Add the tomatoes and the sugar, stir well and simmer for 20 minutes, uncovered.

Add the beans and season to taste. Bring the mixture back to a simmer and cook for a further 5 minutes. Serve immediately.

40 minutes to make
Good source of B group vitamins, vitamin C, potassium

New Orleans Okra

Serve hot over rice or toast.

2 tablespoons olive oil
1 medium onion, chopped
1 small red or green or yellow pepper, chopped
¾lb okra, sliced
1 16oz can chopped tomatoes
1 tablespoon chopped fresh basil or 1 teaspoon dried basil
salt and freshly ground black pepper to taste

Heat the oil in a saucepan and sauté the onion and pepper gently for 5–6 minutes, until lightly browned.

Increase the heat, add the okra and sauté for 5 minutes, stirring constantly.

Reduce the heat and add the tomatoes, herb and seasoning. Stir well, cover the pan and simmer for 15 minutes. Add more liquid, such as tomato juice or vegetable stock, if desired.

30 minutes to make
Good source of vitamin A, vitamin C, calcium

Niçoise Green Beans

Try serving with rice, mashed potatoes or potato pancakes.

2 tablespoons olive oil
1 medium onion, chopped
2 sticks celery, chopped
1lb string beans
1 16oz can chopped tomatoes
4 tablespoons vegetable stock or tomato juice
1 bay leaf
½ cup fresh parsley, chopped
salt and freshly ground black pepper to taste

Heat the oil in a large frying pan and gently sauté the onions and celery until lightly browned.

Boil or steam the beans until tender (about 10 minutes). Drain and set aside.

Add the tomatoes, stock, bay leaf and parsley to the sauté. Stir well and simmer this sauce for 20 minutes, uncovered. Season to taste.

Add the cooked beans to the sauce and stir well. Bring back to a simmer and cook for a further 2 minutes. Serve immediately.

35 minutes to make
Good source of vitamin A, vitamin C

Quiche (p 117) with Breaded Broccoli (p 134), Peas in Cream (p 140) and Herb Bread (p 64)

Orange and Beets

6 medium beets (approx. 1lb)
½ cup water
½ cup orange juice
2 teaspoons grated orange rind
1 tablespoon cider vinegar or rice vinegar or wine vinegar
1 tablespoon brown sugar
2 tablespoons cornstarch
4 tablespoons butter or margarine
pinch of nutmeg
salt and freshly ground black pepper to taste

Cook the beets in boiling water for 20 minutes. Remove from the heat but leave them in the boiled water to keep hot.

Mix the remaining ingredients together in a saucepan. Bring to the boil and simmer, stirring, for about 25 minutes until the cornstarch has cooked and the sauce is clear.

Peel and cube the hot beets and place in a warm serving dish. Pour the sauce over the hot beets and serve immediately.

40 minutes to make
Good source of vitamin C

Peas in Cream

12oz peas, frozen or fresh
4 tablespoons butter or margarine
3–4 scallions, chopped
4 sticks celery, chopped
½ cup cream
2 tablespoons chopped fresh tarragon
salt and freshly ground black pepper to taste

Cook the peas. Melt the butter and sauté the scallions and celery until just tender. Add the cooked peas to the sauté.

Stir in the cream and tarragon. Cook for 5 minutes, uncovered, over a very low heat. Season to taste. Serve immediately.

20 minutes to make
Good source of vitamin A, B group vitamins, vitamin C, calcium

Potato Dumplings with Brown Butter

These quantities should make 12 dumplings.

4 large potatoes, cubed
1 egg, beaten
1¼ cups self-rising flour
salt and freshly ground black pepper to taste
4 tablespoons butter
½ cup dried breadcrumbs

Boil the potatoes until tender, then mash them and allow to cool.

Add the egg, flour, salt and pepper to the potatoes and mix well, using your hands. Shape the mixture into little balls (about ping-pong size).

Drop the dumplings into boiling water and cook gently for 15 minutes. Heat the butter in a pan and allow to brown for a couple of minutes, then mix with the breadcrumbs in a separate bowl.

Remove the dumplings from the water and drain them on a paper towel. Serve immediately with a sprinkling of the breadcrumb mixture.

40 minutes to make
Good source of B group vitamins

Pureed Parsnips

A great favourite – serve with any main course and green vegetable.

6 medium parsnips, peeled and cubed
2 tablespoons butter or margarine
2 tablespoons milk
salt and freshly ground black pepper to taste

Boil the parsnips until tender (about 20 minutes). Drain.

Place the parsnips in a blender with the butter, milk, salt and pepper and puree to a smooth, light consistency. Serve hot.

25 minutes to make
Good source of vitamin C

Raw Mushroom Marinade

Serve with salads or over toast.

3 cups mushrooms, sliced
2 tablespoons olive oil
2 tablespoons vegetable oil
1½ tablespoons wine vinegar
½ tablespoon lemon juice
2 tablespoons chopped fresh tarragon or oregano
salt and freshly ground black pepper to taste

Put the mushrooms in a pretty salad bowl.

Mix the oils, vinegar and lemon juice together in a cup. Add the herbs, salt and pepper and stir well.

Pour the marinade over the mushrooms and leave, covered, in a cool place for 3–6 hours.

5 minutes to make – not including time to marinate
Good source of B group vitamins

Refried Beans

Used in many Mexican recipes, a great filling for tacos.

1lb dried pinto beans, washed and drained
1 quart water
2 medium onions, chopped
1 cup vegetable oil or 1 cup vegetable shortening
salt and freshly ground black pepper to taste

Measure the beans and water into a large saucepan and place over a high heat. Bring the water to the boil, cover the pan, turn off the heat and let the beans soak for 1½ hours.

Add the onions to the beans. Bring the liquid to a boil again, then reduce the heat and simmer, covered, until the beans are very tender, for about 2½–3 hours. Replace any water that is lost through evaporation. (If you want to save time here, use a pressure cooker to cook the beans.)

When the beans are very soft, mash them up (or use a blender) and add the vegetable oil, salt and pepper. Serve hot or cold.

3 hours 45 minutes to make
Good source of protein, B group vitamins, potassium, iron

Sauerkraut

2lb white cabbage (2 small heads), finely shredded
½ cup coarse sea salt
4 cups cider vinegar
2 teaspoons caraway seeds
5 teaspoons whole pickling spice
3 bay leaves

Cover the bottom of a very large mixing bowl with shredded cabbage and sprinkle a layer of salt over it. Continue to layer the cabbage and salt in this way until all the cabbage is used. Make sure that a layer of salt covers the top layer of cabbage.

Cover the bowl with a towel and then a large plate and leave to stand for 12–24 hours. (If you make this one evening, you may finish it the next evening.)

Mix the vinegar and spices together in an enamel pan and bring to a soft boil. Cover the pan and remove it from the heat. Leave this mixture to stand undisturbed for 12–24 hours also.

Drain the cabbage and rinse it very well in cold water to remove the salt. Then pack the cabbage into sterile jars and pour the cool vinegar mixture over until the cabbage is covered. Seal the jars and keep in a cool place until ready to use.

24 hours to make

Savoury Cabbage and Sour Cream

3 tablespoons butter or margarine
1 small cabbage, shredded
1 cup sour cream
1 egg yolk
2 tablespoons lemon juice
salt and freshly ground black pepper to taste

Melt the butter in a large pan. Add the cabbage and stir well. Then cover and cook over a low heat for about 15 minutes, until the cabbage is just tender but not browned.

Beat the sour cream, egg yolk, lemon juice, salt and pepper together in a cup and pour it in with the cabbage.

Bring the mixture to a gentle simmer (not a boil). Spoon into a serving dish and serve immediately.

25 minutes to make

Simple Stuffed Mushrooms

8 large mushrooms
2 tablespoons vegetable oil
1 cup breadcrumbs
4 tablespoons chopped fresh parsley
2 cloves garlic, crushed
1 egg, beaten
salt and freshly ground black pepper to taste

Pre-heat the oven to 350°F (alternatively, you can use the grill). Remove the stems from the mushrooms. Brush the mushroom tops with a little oil. Scoop out some of the mushroom centres and chop finely with the stems.

Mix the remaining ingredients together in a bowl and add the chopped mushroom stems. Season to taste.

Divide this filling between the mushroom tops, then brush with a little more oil.

Place the stuffed mushrooms on a greased baking dish and bake for 10–15 minutes, or place the tray under a hot grill for 10 minutes. Serve immediately.

25 minutes to make
Good source of vitamin A, B group vitamins, vitamin C

Zucchini with Apples

1½lb small zucchinis, thinly sliced
4 tablespoons butter or margarine
1 medium onion, chopped
2 eating apples, chopped
2 fresh tomatoes, peeled and chopped
2 tablespoons chopped fresh parsley
salt and freshly ground black pepper to taste

Set a small pan of water to boil. Drop the zucchini slices into the boiling water for 30 seconds. Remove immediately and drain.

Melt the butter in a frying pan and sauté the onion until it is transparent. Add the apples and stir well to coat with the butter. Add the tomatoes and the blanched zucchini. Stir well, then add the parsley.

Season this mixture and leave it to cook, covered, over a gentle heat for 5–10 minutes, until the zucchinis are soft. Serve hot.

35 minutes to make
Good source of vitamin A, vitamin C

Sour Cream and Beets

1 tablespoon chopped fresh parsley or chives
½ cup sour cream plus more for serving
1 teaspoon mild mustard
1 teaspoon finely chopped onion
salt and freshly ground black pepper to taste
6 medium beets (approx. 1lb), cooked

Mix the parsley, sour cream, mustard, onion and seasoning together in a small saucepan. Bring to a gentle simmer.

Peel and cube the cooked beets and add to the sauce. Return to a simmer and cook for a further 5–10 minutes, until the beets are very hot.

Turn the beets into a hot serving dish and serve topped with extra sour cream, if desired.

30 minutes to make

SAUCES AND SUNDRIES

Learn how to make one or two of the basic sauces I've included here and you'll always be able to whip up a tasty meal. One secret of making a quick meal – almost out of thin air – is to cook leftovers with one of these great sauces. It's amazing, too, how a basic pancake mix can be used in many different ways – if you leave out the lemon and sugar, for instance, you can stuff it with any savoury filling.

Barbecue Sauce

Everyone has their own favourite barbecue sauce, and this is mine. Add (or take away) ingredients according to your family's preferences, and remember to marinate those vegetable burgers and sausages at least 1 hour before grilling for best results.

¾ cup tomato ketchup
½ cup brown sugar
1 cup vinegar
juice of ½ lemon
5 cloves garlic, crushed, or 2 teaspoons garlic powder
2 tablespoons pickle relish
2 tablespoons mild mustard
6 tablespoons vegetable oil
salt and freshly ground black pepper to taste

Pour the ketchup into your largest pan (the pan will be used to marinate all your vegetable burgers, hot dogs etc). Add the remaining ingredients and stir well.

Marinate the burgers, then grill them over the barbecue. You can add extra sauce to them just before serving.

15 minutes to make – not including time to marinate

Béchamel Sauce

1½ cups milk
½ whole onion
6 peppercorns
1 small bay leaf

Put all the ingredients into a pan and bring slowly to the boil. Remove from the heat, cover and leave for 10 minutes.

Strain, and use as required in the Mornay Sauce recipe (page 147), or White Sauce recipe (page 150). For a quick Cheese Sauce, add ½ cup grated cheese once the sauce is cooked, stir to melt the cheese and cook for a further 2–3 minutes.

15 minutes to make

Brown Sauce

3 tablespoons butter or margarine
1 large onion, chopped finely
2 tablespoons plain flour
1½ cups dark vegetable stock
½ teaspoon dried sage
½ teaspoon dried thyme
salt and freshly ground black pepper to taste
1 tablespoon soy sauce

Melt the butter in a frying pan and sauté the onion until lightly browned. Sprinkle the flour over the onions and stir to make a thick paste.

Gradually add the stock to the thick paste, stirring constantly to avoid lumps. Bring the sauce to a boil, add the herbs, salt, pepper and soy sauce. Simmer gently for 3 minutes and use immediately. Makes 1½ cups.

10 minutes to make
Good source of vitamin A

Coleslaw and Mayonnaise

This coleslaw is extremely quick and easy to make, and has a very attractive colour. For best results, prepare it a few hours before you need it, so the flavours can really blend.

1lb white cabbage, shredded
½ cup mayonnaise
juice of ½ lemon
salt to taste

Mix all the ingredients together in a large salad bowl. Serve immediately, or chill or leave to stand for at least 30 minutes before serving so the cabbage can absorb the dressing.

5 minutes to make – unchilled
Good source of vitamin C

Coleslaw and Sour Cream

1 small red or white or green cabbage (12oz–1lb), shredded
1 carrot, grated
6 tablespoons mayonnaise
2 tablespoons sour cream
juice of 1 lemon
salt and freshly ground black pepper to taste

Mix the cabbage and carrot together in a large bowl.

Stir the rest of the ingredients together in a jug and pour over the cabbage. Stir very well. Serve immediately or chill for 30–60 minutes.

10 minutes to make – unchilled
Good source of vitamin A, vitamin C

Cranberry Sauce

These quantities make enough sauce for 8 people. Use less sugar if you prefer a sauce that is not so sweet.

1lb fresh or frozen cranberries
1 large orange
1 cup sugar

Wash the cranberries and pick them over for stems. Put them in a blender.

Slice both ends off the orange, but leave the rest of the peel on. Cut the orange into small pieces and remove the pips. Place the orange pieces in the blender with the cranberries.

Add the sugar to the fruits in the blender and puree to an even consistency (it will be quite chunky).

Turn the sauce into a pretty dish and chill before serving with the festive meal.

15 minutes to make – unchilled

Cucumber, Dill and Sour Cream Sauce

Serve this as a dressing with salads or hot main courses.

½ cup cucumber, peeled and grated
1 teaspoon salt
2 spring onions, chopped
1 tablespoon lemon juice
1 cup sour cream
salt and freshly ground black pepper to taste
6 small sprigs fresh dill weed or 4 tablespoons dried dill

Place the cucumber in a colander, sprinkle with salt and leave for 30 minutes so that some of the excess liquid can drain off.

Place the cucumber and onion in a bowl and pour the lemon juice over.

Stir in the sour cream, salt and pepper. Chop the dill weed and add to the sauce. Stir well and serve immediately. Store any surplus chilled.

40 minutes to make
Good source of vitamin A, vitamin C

Dill Pickles

Although you may have to wait a little while before you can eat these pickles, they only take 30–40 minutes to prepare.

8–12 pickling cucumbers
7 tablespoons sea salt
8 cloves garlic, halved
fresh dill weed to taste
dill seed to taste
equal amounts white cider vinegar and boiling water

Soak the cucumbers overnight in a solution of cold water and 4 tablespoons of the salt.

Drain the cucumbers and arrange them in large pickling jars. Add the garlic pieces to the cucumbers at even intervals.

Pack the dill weed evenly around the cucumbers, and sprinkle the dill seed over the top cucumbers, when the jar is full.

Mix the vinegar and boiling water together and dissolve the remaining salt in it. Pour this brine over the cucumbers until they are covered. Cover the jars and leave the pickles in the refrigerator or cool place for at least a week before serving.

Good source of vitamin C, potassium

Egg and Mushroom Cheese Sauce

Serve over potatoes, steamed broccoli, cauliflower or vegetable burgers.

> *3 cups thin White Sauce (see page 150)*
> *¾ cup Cheddar cheese, grated*
> *6 eggs*
> *2 tablespoons butter or margarine*
> *½lb mushrooms, sliced*
> *1 tablespoon chopped fresh parsley*
> *salt and freshly ground black pepper to taste*

Make up the white sauce and stir in the grated cheese. Leave the sauce over a very low heat, stirring occasionally, while the cheese melts.

Hard-boil the eggs and, when cool enough to handle, peel and thickly slice them. Melt the butter in a frying pan and sauté the mushrooms.

Add the hard-boiled eggs, mushrooms, parsley, salt and pepper to the cheese sauce. Fold gently and serve immediately.

20 minutes to make
Good source of protein, B group vitamins, calcium

Fresh Herb Dip

This makes a tasty party dip for 8 people – serve with raw vegetables, crisps or crackers.

> *12oz soft cream cheese*
> *1 cup sour cream*
> *2 scallions, chopped*
> *2 tablespoons chopped fresh parsley*
> *salt and freshly ground black pepper to taste*
> *½ clove garlic, crushed*
> *1 tablespoon chopped fresh tarragon or mint (optional)*
> *1 teaspoon lemon juice (optional)*
> *3 teaspoons capers (optional)*

Let the cream cheese stand until it is at room temperature then mix with the sour cream and blend to a light consistency with a fork or whisk.

Add the remaining ingredients to the cheese mixture. Blend, then turn the dip into a serving bowl.

Cover and chill in the refrigerator, or serve immediately.

10 minutes to make – unchilled
Good source of vitamin A, B group vitamins, vitamin C

Fresh Herb Mayonnaise

> *1 tablespoon chopped mixed fresh herbs or 1 teaspoon mixed dried herbs*
> *½ cup mayonnaise*
> *1 teaspoon lemon juice*
> *4 tablespoons sour cream*
> *salt and freshly ground black pepper to taste*

Blend all the ingredients together in a bowl. Serve immediately.

5 minutes to make

Fresh Tomato Sauce

Serve over pasta, mashed potatoes or rice.

> *1lb tomatoes*
> *1 medium onion, chopped*
> *8 tablespoons chopped fresh basil*
> *2 cloves garlic, crushed*
> *salt and freshly ground black pepper to taste*
> *½ cup vegetable stock or water or tomato juice*
> *¼ teaspoon sugar*
> *2 tablespoons olive oil or vegetable oil*

Peel the tomatoes by plunging them into boiling water, leave them for 1 minute, plunge them into cold water, then peel off the skins.

Put the remaining ingredients, except the oil, into a large saucepan and stir well.

Bring the mixture to a gentle boil, then cover, reduce the heat and simmer for 40 minutes.

Add the oil and remove the sauce from the heat.

45 minutes to make
Good source of vitamin A, vitamin C

Garlic Dressing

½ teaspoon mild mustard
pinch of sugar
salt and freshly ground black pepper to taste
1 clove garlic, crushed
2 tablespoons tarragon vinegar
3 tablespoons lemon juice
⅔ cup olive oil
2 teaspoons honey (optional)

Mix the mustard, sugar, salt and pepper together in a cup or large jar. (Omit the sugar if using honey, and add honey with the liquid ingredients.)

Add the liquid ingredients to the mixture and stir well. If using a jar, put the lid on and shake the jar vigorously. Serve over salad.

10 minutes to make

Garlic Herb Sauce

Serve over pasta.

3 tablespoons chopped fresh basil or parsley
⅔ cup olive oil
3 cloves garlic, crushed

Heat the oil in a pan, add the garlic and stir over a low heat for 2–3 minutes. Remove the pan from the heat and add the fresh herbs.

10 minutes to make
Good source of vitamin A, calcium, iron

Hollandaise Sauce

Serve hot over asparagus, green beans, artichoke hearts or any vegetable of your choice.

½ cup butter or margarine
3 egg yolks, well beaten
1 tablespoon lemon juice
salt and freshly ground black pepper to taste

Divide the butter into 3 equal portions. Melt one portion in the top of a double boiler. Add the beaten yolks and stir constantly.

Add the second portion of the butter to the hot mixture and stir as it melts. Then add the third portion and continue to stir as the mixture comes to a very low boil. Remove from the heat and continue to stir for approximately 5 minutes as it cools.

Add the lemon juice, salt and pepper and place the sauce over the heat once again. Whisk the mixture to prevent curdling. (Add 2 teaspoons of boiling water if it does begin to curdle.) Serve hot.

20 minutes to make
Good source of vitamin A

Home-made Tomato Sauce

1 tablespoon olive oil
1 clove garlic, crushed
1 onion, chopped
1 16oz can chopped tomatoes
1 small can tomato paste
½ cup tomato juice
1 teaspoon oregano
salt and freshly ground black pepper to taste

Heat the olive oil in a saucepan, add the garlic and onion and sauté lightly.

Add the remaining ingredients and stir well. Bring the sauce to a boil, cover the pan, then reduce the heat and simmer for 30 minutes. Stir occasionally.

40 minutes to make
Good source of vitamin A, vitamin C

Mornay Sauce

For a less rich sauce, use half milk and half stock in the basic béchamel. For a creamier version, add 1–2 tablespoons cream to the cooked sauce.

1½ cups Béchamel Sauce (see page 143)
1 tablespoon grated Parmesan cheese
1 tablespoon grated Swiss or Cheddar cheese
2 tablespoons butter or margarine

Prepare the béchamel sauce and keep it over a low heat. Add the cheeses and stir constantly as they melt. Then add the butter, stir well and use immediately with vegetables, pancakes or pasta.

12 minutes to make
Good source of calcium

147

Cranberry Sauce (p 144), Dill Pickles (p 144), Pesto (p 148), Vinaigrette Dressing (p 150)

Pancake Mix

Makes 6.

1 egg, beaten
1 cup milk
2 cups plain flour
pinch of salt
1 tablespoon butter or margarine

to serve:
lemon juice
sugar

Beat the egg and milk together in a small bowl. Measure the flour and salt into a mixing bowl and stir. Make a hollow in the flour and add the egg and milk mixture. Stir the mixture slowly into the flour to make a smooth batter.

Leave the batter to stand, covered, for up to 2 hours in a cool place.

Melt the butter in an 8 inch frying pan, over a medium heat, so that the flat bottom is thinly and evenly coated, tip out any excess. Spoon 2 tablespoons of the pancake batter into the pan and spread it to the edges by tilting the pan. Cook until small bubbles appear on the surface.

Use a spatula to lift the edges of the pancake, then flip it and cook its other side. Serve hot, rolled, with lemon juice and sugar.

10 minutes to make – not including standing time

Parsley and Mushroom Cream Sauce

1 tablespoon butter or margarine
4 cups mushrooms, sliced
1½ cups medium White Sauce (see page 150)
2 tablespoons chopped fresh parsley
salt and freshly ground black pepper to taste

Melt the butter in a saucepan and sauté the mushrooms until lightly browned. Remove from the heat and add the white sauce, parsley, salt and pepper. Stir well, and return to the heat for 2–3 minutes. Serve immediately.

15 minutes to make
Good source of B group vitamins, calcium

Pesto

Delicious served mixed into fresh-cooked pasta.

1½ cups fresh basil (leaves, not stems)
4 cloves garlic, crushed
½ cup pine nuts
¾ cup olive oil
1 cup Parmesan cheese, grated
salt and freshly ground black pepper to taste

Place the basil, garlic, nuts and oil in a blender and blend for 2–3 minutes, until creamy. Then blend in the grated cheese. Season to taste. Serve immediately.

10 minutes to make
Good source of protein, calcium, iron, zinc

Plain Dumplings

Serve with hot winter dishes or in a bowl of soup.

2 eggs
2 tablespoons milk
1 cup self-rising flour
pinch of salt
1 clove garlic, crushed
1–2 tablespoons chopped fresh parsley
salt and freshly ground black pepper to taste

Beat the eggs well in a mixing bowl. Add the milk, salt and pepper, and slowly stir in the flour to make a smooth batter with no lumps.

Boil about 8 cups of salted water, and, when boiling, take spoonful of the dough and drop them into the water. Cover, let them boil for about 10 minutes until well cooked, then drain.

20 minutes to make

Puff Pastry

1 cup butter or margarine or vegetable shortening (must be as cold as possible)
2 cups plain flour
up to 1 cup iced water

Divide the butter into 3 equal portions. Coarsely rub one-third of the butter into the flour, then add a little water and mix into a smooth dough. Don't add too much water, or the mixture will become sticky.

Mould the second portion of the butter into a small lump (keep it as cold as you can). Roll the pastry into a square.

Place the butter on one side of the pastry, and fold the edges over to create a little envelope of pastry with the butter in the middle. Press the edges down to seal them. Roll the pastry out on a floured surface to make a long strip. Now roll the strip up like a Swiss roll.

Roll the pastry into a square again, repeating the process described above: place the third portion of butter in the centre of the pastry, fold the edges over and press them together. Roll the pastry into a long strip. Now roll the strip up Swiss roll style, and finish by rolling it into a square. Chill the finished pastry for 1 hour before you use it.

15 minutes to make – unchilled

Shortcrust Pastry

1½ cups self-rising flour
pinch of salt
6 tablespoons butter or margarine
3 tablespoons cold water

Mix the flour and salt together in a large mixing bowl.

Cut the butter into small pieces and drop them into the flour mix. Use your fingertips to rub the butter into the flour until it has reached the consistency of breadcrumbs.

Sprinkle the very cold water over the mixture, and mix with a wooden spoon to form a ball.

Lightly flour a board and your rolling pin, and roll the dough into a thin circle.

Place in a lightly-greased glass, enamel or metal pie dish, leaving some pastry overhanging the edges. This can be trimmed off cleanly with a knife.

If baking the pastry without filling (blind baking), prick the pastry with a fork to prevent it bubbling, then line with greaseproof paper and pour in some raw rice or beans to a depth of 1 inch.

15 minutes to make

Spaghetti Sauce Bolognaise

This is another all-time favourite. Serve it with a good, tasty spaghetti (try experimenting with whole-wheat varieties), or use another type of pasta, such as macaroni, tagliatelle or fettuccine. Cooking spa-ghetti is very easy, just follow the simple instructions on the packet, and remember when it's cooked to rinse immediately in cold water in a colander. This halts the cooking and washes the starch away. Spaghetti should always be served 'al dente', in other words, not mushy.

2 tablespoons olive oil
2 onions, chopped
2 cloves garlic, crushed
1 4½oz packet TVP mince or 4 vegetable burgers, crumbled
1 cup mushrooms, sliced
2 16oz cans chopped tomatoes
4–5 tablespoons tomato paste
fresh basil to taste
1 cup water or vegetable stock (if using protein mince)

Heat the oil in a frying pan and sauté the onions and garlic until lightly browned.

Add the TVP mince and mushrooms and cook for 2 minutes, stirring often.

Add the tomatoes, tomato paste and basil (and water if using TVP mince) and simmer, covered, for 1 hour (it may be ready sooner, but the longer it simmers, the better the flavour). Add a little water or vegetable stock if the sauce becomes too thick.

1 hour 5 minutes to make
Good source of protein, vitamin A, vitamin C

Special Gravy

People are always surprised by the taste of this wonderful old-fashioned gravy.

2 cups mushrooms, finely chopped
2 tablespoons vegetable oil
4 heaped teaspoons vegetarian gravy powder
½ cup water or vegetable stock
1 clove garlic, crushed
4 tablespoons vegetable extract or soy sauce

Sauté the mushrooms in the oil until lightly brown. Add a small amount of cold water to the gravy powder and mix into a smooth paste in a cup.

Add the pint of water to the sautéd mushrooms, and any extra oil or juices from your roasting pan.

Add the gravy paste, garlic and vegetable extract and bring to a slow boil, stirring constantly. Add a little extra water or gravy powder, if necessary, to produce an ideal pouring consistency, then pour into a sauce boat and serve.

15 minutes to make

Tomato and Mushroom Sauce

3 tablespoons olive oil
1 medium onion, chopped
2 sticks celery, chopped (optional)
1 clove garlic, crushed
2 cups mushrooms, sliced
2 16oz cans chopped tomatoes
2–3 tablespoons tomato paste
1 teaspoon dried oregano
salt and freshly ground black pepper to taste

Heat the oil in a saucepan and sauté the onion, celery and garlic in the oil until lightly browned.

Add the mushrooms and stir for 2 minutes.

Add the tomatoes, tomato paste and oregano, and simmer for 20 minutes. Add seasoning.

30 minutes to make
Good source of vitamin A, vitamin C, potassium

Tomato and Onion Sauce Italian Style

You can make this sauce in much less than 2 hours, but the longer you let it simmer, the more the flavour improves, so it's a pity to rush it.

3 tablespoons olive oil
1 large onion, chopped
2 cloves garlic, crushed
1 16oz can chopped tomatoes
2–3 tablespoons tomato paste
1 cup tomato juice
½ cup water
1 tablespoon chopped fresh oregano or 1½ teaspoons dried
salt and freshly ground black pepper to taste

Heat the oil in a saucepan and sauté the onion and garlic until tender. Add the chopped tomatoes, tomato paste, tomato juice and water. Stir well over a medium heat to bring the sauce to a gentle simmer.

If using dried oregano, add now. If using fresh oregano, add 10 minutes before serving.

Keep the sauce covered and simmering gently for 1½–2 hours, stirring occasionally. Season to taste. Add a little more water or tomato juice if a less thick sauce is desired. Makes 2 cups.

2 hours 10 minutes to make
Good source of vitamin C

Vinaigrette Dressing

This dressing can be varied in countless ways. Here are some suggested additions, according to taste:

crushed garlic, chopped fresh parsley, cream, tarragon or other chopped fresh herbs, chopped scallion, capers, sour cream, curry powder, Roquefort or blue cheese, mild mustard.

4 tablespoons white wine vinegar or cider vinegar or 1 tablespoon lemon juice and 2 tablespoons vinegar
4 tablespoons vegetable oil
3 tablespoons olive oil
a little salt

Mix all the ingredients together in a cup or glass jar, adding extra ingredients if desired.

Stir or shake the mixture very well until an emulsion is created. Pour over the salad of your choice.

5 minutes to make

White Sauce

This is the 'mother' of countless variations – just add flavourings of your choice.

for thin sauce:
2 cups milk
1 tablespoon plain flour
salt and freshly ground black pepper to taste
1 tablespoon butter or margarine

for medium sauce:
2 cups milk
2 tablespoons plain flour
salt and freshly ground black pepper to taste
4 tablespoons butter or margarine

for thick sauce:
2 cups milk
4 tablespoons plain flour
salt and freshly ground black pepper to taste
5 tablespoons butter or margarine

Pour the milk into a saucepan and bring it to the boil. Mix the flour, salt and pepper together in a small bowl.

In a separate saucepan, melt the butter and sprinkle the flour mixture over it, stirring constantly. When a thick paste has formed, gradually add the hot milk, stirring constantly to make a smooth sauce. Bring to boiling point, then simmer for 4–5 minutes.

Keep the white sauce over a very low heat until ready to use. Makes 2 cups.

15 minutes to make

Niçoise Green Beans (*p 138*)

DESSERTS, CAKES AND COOKIES

I don't know anything that can attract the family as quickly as the aroma of a home-made cake – wherever they are, one whiff and they start to congregate in the kitchen. Like most people, I've learned one or two tricks over the years. Most cakes need to sit in the pan for about 15 minutes before you turn them out on to a rack to cool. I grease and flour my cake pan to stop the cake sticking. If your cakes sink in the middle, try reducing the amount of liquid in the mix. Always use the hottest position inside the oven to bake in – and *don't* open the door halfway through! To test if my cake has finished baking, I stick a piece of uncooked spaghetti into the centre – if nothing sticks, the cake is ready. Remember that richer cakes – such as fruit cakes and Christmas cakes – often improve in flavour if they're kept in a cake pan for a few days before eating.

Almond Cake

8 tablespoons butter or margarine
¾ cup sugar
2 eggs, separated
1 teaspoon vanilla extract
1½ cups self-rising flour
½ teaspoon baking powder
½ cup milk
½ cup finely ground almonds

Pre-heat the oven to 350°F and line an 8 inch cake pan with greaseproof paper.

Cream the butter and sugar together in a large mixing bowl. Beat in the egg yolks and add the vanilla extract.

Sift the flour with the baking powder into another bowl, then mix the creamed ingredients into it. Add the milk and almonds and mix well.

In another bowl, beat the egg whites until stiff (but not dry) then gently fold them into the cake batter. Spoon the mixture into the cake pan and bake for 1 hour. Leave to cool, then cut into three horizontally and sandwich the layers back together with Butter Icing (page 156).

1 hour 20 minutes to make

Apple Brown Betty

Serve hot with Brandy Butter (see page 155) or cream.

2 tablespoons butter or margarine
1¼ cups dried breadcrumbs
½ cup crushed cornflakes
½ cup sugar
¼ teaspoon ground nutmeg
¼ teaspoon ground cinnamon
juice and grated rind of 1 lemon
1lb cooking apples, peeled, cored and chopped
½ cup water

Pre-heat the oven to 375°F. Melt the butter in a saucepan and add the breadcrumbs, cornflakes, sugar, spices and lemon rind and mix together.

Grease a baking dish and spoon about one-third of this mixture into it, then add half of the chopped apples.

Cover the apples with another third of the breadcrumb mixture, add another layer of apples, and finish off with the remaining breadcrumb mixture.

Pour over the lemon juice and water, cover the dish and bake for 45 minutes. Remove the cover for the last 15 minutes to brown the topping.

1 hour 15 minutes to make

Apple Sauce Cake

You can serve this hot or cold, with a generous serving of vanilla ice cream.

for the apple sauce:
1lb apples, peeled and chopped
¾ cup water
1 teaspoon chopped lemon peel
½ teaspoon ground cinnamon
4 tablespoons sugar (optional)

for the cake mixture:
¼lb butter or margarine
½ cup sugar
1 teaspoon vanilla extract
1 egg, beaten
2 cups plain flour
2 teaspoons baking soda
pinch of salt
⅔ cup broken pecan nuts
1 generous cup mixed dried fruit
½ teaspoon ground cinnamon
½ teaspoon ground nutmeg

Pre-heat the oven to 350°F, and lightly grease and flour an 8 inch cake tin.

Put all the apple sauce ingredients together in a pan, just cover with water and bring to the boil. Then reduce the heat and simmer, stirring occasionally, until the sauce has thickened.

Cream the butter and sugar together in a mixing bowl. When fluffy gradually add the vanilla and egg, beating thoroughly after each addition.

Mix in the apple sauce. Sift the flour, baking soda and salt together into a separate bowl. Add the remaining ingredients to the flour mixture and stir well.

Stir the dry mixture into the creamed mixture to make a smooth batter. Transfer to the prepared cake tin, spread evenly and bake for 1 hour.

1 hour 20 minutes to make

Baked Apples

A traditional, tasty autumn dish, best served piping hot with cream.

4 large cooking apples
4 tablespoons brown sugar
¼ cup raisins or sultanas
½ cup butter or margarine

Pre-heat the oven to 350°F and grease a baking dish. Set this dish in a shallow pan full of water.

Wash the apples and remove their cores. Cut a very shallow slit around the centre of each apple (to prevent them exploding) and place them in the greased baking dish.

Mix the sugar and raisins together in a small bowl, then spoon this mixture into the hollow core of each apple. Cut the butter into four pieces and place one piece over the raisin and sugar filling of each apple. Bake for 50–60 minutes, then serve immediately.

1 hour 15 minutes to make

Baked Custard

2 cups milk
3 eggs
¼ cup sugar
2–3 drops vanilla extract
½ teaspoon ground nutmeg

Pre-heat the oven to 325°F. Warm the milk until just short of boiling point.

Beat the eggs and sugar together until smooth, then add the hot milk and vanilla extract and continue beating for a minute or so. Pour the mixture into an oven-proof dish and sprinkle with the nutmeg.

Place the dish inside another shallow baking dish half filled with water, and bake for 50–60 minutes. Insert a piece of uncooked spaghetti a little way into the custard – if any mixture sticks to the spaghetti when you pull it out, it hasn't quite finished cooking.

1 hour 15 minutes to make

Banana Cake

¼lb butter or margarine
⅔ cup sugar
2 eggs, beaten
3 medium bananas
1 teaspoon baking soda
1 tablespoon sour cream
2 teaspoons vanilla extract
2 cups self-rising flour
1 cup broken pecan nuts

Pre-heat the oven to 350°F. Cream the butter and sugar together in a mixing bowl, then gradually add the eggs, beating between each addition.

Mash the bananas with a fork and add them to the mixture. Add the baking soda, sour cream and vanilla extract, and mix well.

Finally add the flour and the pecan nuts to the mixture, stirring constantly. Grease and flour an 8 inch cake pan and pour in the batter.

Bake for 1 hour 15 minutes, until cooked through. Remember to let the cake cool on a wire rack before serving.

1 hour 30 minutes to make

Blueberry Muffins

These gorgeous muffins are a treat at any time, but particularly for a relaxed weekend breakfast. Serve them with butter and honey.

¼ cup sugar
3 cups self-rising flour
½ teaspoon salt
1½ cups milk
1 egg
4 tablespoons butter or margarine
1½ cups fresh or frozen blueberries or berries of your choice

Pre-heat the oven to 400°F and lightly grease two muffin tins. Grease a large mixing bowl, then mix the sugar, flour and salt together in it.

Beat the milk and egg together in a small mixing bowl. Pour this into the centre of the dry mix, and stir briefly.

Melt the butter, add it to the batter mixture and stir well. Drain the berries, then take a little flour and sprinkle it lightly over them to coat each one. Add the berries to the batter and stir well.

Spoon the batter into the muffin tins and bake for 20–25 minutes, until lightly golden on top. Makes 18 muffins.

35 minutes to make

Blueberry Pancakes

Serve with ice cream, maple syrup, honey or with sugar and a touch of lemon – great for Saturday morning breakfast. Makes 8.

2 cups self-rising flour
1 egg, beaten
1 cup milk
¾ cup fresh or frozen blueberries
1 tablespoon butter or margarine

Measure the flour in a mixing bowl, add the egg and milk and gradually stir to a smooth consistency.

Drain the blueberries, add them to the batter and continue mixing. Melt the butter in an 8 inch frying pan and when hot, spoon enough of the pancake mixture into the pan to make thick pancakes. Brown on both sides.

20 minutes to make

Brandy Butter

Serve with Christmas Pudding, or Apple Brown Betty.

6 tablespoons butter or margarine at room temperature
½ cup sugar
1 teaspoon brandy (or to taste)

Whip the butter and sugar together in a bowl. Add the brandy and stir well. Chill.

5 minutes to make

Brown Sugar Loaf Cake

¼lb butter or margarine
½ cup brown sugar
2 eggs, separated
1½ cups self-rising flour
1 teaspoon baking powder
1 teaspoon ground cinnamon
½ teaspoon mixed spice
1 cup milk
½ cup broken pecan nuts
1 teaspoon vanilla extract

Pre-heat the oven to 350°F and grease and line a 2lb loaf tin. Cream the butter and sugar together until fluffy, then add the egg yolks and mix well.

Combine the flour, baking powder, cinnamon and spice together in a separate bowl. Add the dry mixture to the creamed mixture, alternately with the milk. Beat after each addition.

Add the pecan nuts and vanilla and beat well. In a separate bowl, beat the egg whites until they stand as stiff peaks, then fold into the cake mixture.

Pour into the loaf tin and bake for 45 minutes. Let the cake cool on a rack for 15 minutes, then remove from the tin and cool completely before serving.

1 hour 10 minutes to make

Banana Cake (*p 153*)

Brownies

This recipe makes about 12 Brownies. If you can't find pecan nuts, use walnuts instead. Great with a cold glass of skimmed milk.

¼lb butter or margarine
3oz baker's chocolate
2 large eggs
1½ cups sugar
1 teaspoon vanilla extract
½ cup self-rising flour
¼ cup broken pecans nuts

Pre-heat the oven to 350°F and lightly grease and flour a 12 inch cake tin. Melt the butter and chocolate, using a double saucepan over a medium heat. Stir constantly to prevent burning. Remove from the heat when both ingredients are melted.
Beat the eggs in a large mixing bowl, add the sugar and vanilla and beat until thick.
Stir the butter and chocolate into the egg and sugar mixture.
Sift the flour into this mixture and add the nuts. Stir very well and pour into the cake tin. Bake for 20–25 minutes or until just set, then cut into squares. The brownies should be moist and sticky, and should be served when cool (if you can wait!).

40 minutes to make

Butter Cookies

This is an excellent recipe for Christmas cookies and children's birthday parties. Makes about 3 dozen.

½lb butter or margarine
¾ cup sugar
2 eggs, separated
grated rind and juice of ½ lemon
4 cups self-rising flour
½ cup almonds, very finely chopped

Pre-heat the oven to 350°F. Cream the butter and sugar together in a large mixing bowl.
Add the egg yolks to the creamed mixture and beat well. Then add the lemon rind and juice. Add the flour and mix well, then chill the dough for 2 hours in the refrigerator.
Lightly beat the egg whites. Grease a baking tray. Roll out the dough to ¼ inch thickness and cut into cookie shapes. Brush each cookie with a little egg white, then sprinkle with a little extra sugar and the

the chopped almonds. Bake for 10–12 minutes, then cool on a wire rack.

2 hours 10 minutes to make – including chilling

Butter Icing

This amount of icing will cover an average 8 inch cake – for a two-layer cake, double the quantities listed here. If you want chocolate icing, melt some dark chocolate into the mixture. Other flavours include coffee, lemon peel and lemon juice, orange peel and juice, and maple syrup. Leave out the vanilla if you're using any of these flavourings.

2 tablespoons butter or margarine
½ cup confectioners sugar, sifted
1 tablespoon milk
2–3 drops vanilla extract

Cream the butter and sugar together in a mixing bowl. Add enough milk to make the mixture smooth. Then add the vanilla and beat well. Smooth the icing over the cake and chill before serving.

5 minutes to make – unchilled

Cherry Cake

6oz glacé cherries
⅔ cup broken pecan nuts
2 cups self-rising flour
½lb butter or margarine
1 cup sugar
4 eggs, separated
¾ tablespoon milk

Pre-heat the oven to 350°F, and line and flour a 9 inch ring mould. Measure the cherries and nuts into a small mixing bowl and sift 1oz of the flour over them.
Cream the butter and sugar together in a large mixing bowl. Add the egg yolks to the butter and sugar, beating well after each addition.
Fold in the flour. Then add the cherries and nuts, together with enough milk to make a soft dough.
Beat the egg whites to the stiff-peak stage and fold them gently into the batter. Spoon the batter into the cake tin and bake for 1¼ hours.

1 hour 30 minutes to make

Chocolate Mousse

A tasty treat for any dinner party or special occasion. Try garnishing with candied violets or rose petals, and serve with whipped cream.

8oz dark chocolate
3 tablespoons sugar
4 tablespoons water
4 eggs, separated
½ cup whipped cream
1 teaspoon vanilla extract

Melt the chocolate in a double boiler over a low heat and add the sugar and water, stirring often.

Remove the sauce from the heat and allow to cool. Beat the egg yolks and add them, little by little, to the cool sauce. Stir constantly.

Beat the egg whites to a stiff-peak consistency and fold, with the whipped cream and vanilla, into the chocolate mixture.

Pour the mixture into individual dessert bowls or one large, pretty bowl and refrigerate for 4–12 hours. The mousse will set firm.

4 hours to make – chilled

Chocolate and Pecan Nut Cookies

A great favourite with the kids. Makes 2 dozen.

¼lb butter or margarine
⅓ cup sugar
1 egg, beaten
½ teaspoon vanilla extract
1½ cups self-rising flour
1 cup broken pecan nuts
4oz plain chocolate chips or plain chocolate broken into
*   small pieces*

Pre-heat the oven to 325°F and grease a baking tray. Cream the butter and sugar to a light consistency in a mixing bowl. Add the egg, vanilla extract, flour, nuts, and chocolate and continue mixing until well blended.

Spoon the batter in small drops onto the baking tray and flatten with a fork or the bottom of a glass, then bake for about 20 minutes until they are light brown in colour.

30 minutes to make

Chocolate Pudding

Serve with cream.

4oz baker's chocolate
½ cup sugar
1½ cups milk
3 tablespoons cornstarch

Melt the chocolate in a double boiler over a low heat and add the sugar. Stir until the sugar is dissolved and the mixture is smooth.

Take 3 tablespoons of the cold milk and mix it with the cornstarch to make a smooth, lump-free paste. Add the rest of the milk to the chocolate mixture and stir well.

Add the cornstarch paste to the chocolate mixture. Continue to stir thoroughly and cook over a low heat for about 15 minutes, until nice and thick. Pour into individual cups or moulds and chill for 1 hour.

1 hour and 35 minutes to make – chilled

Chocolate Soufflé

Serve with whipped cream.

2 tablespoons butter or margarine
2 tablespoons plain flour
1 cup milk
3oz baker's chocolate
⅓ cup sugar
½ teaspoon vanilla extract
4 egg yolks
5 egg whites

Pre-heat the oven to 375°F. Grease and flour a 2 cups soufflé dish. Melt the butter in a saucepan and sprinkle the flour over it. Stir well to make a thick, smooth paste.

Bring the milk to a boil and gradually add it to the paste, stirring well to make a thick white sauce. Melt the chocolate and sugar together in a small pan, and stir this mixture into the white sauce. Remove from the heat and add the vanilla.

Beat the egg yolks and add them to the chocolate sauce when it has cooled slightly. Beat the egg whites to a stiff-peak consistency and, when the sauce is quite cool, gently fold them in.

Turn the mixture into the soufflé dish, sprinkle with a little extra sugar and bake for 40 minutes, until light brown. Serve immediately.

1 hour to make

Christmas Pudding

I always make two of these family-sized puddings because there is always someone I know who loves to be given one! The best puddings are those that are made in the early autumn and allowed to mature until Christmas Day. Be sure to steam the pudding for 2 hours just before you eat it.

1 cup raisins, chopped
1 cup sultanas, chopped
1 cup currants, chopped
3oz chopped peel
rind of 1 lemon, grated
1 cooking apple, peeled and chopped
2/3 cup plain flour
1/4 teaspoon mixed spice
1/4 teaspoon ground nutmeg
1/4 teaspoon ground cinnamon
1 cup breadcrumbs
6oz vegetable shortening or butter or margarine
1 1/4 cups sugar
4 tablespoons fruit juice or sherry or brandy
juice of 1/2 lemon
3 eggs, beaten
2 tablespoons honey
pinch of salt
3/4 cup pine nuts
3/4 cup brazil nuts, broken or chopped
3/4 cup sweet almonds, peeled and chopped

Grease two 1 quart pudding steamers and place two saucepans of water over a medium heat.

Mix the raisins, sultanas and currants together with the chopped peel, lemon rind and apple.

Mix the flour, spices and breadcrumbs together in a separate bowl and add in the shortening or butter, then the contents of this bowl to the fruit mixture. Use your hands or a wooden spoon to mix everything together very well. Add the remaining ingredients and work to an even consistency.

Put the mixture into the steamers, cover them with greased greaseproof paper and finish off with a pudding cloth tied round the rim of the steamer. Put each pudding into a pan of simmering water (make sure the water doesn't come over the rim) and steam, with a lid, for 5–6 hours. Take care that the pans do not boil dry. When you refill them, use boiling water from the kettle. Allow the puddings to cool then store in a cool, dry place until Christmas.

6 hours to make

Cocoa Cake

Ice with chocolate Butter Icing (see page 156).

2 tablespoons butter or margarine
1 cup sugar
4 tablespoons cocoa
1 egg, beaten
2 cups self-rising flour
1 teaspoon baking powder
1 cup milk
1 teaspoon vanilla extract
1 teaspoon baking soda

Pre-heat the oven to 350°F and grease and flour two 9 inch cake pans. Cream the butter and sugar together in a mixing bowl. Add the cocoa and mix well.

Add the egg to the batter. Mix the flour and baking powder together and gradually add to the batter, alternately with the milk. Stir well after each addition.

Stir in the vanilla and the baking soda. Pour into the cake pans and bake for 25 minutes. Allow to cool in the pan, then tip out and cool on a wire rack.

45 minutes to make

Coconut Cream Pie

1 8 inch pastry shell
1/2 cup milk
1 tablespoon butter or margarine
1/2 cup sugar
3 tablespoons cornstarch
1 teaspoon vanilla extract
3oz fresh grated or canned coconut
2 eggs, separated

Pre-heat the oven to 350°F. Bake the pastry shell for 7 minutes. Warm the milk with the butter in a pan. Mix half the sugar with the cornstarch in a bowl, and gradually add the warmed milk and butter, stirring constantly. Return to the pan and cook gently until thick and smooth.

Add the vanilla, coconut (reserving a little) and egg yolks to the mixture, beat well, then turn it into the pastry shell.

Beat the egg whites with the rest of the sugar to the stiff-peak stage. Spread over the pie filling and sprinkle the reserved coconut over the meringue. Bake for 15 minutes, until the meringue is brown.

35 minutes to make

Coconut Custard

1½ cups milk
½ cup sugar
3 eggs, separated
1 tablespoon cornstarch
½ cup cream
pinch of salt
1 cup confectioners sugar
3oz fresh grated or canned coconut
1 teaspoon vanilla extract

Pre-heat the oven to 325°F, and grease a baking dish. Put 2 tablespoons of the milk aside, and heat the remainder in a saucepan with the sugar. Beat the egg yolks into the milk mixture. Mix the cornstarch with the remaining 2 tablespoons of milk and add to the egg and milk mixture.

Add the cream and a pinch of salt, and gently cook until quite thick. Then pour into the baking dish.

Beat the egg whites with the confectioners sugar until very stiff. Stir in the grated coconut and vanilla extract. Spread this mixture over the top of the custard and bake for 20–25 minutes until the meringue is cooked and lightly browned.

35 minutes to make

Empire Biscuits

½ cup butter or margarine
2½ cups self-rising flour
1 cup confectioners sugar
2 tablespoons cornstarch
1 teaspoon vanilla extract
½ cup and 2 tablespoons skimmed milk

Pre-heat the oven to 300°F. Mix all the ingredients together in a bowl. Grease and flour a baking tray then, using a teaspoon, drop walnut-sized pieces of dough onto the tray and smooth down into a cookie shape. Bake for 25–30 minutes. Cool on a wire rack and serve.

45 minutes to make

Fluffy Lemon Pie

6 egg whites
2 cups sugar
1½ teaspoons lemon juice

for the filling:
6 egg yolks
⅔ cup sugar
6 tablespoons lemon juice
3 tablespoons grated lemon rind
1 heaped teaspoon cornstarch
1 cup whipped cream

Pre-heat the oven to 300°F. Line a large round baking tray or flan dish with greaseproof paper, grease it and dust it with confectioners sugar. Beat the egg whites, adding the sugar about 1oz at a time, and the lemon juice. Continue beating the whites to the stiff-peak stage. Spread this mixture on the baking tray and bake for 1½ hours, until lightly browned.

For the filling, beat the egg yolks in a double boiler over a low heat and add the sugar, lemon juice and lemon rind. Dissolve the cornstarch in 2 teaspoons of cold water, and add to the mixture. Cook for 8 minutes over a medium heat, stirring constantly until the mixture thickens.

Cool this mixture, then fold in the whipped cream. Spoon over the baked meringue and chill before serving.

2 hours to make – unchilled

Gingerbread Cake

½ cup butter or margarine
⅔ cup sugar
1 egg, beaten
2 cups self-rising flour
½ teaspoon ground cinnamon
2 teaspoons ground ginger
¼ teaspoon ground nutmeg
½ cup milk
2 tablespoons molasses

Pre-heat the oven to 325°F and lightly grease and flour an 8 inch cake pan.

Cream the butter and sugar together in a large mixing bowl. Add the egg a little at a time, beating between each addition.

Mix all the dry ingredients together and add them to the butter mixture. Gradually add the milk, stirring to make a smooth batter. Warm the molasses slightly and then beat it into the batter.

Transfer the batter to the cake pan and bake for 40–45 minutes.

55 minutes to make

Glacé Icing

1¼ cups confectioners sugar, sifted
5 tablespoons warm water
½ teaspoon vanilla extract or flavouring of your choice

Mix the ingredients together in a saucepan and place over a low heat. Stir the icing constantly with a wooden spoon until it is warm but not hot.

The icing is ready when it coats the back of the spoon evenly. Pour over the cake or sponge and serve after it has cooled.

20 minutes to make

Heather's Lemon Pudding Cake

2 tablespoons butter or margarine
⅔ cup sugar
⅓ cup self-rising flour
3 eggs, separated
1¼ cups milk
6 tablespoons fresh lemon juice
1½ teaspoons freshly grated lemon rind

Pre-heat the oven to 400°F and lightly grease a 5 cup baking dish. Melt the butter. Blend the sugar, flour and melted butter together in a mixing bowl.

Beat the yolks and continue stirring as you add the milk to them. Pour this liquid into the flour mixture and stir into a batter.

Add the lemon juice and rind, and mix well.

Beat the egg whites to the stiff-peak stage and fold gently into the batter. Pour the batter into the baking dish, place inside a large, shallow pan of water and bake for 45 minutes. Let the baking dish cool to blood temperature, then turn the cake out on to its serving dish.

1 hour 10 minutes to make

Honey Steamed Pudding

3 tablespoons honey
6 tablespoons butter or margarine
½ cup sugar
2 eggs
½ cup self-rising flour
½ teaspoon baking powder
2 tablespoons milk

Grease a 3 cup pudding steamer and pour 1 tablespoon of the honey into the bottom.

Cream the butter and sugar together well in a mixing bowl and whisk in the remaining honey. Then beat in the eggs one at a time. Mix the flour and baking powder together in a separate bowl, then add to the creamed mixture.

Add the milk, while stirring, to make a medium soft dough.

Spoon the mixture into the pudding steamer, cover with greaseproof paper and steam for 1 hour 30 minutes. Turn out on to a serving plate.

2 hours to make

Ice Cream Cake

Friends always ask me for this recipe, as it's great for any birthday party, no matter what age. Decorate for fun!

1 madeira or sponge cake
3 flavours and colours of ice cream (e.g. vanilla, chocolate, strawberry), approximately 4oz of each flavour

Line an 8 inch cake pan with greaseproof paper so that it overhangs the edges. Slice the cake into ½ inch thick pieces and press them on to the paper to cover the whole cake pan.

Fill the cake-lined pan with ice cream. Arrange it according to colour, and really press it down into the cake so that as much ice cream as possible is used. Place the cake in the freezer.

When the cake is frozen, pull on the greaseproof paper to remove the cake from the pan. Turn it upside down on to a serving dish.

Ice and decorate it as you would a normal cake, and serve immediately.

1 hour to make – chilled

Lemon Bread Cake

Serve with a dash of lemon juice, if you like, together with a sprinkling of sugar and a touch of fresh cream. A tangy cake which children and adults love as a dessert or with a cup of tea.

2 cups sugar
½ cup vegetable shortening
rind of 1 lemon
2 eggs, beaten
1½ cups flour
1 teaspoon baking powder
1 cup pecan nuts, chopped
½ cup skimmed milk

for the topping:
1½ tablespoons lemon juice
1 cup confectioners sugar

Pre-heat the oven to 350°F. In a mixing bowl, cream the sugar, vegetable shortening and lemon rind together. Add the eggs and mix well. Mix the flour with the baking powder and add to the mixture. Add the nuts, then the milk and stir well.

Pour into a small (1lb) greased and floured loaf pan and bake for 30 minutes. Reduce the heat to 275°F and bake for a further 30 minutes. Turn the bread out of the loaf tin, mix the lemon juice with the icing sugar, and pour over the loaf while still hot.

1 hour 15 minutes to make

Lemon Meringue Pie

⅓ cup cornstarch
1½ cups sugar
1¼ cups boiling water
3 tablespoons butter or margarine
6 eggs, separated
grated rind of 2 lemons
8 tablespoons lemon juice
1 8 inch shortcrust pastry shell, cooked

Pre-heat the oven to 300°F. Mix the cornstarch and sugar in a pan and slowly add the boiling water. Stir constantly over a low heat until the mixture is boiling and clear.

Add the butter. Beat the egg yolks and add a little at a time. Cook over a low heat until thick, stirring constantly.

Add the lemon rind and juice and mix well. Cool the sauce, then pour into the shell. Whip the egg whites to the stiff-peak stage, and pile on top of the filling. Bake for 15 minutes. Serve hot or cold.

30 minutes to make

Mixed Fruit Pudding

⅔ cup raisins
½ cup currants
1 tablespoon candied peel
¼ cup vegetable shortening
¼ cup self-rising flour
½ cup breadcrumbs
½ teaspoon mixed spice
½ teaspoon ground ginger
¼ cup brown sugar
1 egg, beaten
4 tablespoons milk

Grease a 4 cups pudding steamer. Mix the dried fruit and peel in a large bowl, and add the vegetable shortening. Add the flour, breadcrumbs, spices and sugar and mix well.

Beat the egg and milk together and add to the dry ingredients, mixing thoroughly.

Press the mixture into the steamer, cover with greaseproof paper and foil, then steam for 3–4 hours.

4 hours to make

New Year Pudding

This is a great festive pudding to bring in the New Year. Serve with Brandy Butter (see page 155).

6 cups fine, fresh breadcrumbs
1 teaspoon salt
1½ teaspoons ground cinnamon
1½ teaspoons ground nutmeg
1 teaspoon mixed spice
1½ cups brown sugar
1¼ cups milk
12 eggs, beaten
1¼ cups vegetable shortening
1 cup apples, chopped
3¼ cups seedless raisins, chopped
1 cup currants, chopped
½ cup dates, chopped
½ cup candied peel, chopped
½ cup glacé cherries, quartered
4 tablespoons brandy

Mix the breadcrumbs, salt, spices and sugar together in a large mixing bowl. Heat the milk in a small saucepan and pour it over the dry ingredients. Mix well and allow to cool.

Crumble the vegetable shortening into the breadcrumb mixture, add the beaten eggs and stir the mixture very well.

Add all the fruit and the brandy to the pudding mix and stir very well.

Turn the mixture into two 1 quart pudding steamers and cover with baking foil. Place each steamer in a pan with 2 inches of water and steam for 4–6 hours. Add more water if necessary.

5 hours to make

Orange Custard

3 eggs
½ cup sugar
1 cup heavy cream
1 cup fresh orange juice
2 teaspoons grated orange rind

Pre-heat the oven to 350°F. Beat the eggs in a mixing bowl. Gradually add the sugar, cream, orange·juice and rind and continue beating to an even consistency.

Pour the mixture into individual custard dishes or one large, pretty dish and place in a pan of hot water inside the oven.

Bake for 40–50 minutes, until a piece of raw spaghetti inserted into the custard comes out clean. Serve hot or cold.

1 hour to make

Pavlova

Serve this delicious classic with whipped cream, and top with fresh strawberries, kiwi fruit, mandarin oranges, raspberries, any other fresh fruit or a chocolate sauce.

6 egg whites
2 cups sugar
1 teaspoon cornstarch
1 teaspoon vanilla extract
½ teaspoon vinegar

Pre-heat the oven to 275°F. Line a baking tray (or a special pavlova pan, if you have one) with grease-proof paper (or grease it and dust it with confectioners sugar).

Lightly beat the egg whites, then add half the sugar and beat the mixture to a stiff-peak consistency.

Fold in the cornstarch, vanilla, vinegar and remaining sugar. Pile the beaten mixture on to the pan in whatever shape you like.

Bake for 1½ hours, until light brown. Cool it in a draught-free place to avoid sinking.

1 hour 45 minutes to make

Pecan Cake

½ cup butter or margarine
1 cup brown sugar
2 eggs, separated
1½ cups self-rising flour
⅔ cup milk
1 teaspoon vanilla extract
1 cup pecan nuts, chopped
½ teaspoon baking powder

Pre-heat the oven to 350°F. Cream the butter and sugar together. Gradually add the egg yolks, beating thoroughly between each addition.

Sift the flour into the mixture. Add the remaining ingredients, except the egg whites, and stir well.

Beat the egg whites until stiff and fold them into the mixture. Transfer to a greased and floured 8 inch cake pan and bake for 50 minutes.

1 hour 15 minutes to make

Pecan Cookie Balls

½ cup butter or margarine
⅔ cup self-rising flour
½ cup sugar
½ teaspoon vanilla extract
1 cup pecan nuts, chopped
confectioners sugar to coat

Mix all the ingredients (apart from the confectioners sugar) together in a large bowl and work to an even consistency. Chill the dough in the refrigerator for about 30 minutes. Pre-heat the oven to 350°F and mould the chilled cookie mixture into little ball shapes. Place them on a greased and floured baking sheet in the oven for 15 minutes, until lightly browned. Remove from the oven, roll each one in confectioners sugar, cool and serve.

1 hour to make

Pineapple Upside-Down Cake

8 tablespoons butter or margarine
¼ cup brown sugar
1 16oz can pineapple rings or pears or peaches
⅓ cup broken pecan nuts
2oz glacé cherries, chopped roughly
4 eggs, separated
1¼ cup sugar
1 cup self-rising flour

Pre-heat the oven to 350°F. Melt the butter in a saucepan and pour it into a heavy 9 inch shallow pan (1½ inch deep).

Sprinkle the brown sugar over the butter and place one slice of pineapple in the centre of the cake pan. Cut the remaining pineapple rings in half and arrange them around the centre slice like the spokes of a wheel. Fill the spaces between the pineapple with the pecans and cherries.

Beat the egg yolks and sugar together to a light and creamy consistency. Fold the flour into this mixture. Beat the egg whites to the stiff-peak stage and fold them gently into the cake batter.

Pour the batter over the pineapple base and bake for 30 minutes. Turn the cake upside-down on to a serving dish immediately it is removed from the oven, so that the caramel pineapple mixture is on top. Let the cake cool before serving.

55 minutes to make

Pound Cake

Called 'Pound Cake' because it uses a pound weight of all its main ingredients. This recipe makes several cakes which can be frozen or given to friends. The cake goes well with afternoon tea or as a dessert with sorbet.

1lb butter or margarine
2⅔ cups sugar
10 eggs
1 teaspoon vanilla extract
4 cups self-rising flour

Pre-heat the oven to 350°F, and grease and flour three 1 lb cake/loaf pans. Cream the butter and sugar together in a large mixing bowl, until fluffy.

Beat the eggs and gradually add them to the mixture, beating after each addition.

Gradually add the vanilla extract and flour,

stirring constantly. Pour the mixture into the baking pans and bake until cooked through (about 1 hour 20 minutes).

1 hour 30 minutes to make

Pumpkin Pie

This traditional American pie is customarily eaten at Thanksgiving, but goes down just as well on Guy Fawkes night, Halloween, or any other autumn celebration.

1 9 inch shortcrust pastry shell, uncooked
1¼ cups sugar
pinch of salt
½ teaspoon ground ginger
1 teaspoon ground cinnamon
½ teaspoon ground cloves
2 cups fresh-cooked pumpkin or canned
½ teaspoon vanilla extract
2 eggs, beaten
grated rind of 1 lemon
½ cup milk
½ cup cream

Pre-heat the oven to 425°F. Prepare the pie shell and bake it for 5 minutes.

Mix the sugar, salt and spices together in a large mixing bowl. Add the pumpkin, vanilla, eggs and lemon and mix these together very well.

Add the milk and cream and stir well to a very thick soupy consistency.

Pour the pumpkin filling into the pie shell and bake for 20 minutes. Then reduce the oven temperature to 275°F and bake for a further 40 minutes. A knife or piece of raw spaghetti inserted in the filling should come out clean when the pie is finished. Remove, allow to cool and serve chilled.

1 hour 20 minutes to make

Rice Pudding

½ cup short grain rice
⅓ cup sugar
4 cups milk
4 tablespoons butter or margarine
1 teaspoon ground cinnamon (optional)

Pre-heat the oven to 325°F and lightly grease a 9 inch baking dish. Wash the rice and put it in the dish.

Sprinkle the sugar over the rice, then pour the milk on top. Cut the butter into small pieces and dot these on to the milk. Sprinkle the cinnamon over the pudding, if desired.

Bake for 30 minutes, then stir the pudding gently and return it to the oven. Stir it again 30 minutes later.

After 1½ hours baking, the pudding should have a light golden crust. Serve immediately.

1 hour 45 minutes to make

Rich Fruit Cake

1 cup butter or margarine
1¼ cups sugar
1¼ cups brown sugar
4 eggs, beaten
2 teaspoons mixed spice
2 cups self-rising flour
juice of ½ lemon
4oz glacé cherries
1½ cups sultanas
1½ cups raisins
1½ cups currants
1 cup almonds, chopped
½ cup mixed peel
grated rind of 1 lemon

Pre-heat the oven to 275°F. Grease a 9 inch cake pan and line it with a double layer of greaseproof paper, then tie brown paper around the outside.

Cream the butter and sugars together in a large mixing bowl. Whisk the eggs gradually into the creamed mixture. Mix the spice into the flour. Add the lemon juice to the cake mixture, a little at a time, adding a spoonful of the flour mixture with each addition to prevent curdling.

Add the fruit, nuts, peel and lemon rind to the cake mixture. Spoon the mixture into the cake pan and bake for 4½–5 hours or until golden brown. Cover the cake with greaseproof paper towards the end of cooking to help prevent it from becoming too browned. If you stick a knife into the cake it should come out clean when the cake is properly baked.

5 hours to make

Sour Cream Cake

8 tablespoons butter or margarine
1 cup sugar
2 eggs, beaten
1 teaspoon vanilla extract
1½ cups self-rising flour
½ teaspoon baking powder
2 teaspoons ground cinnamon
⅔ cup sour cream
1 cup pecan nuts, chopped

Pre-heat the oven to 350°F and grease and flour an 8 inch baking pan.

Cream the butter and sugar together, then beat in the eggs little by little. Pour in the vanilla extract.

Sift the flour with the baking powder and cinnamon and mix into the creamed ingredients, then add the sour cream and chopped pecans. Mix well.

Spoon the mixture into the pan and bake for 55–65 minutes. Leave to cool for 15 minutes before turning out.

1 hour 15 minutes to make

Spice Cake

8 tablespoons butter or margarine
1 cup sugar
1 cup brown sugar
3 eggs, beaten
1¼ cups mixed dried fruit
⅔ cup pecan nuts, chopped
2½ cups self-rising flour
½ teaspoon ground cinnamon
½ teaspoon mixed spice
1⅔ cups heavy cream

Pre-heat the oven to 350°F and grease and flour an 8 inch round cake pan.

Cream the butter and sugars together, then gradually add the eggs, beating well after each addition.

Mix all the remaining ingredients except the cream into the egg and butter mixture. Then add the cream and mix well. Spoon the mixture into the cake pan and bake for 1 hour, or until a knife inserted into the cake comes out clean.

1 hour 15 minutes to make

Strawberry Mousse

1lb strawberries, washed and cleaned
2 cups confectioners sugar
1½ cups heavy cream, whipped
1 teaspoon vanilla extract

Mash the strawberries with the sugar in a mixing bowl. Fold in the cream, and add the vanilla extract, then turn into small bowls, chill, and serve.

30 minutes to make – including chilling time

Strawberry Shortcake

1 Victoria Sponge cake (see this page)
½ pint whipping cream
1 tablespoon sugar
1 teaspoon vanilla extract
2 baskets fresh strawberries

Let the victoria sponge cake cool, then whip the cream with the sugar and vanilla extract in a mixing bowl.

Wash and clean the strawberries and allow them to drain.

Mash half of the strawberries and fold them into the mixture. Ice each portion with the strawberry and cream whip, then top with whole strawberries and serve immediately.

15 minutes to make

Syrup Steamed Pudding

Serve warm, with more golden syrup spooned over the pudding.

4 tablespoons corn syrup, plus extra for serving
1 cup self-rising flour
½ cup sugar
1 cup breadcrumbs
½ teaspoon ground ginger
1 teaspoon mixed spice (optional)
1 teaspoon baking soda
pinch of salt
8 tablespoons vegetable shortening
1 egg
1 cup milk

Grease a 4 cup pudding steamer and pour 2 tablespoons of golden syrup in to the bottom.

Mix the flour, sugar, breadcrumbs, spices, soda and salt together in a large mixing bowl. Break the vegetable shortening over the dry mixture.

Beat the remaining syrup, the egg and half the milk together in a cup. Gradually beat this liquid into the dry mix. Add more milk, if necessary, to make a dough of a dropping consistency.

Press the mixture into the pudding steamer, cover and steam for 2 hours.

2 hours 20 minutes to make

Tapioca Cream

1 cup instant cooking tapioca
1½ cups milk
2 eggs, separated
⅓ cup sugar
1 teaspoon vanilla extract

Gently heat the tapioca and milk in a saucepan over a low heat until the mixture becomes thick, stirring all the time.

Remove the saucepan from the heat and beat in the egg yolks and sugar, then let it cool for 5 minutes. Stir in the vanilla.

Whisk the egg whites until they are stiff, then fold them into the mixture. Serve in pretty bowls with a dollop of jam in the middle.

20 minutes to make

Victoria Sponge

For some variations on this dependable recipe, try adding 1 tablespoon of cocoa powder, or the juice and rind of an orange or lemon (and leave out the vanilla extract).

½ cup butter or margarine
⅔ cup sugar
2 eggs, beaten
2–3 drops vanilla extract
1 cup self-rising flour

Pre-heat the oven to 350°F and grease and flour two 8 inch sponge pans.

Cream the butter and sugar together in a mixing bowl. Add the eggs, a little at a time, to the creamed mixture. Beat well after each addition. Then add the vanilla. Sift the flour and fold it in. (If a chocolate cake is desired, add the cocoa with the flour.) The mixture should drop off the spoon: if it doesn't, add a little hot water.

Divide the batter between the two cake pans and bake for 20–25 minutes. Leave them in the pans for 5 minutes before turning out on to a wire rack to finish cooling.

40 minutes to make

INDEX

acorn squash, 22
aduki beans, 43
almonds, 32
    Almond Cake, 152
apples, 35
    Apple Sauce Cake, 152–3
    Apples Brown Betty, 152
    Baked Apples, 153
    Zucchini with Apples, 142
apricots, 35
artichokes, 22
    Hearts of Artichoke with
      Mushroom Sauce, 101
    Jerusalem Artichokes in
      Lemon Parsley Sauce, 137
asparagus, 22
    Asparagus Casserole with
      Sour Cream, 80
    Asparagus with Cheese, 81
    Asparagus in Divine Sauce,
      81
    Asparagus and Egg
      Casserole, 80
    Rice with Asparagus, 118
aubergines, 22–3
    Aubergine Caponata, 81
    Aubergine Casserole, 83
    Aubergine Fritters, 83
    Aubergine Parmigiano, 83
    Aubergine and Pasta, 84
    Mince and Aubergine
      Casserole, 109
    Moussaka, 109–10
avocados, 23
    Avocado and Dill Soup, 51
    Avocado and Green Chili
      Soup, 51
    Guacamole, 64
bananas, 35
    Banana Cake, 153, 155
basil, 44, 48
    Tomatoes stuffed with
      Cottage Cheese and Basil,
      77
bay leaves, 44, 48
bean sprouts, 48
beans, 41
    Bean Tacos, 85
    Green Bean Savoury, 137
    Green Beans and Mushrooms
      in Sour Cream, 136–7
    New Orleans Broad Beans,
      138
    Niçoise Green Beans, 138
    Pasta Flageolet Soup, 57
    Refried Bean Dip, 67
    Refried Beans, 141
    Rice and Beans, 118
beer,
    Beer Fondue, 88

Beer Rarebit, 88
beets, 23
    Beet and Celery Salad, 70
    Beet and Onion Salad, 70
    Bortsch Soup, 52
    Harvard Beets, 137
    Orange and Beets, 140
    Potato and Carrot Bortsch, 57
    Sour Cream and Beets, 142
blackberries, 35
black-eyed peas, 41
blueberries, 36
    Blueberry Muffins, 155
    Blueberry Pancakes, 155
borlotti beans, 41
brazil nuts, 32
bread,
    Cheese and Green Chili
      Corn Bread, 93
    Corn Bread, 61
    Corn Bread Mexican Style, 63
    Garlic Bread, 63
    Herb Bread, 64
    Hot Mozzarella Sandwich,
      103
    Irish Brown Bread, 64
    Mexican Corn Bread, 64–5
    Mozzarella French Loaf, 110
    Pizza Bread, 65
broad beans, 43
broccoli, 23–4
    Breaded Broccoli, 134
    Broccoli Cream Soup, 52
brussels sprouts, 24
buckwheat, 40
bulgur wheat, see cracked
    wheat
burgers, see vegetable
    burgers
butter beans, 42, 43
cabbage, 24
    Cabbage and Caraway Seed
      Salad, 70
    Coleslaw, 73
    Coleslaw and Mayonnaise,
      144
    Coleslaw and Sour Cream,
      144
    Lemon Coleslaw, 75
    Maine Sauerkraut, 105
    Sauerkraut, 141
    Sauerkraut and Veggy Dogs,
      67
    Savoury Cabbage and Sour
      Cream, 141
cakes,
    Almond Cake, 152
    Apple Sauce Cake, 152–3
    Banana Cake, 153
    Brown Sugar Loaf Cake, 155

    Brownies, 156
    Cherry Cake, 156
    Cocoa Cake, 158
    Gingerbread Cake, 160
    Heather's Lemon Pudding
      Cake, 161
    Ice Cream Cake, 161
    Lemon Bread Cake, 162
    Pecan Cake, 163
    Pineapple Upside-Down
      Cake, 164
    Pound Cake, 164
    Rich Fruit Cake, 165
    Sour Cream Cake, 165
    Spice Cake, 165
    Victoria Sponge, 166
calcium, 8-9
capers,
    Cheese and Caper Dip, 61
caraway seeds, 45–6
carbohydrates, 7
carrots, 24
    Carrot Cream Soup, 53
    Carrot and Turnip Purée, 134
    Glazed Carrots, 136
    Moroccan Carrot Salad, 76
    Potato and Carrot Bortsch, 57
    Turnip, Carrot and Split-Pea
      Soup, 58
cashew nuts, 32
casseroles,
    Asparagus Casserole with
      Sour Cream, 80
    Asparagus and Egg
      Casserole, 80
    Aubergine Casserole, 83
    Beefless Rice Casserole, 86
    Cheese and Noodle
      Casserole, 93
    Cheese and Tomato
      Casserole, 94
    Mince and Aubergine
      Casserole, 109
    Oriental Beefless Casserole,
      115
cauliflower, 24
    Cauliflower Gratin, 91
    Cauliflower Mexican Style, 92
cayenne, 46
celeriac,
    Celeriac Salad, 72
celery, 24–5
    Beet and Celery Salad, 70
    Celery and Rice Salad, 72
    Cream of Celery, 136
    Cream of Celery Soup, 53
    Parsley, Celery and Green
      Pea Soup, 57
cheese,
    Asparagus with Cheese, 81

Baked Macaroni Cheese, 84
Beer Fondue, 88
Beer Rarebit, 88
Cheddar Cheese Bake, 92
Cheddar Cheese Pie, 92
Cheddar Cheese Rolls, 61
Cheese and Caper Dip, 61
Cheese and Green Chilli
    Corn Bread, 93
Cheese with Herbs and
    Pasta, 93
Cheese and Noodle
    Casserole, 93
Cheese Soufflé, 94
Cheese and Tomato
    Casserole, 94
Cottage Cheese Pie, 96
Egg and Cheese Salad, 73
Egg and Mushroom Cheese
    Sauce, 145
Fried Mozzarella, 99
Herby Cheese and Rice Bowl,
    101
Hot Mozzarella Sandwich,
    103
Lentil Cheese Loaf, 104
Linda's Lasagna, 104–5
Mexican Rarebit, 109
Mozzarella Croquettes, 110
Mozzarella French Loaf, 110
Pizza Bread, 65–6
Quiche, 117
Spinach Cheese Dumplings,
    124
Stilton Pâté, 68
Swiss Fondue, 127
Tomatoes stuffed with
    Cottage Cheese and Basil,
    77
Welsh Rarebit, 69
cherries, 36
    Cherry Cake, 156
chestnuts, 32
chick peas, 41, 42
    Chick Pea Salad, 73
    Hummus, 64
chili powder, 46
chilies,
    Avocado and Green Chili
      Soup, 51
    Cheese and Green Chili
      Corn Bread, 93
    Chili Non Carne, 94–5
    Green Chili and Rice, 101
chives, 44, 49
chocolate,
    Brownies, 156
    Chocolate Mousse, 157
    Chocolate and Pecan Nut
      Cookies, 157

Chocolate Pudding, 157
Chocolate Soufflé, 157
Cocoa Cake, 158
cinnamon, 46
cloves, 46
coconuts, 32–3
Coconut Cream Pie, 158
Coconut Custard, 160
coleslaw, 73
cookies,
Butter Cookies, 156
Chocolate and Pecan Nut
Cookies, 157
Empire Biscuits, 160
Pecan Cookie Balls, 163
cooking methods, 14–17
corn, see sweet corn
couscous, 40
cracked wheat, 40
Tabouli Salad, 77
Cranberry Sauce, 144
cucumber, 25
Cucumber, Dill and Sour
Cream Sauce, 144
Cucumber Salad, 73
Dill Pickles, 144–5
cumin seeds, 46
currants, black and red, 35–6
curries,
Curried Eggs, 97
Curried Lentils, 97
Madras Onion Curry, 105
Stuffed Curried Eggs, 68
Super Curried Eggs Indian
Style, 127
Vegetable Curry, 132
curry powder, 46
desserts,
Apple Brown Betty, 152
Baked Apples, 153
Baked Custard, 153
Chocolate Mousse, 157
Chocolate Pudding, 157
Chocolate Soufflé, 157
Christmas Pudding, 158
Coconut Cream Pie, 158
Coconut Custard, 160
Fluffy Lemon Pie, 160
Heather's Lemon Pudding
Cake, 161
Honey Steamed Pudding,
161
Lemon Meringue Pie, 162
Mixed Fruit Pudding, 162
New Year Pudding, 162–3
Orange Custard, 163
Pavlova, 163
Pumpkin Pie, 164
Rice Pudding, 165
Strawberry Mousse, 166
Syrup Steamed Pudding, 166
Tapioca Cream, 166
dill, 44
Avocado and Dill Soup, 51
Cucumber, Dill and Sour
Cream Sauce, 144
Dill Pickles, 144–5
dips,
Cheese and Caper Dip, 61
Fresh Herb Dip, 145
Refried Bean Dip, 67

dressings
Garlic Dressing, 146
Vinaigrette Dressing, 150
eggs,
Asparagus and Egg
Casserole, 80
Curried Eggs, 97
Devilled Eggs, 63
Egg and Cheese Salad, 73
Egg and Mushroom Cheese
Sauce, 145
Egg and Potato Salad, 75
Egg Salad Sandwich Spread,
63
Eggs Florentine, 97
Eggs Au Gratin, 97
French Baked Eggs, 99
Mexican Omelette, 108
Omelette, 65
Pavlova, 163
Pressed Egg and Tomato, 67
Scrambled Eggs, 68
Shirred Eggs, 68
Spaghetti Omelette, 121
Spanish Omelette, 123
Spicy Eggs, 123
Spinach and Sour Cream
Omelette, 124
Stuffed Curried Eggs, 68
Stuffed Eggs and Tomato, 126
Super Curried Eggs Indian
Style, 127
Tarragon and Herb Eggs, 128
Tomato Soufflé, 129
eggplants, see aubergines
fibre, 7
figs, 36
fondues,
Beer Fondue, 88
Swiss Fondue, 127
frankfurters, see vegetable
frankfurters
fritters,
Aubergine Fritters, 83
Corn Fritters, 96
garlic, 25, 44–5
Garlic Bread, 63
Garlic Dressing, 146
Garlic Herb Sauce, 147
Noodles and Garlic, 113
ginger, 46
Gingerbread Cake, 160
gooseberries, 36
grains, 40–1
grapefruit, 36
grapes, 36
green beans, 23
green peas, 41
Parsley, Celery and Green
Pea Soup, 57
haricot beans, 41, 43
hazel nuts, 33
herbs, 44–5, 48–9
Cheese with Herbs and
Pasta, 93
Fresh Herb Dip, 145
Fresh Herb Mayonnaise, 145
Garlic Herb Sauce, 147
Herb Bread, 64
Herby Cheese and Rice Bowl,
101

Pasta with Herbs, 115
Tarragon and Herb Eggs, 128
ice cream,
Ice Cream Cake, 161
icings,
Butter Icing, 156
Glacé Icing, 161
iodine, 9
iron, 9
kidney beans, 41, 43
kiwi fruit, 36
lasagna,
Lasagna Italiano, 104
Linda's Lasagna, 104–5
leeks, 25
Leeks Vinaigrette, 137–8
Vichyssoise, 60
legumes, 41, 43
lemons, 36–7
Fluffy Lemon Pie, 160
Heather's Lemon Pudding
Cake, 161
Jerusalem Artichokes in
Lemon Parsley Sauce, 137
Lemon Bread Cake, 162
Lemon Coleslaw, 75
Lemon Meringue Pie, 162
Lemon Rice Salad, 75
lentils, 41, 43
Curried Lentils, 97
Lentil Cheese Loaf, 104
Lentil Soup, 56
Lentil and Steaklets Stew, 104
lettuce, 25
lima beans, 43
macaroni, see pasta
magnesium, 9
mangoes, 37
marjoram, 45, 49
mayonnaise,
Fresh Herb Mayonnaise, 145
Meatless Loaf, 106
melons, 37
Mexican dishes,
Bean Tacos, 85
Cauliflower Mexican Style, 92
Chili Non Carne, 94–5
Corn Bread Mexican Style, 63
Mexican Corn Bread, 64–5
Mexican Corn Pudding, 108
Mexican Loaf, 108
Mexican Omelette, 108
Mexican Rarebit, 109
Refried Beans, 141
microwave cooking, 21
minerals, 7–9
mint, 45, 49
mixed herbs, 45
mixed spice, 46
mousses,
Chocolate Mousse, 157
Strawberry Mousse, 166
Tomato and Potato Mousse,
69
muffins,
Blueberry Muffins, 155
mung beans, 43
mushrooms, 26
Bisque of Mushroom, 52
Egg and Mushroom Cheese
Sauce, 145

Green Beans and Mushrooms
in Sour Cream, 136–7
Hearts of Artichoke with
Mushroom Sauce, 101
Mushroom Loaf, 112
Mushroom Pie, 112
Mushroom and Rice, 112
Mushroom Risotto, 113
Mushrooms and Onions in
Sherry, 113
Parsley and Mushroom
Cream Sauce, 148
Raw Mushroom Marinade,
141
Simple Stuffed Mushrooms,
142
Sour Cream, Paprika and
Mushrooms, 121
Stuffed and Broiled
Mushrooms, 125
Tomato and Mushroom
Sauce, 150
mustard, 46
mustard and cress, 49
nectarines, 37
noodles, see pasta
nutmeg, 46–7
nuts, 31–3
oats, 40
okra, 26
New Orleans Okra, 138
olives,
Olive and Steaklet Bake, 115
omelettes, see eggs
onions, 26
Beet and Onion Salad, 70
Burgers with Fried Onion, 91
Madras Onion Curry, 105
Mushrooms and Onions in
Sherry, 113
Tomato and Onion Sauce
Italian Style, 150
oranges, 37
Orange and Beets, 140
Orange Custard, 163
oregano, 45
Pancake Mix, 148
Blueberry Pancakes, 155
paprika, 47
parsley, 45, 49
Burgers with Parsley Butter,
91
Jerusalem Artichokes in
Lemon Parsley Sauce, 137
Parsley, Celery and Green
Pea Soup, 57
Parsley and Mushroom
Cream Sauce, 148
parsnips, 26
Puréed Parsnips, 140
pasta,
Aubergine and Pasta, 84
Baked Macaroni Cheese, 84
Cheese with Herbs and
Pasta, 93
Cheese and Noodle
Casserole, 93
Noodle Salad, 76
Noodles and Garlic, 113
Noodles German Style, 113
Pasta Flageolet Soup, 57

Pasta with Herbs, 115
Penne with Vodka, 116
pastry,
    Puff Pastry, 148–9
    Shortcrust Pastry, 149
pâtés,
    Stilton Pâté, 68
peaches, 37
peanuts, 33
pears, 37
peas, 126–8
    Peas in Cream, 140
    Wild Rice and Peas, 133
pecan nuts, 33
    Chocolate and Pecan Nut
        Cookies, 157
    Pecan Cake, 163
    Pecan Cookie Balls, 163
pepper, 47
    Pepper Steaklets, 116
peppers, 28
    Steaklets Pepper, 125
    Stuffed Peppers, 126
phosphorus, 9
pies,
    Beefless Pie, 85
    Cheddar Cheese Pie, 92
    Coconut Cream Pie, 158
    Cottage Cheese Pie, 96
    Fluffy Lemon Pie, 160
    Lemon Meringue Pie, 162
    Mushroom Pie, 112
    Pumpkin Pie, 164
    Shepherd's Pie, 120
    Spinach Pie, 124
    Tomato Pie, 128–9
pine nuts, 33
pineapples, 38
    Pineapple Upside-Down
        Cake, 164
pinto beans, 43
pistachio nuts, 33
Pizza Bread, 65, 67
plums, 38
poppy seeds, 33
potassium, 9
potatoes, 28
    Egg and Potato Salad, 75
    German Potato Salad, 75
    Gnocchi, 100
    New Potato Salad, 76
    Potato and Carrot Bortsch, 57
    Potato Dumplings with
        Brown Butter, 140
    Potato Salad and
        Mayonnaise, 76
    Potato Salad Vinaigrette, 77
    Potato Torte à la Faranto, 117
    Simple Beefless Hash, 120
    Tomato and Potato Mousse,
        69
protein, 7
Pumpkin Pie, 164
pumpkin seeds, 33
purées,
    Carrot and Turnip Purée, 134
    Puréed Parsnips, 140
Quiche, 117
radishes, 28
raspberries, 38
rhubarb, 38

rice, 40–1
    Beefless Rice Casserole, 86
    Celery and Rice Salad, 72
    Fried Rice, 99
    Green Chili and Rice, 101
    Herby Cheese and Rice
        Bowl, 101
    Lemon Rice Salad, 75
    Mushroom and Rice, 112
    Mushroom Risotto, 113
    Rice with Asparagus, 118
    Rice and Beans, 118
    Rice Pudding, 165
    Rice in Tasty Vegetable Stock,
        118
    Rice and Vegetables in Wine,
        119
    Savoury Rice, 119
    Stuffed Peppers, 126
    Tomato Rice, 129
    Wild Rice and Peas, 133
risottos,
    Mushroom Risotto, 113
rosemary, 45
rutabagas, 28
sage, 45
salads,
    Beet and Celery Salad, 70
    Beet and Onion Salad, 70
    Cabbage and Caraway Seed
        Salad, 70
    Caesar Salad, 72
    Celeriac Salad, 71
    Celery and Rice Salad, 71
    Chef's Salad, 71
    Chick Pea Salad, 73
    Cucumber Salad, 73
    Egg and Cheese Salad, 73
    Egg and Potato Salad, 75
    Four Seasons Salad, 75
    German Potato Salad, 75
    Lemon Rice Salad, 75
    Moroccan Carrot Salad, 76
    New Potato Salad, 76
    Noodle Salad, 76
    Potato Salad and
        Mayonnaise, 76
    Potato Salad Vinaigrette,
        77
    Spinach Salad, 77
    Tabouli Salad, 77
    Watercress and Lettuce
        Salad, 78
salt, 47
sauces,
    Barbecue Sauce, 143
    Béchamel Sauce, 143
    Brown Sauce, 143
    Cranberry Sauce, 144
    Cucumber, Dill and Sour
        Cream Sauce, 144
    Egg and Mushroom Cheese
        Sauce, 145
    Fresh Tomato Sauce, 145
    Garlic Herb Sauce, 147
    Hollandaise Sauce, 147
    Home-made Tomato
        Sauce, 147
    Mornay Sauce, 147
    Parsley and Mushroom
        Cream Sauce, 148

Pesto, 148
    Spaghetti Sauce Bolognaise,
        149
    Tomato and Mushroom
        Sauce, 150
    Tomato and Onion Sauce
        Italian Style, 150
    White Sauce, 150
Sauerkraut, 141
    Maine Sauerkraut, 105
    Sauerkraut and Veggy Dogs,
        67
sausages, *see* vegetable
    sausages
schnitzels, *see* vegetable
    schnitzels
seeds, 31–3
sesame seeds, 33
soufflés,
    Cheese Soufflé, 94
    Chocolate Soufflé, 157
    Corn Soufflé, 96
    Sour Cream Soufflé, 121
    Tomato Soufflé, 129
soups,
    Avocado and Dill Soup, 51
    Avocado and Green Chili
        Soup, 51
    Bisque of Mushroom, 52
    Bortsch Soup, 52
    Broccoli Cream Soup, 52
    Carrot Cream Soup, 53
    Cream of Celery Soup, 53
    Cream of Tomato Soup, 53
    Delicious Watercress Soup,
        55
    French Carrot Soup, 55
    Gazpacho, 55
    Lentil Soup, 56
    Minestrone, 56
    Parsley, Celery and Green
        Pea Soup, 57
    Pasta Flageolet Soup, 57
    Potato and Carrot Bortsch, 57
    Sweet Corn Noodle Soup, 58
    Turnip, Carrot and Split-Pea
        Soup, 58
    Vegetable Soup, 58
    Vichyssoise, 60
    Wine and Vegetable Soup, 60
sour cream,
    Asparagus Casserole with
        Sour Cream, 80
    Burgers in Sour Cream and
        Red Wine, 91
    Coleslaw and Sour Cream,
        144
    Cucumber, Dill and Sour
        Cream Sauce, 144
    Green Beans and Mushrooms
        in Sour Cream, 136–7
    Savoury Cabbage and Sour
        Cream, 141
    Sour Cream and Beets, 142
    Sour Cream Cake, 165
    Sour Cream, Paprika and
        Mushrooms, 121
    Sour Cream Soufflé, 121
    Sour Cream Steaklet Chunks,
        121
    Spinach and Sour Cream

Omelette, 124
soya beans, 43
spaghetti,
    Spaghetti Omelette, 121
spices, 45–7
spinach, 29
    Eggs Florentine, 97
    Spinach Cheese Dumplings,
        124
    Spinach Pie, 124
    Spinach Salad, 77
    Spinach and Sour Cream
        Omelette, 124
split peas, 43
    Turnip, Carrot and Split Pea
        Soup, 58
squash, *see* acorn squash
steaklets, *see* vegetable steaklets
stews,
    Beefless Stew, 86
    Greek Beefless Stew, 100–1
    Lentil and Steaklets Stew, 104
    Vegetable Burger Stew with
        Tomatoes, Peas and
        Cheese Topping, 130
strawberries, 38
    Strawberry Mousse, 166
    Strawberry Shortcake, 166
sunflower seeds, 33–4
sweet corn, 29
    Baked Sweet Corn, 85
    Cheese and Green Chili
        Corn Bread, 93
    Corn Bread, 61
    Corn Bread Mexican Style, 63
    Corn Fritters, 96
    Corn Soufflé, 96
    Mexican Corn Bread, 64–5
    Mexican Corn Pudding, 108
    Mexican Loaf, 108
    Sweet Corn Noodle Soup, 58
sweet potatoes, 29
    Baked and Creamed Sweet
        Potatoes, 134
tapioca,
    Tapioca Cream, 166
tarragon, 45
    Tarragon and Herb Eggs, 128
Textured Vegetable Protein, 12
    Beefless Pie, 85
    Beefless Rice Casserole, 86
    Beefless Stew, 86
    Burgers Bourguignonne, 89
    Chili Non Carne, 94–5
    Festive Roast with Savoury
        Stuffing, 98
    Lentil and Steaklets Stew, 104
    Linda's Lasagna, 104–5
    Madras Onion Curry, 105
    Maine Sauerkraut, 105
    Meatless Loaf, 106
    Mexican Loaf, 108
    Mince and Aubergine
        Casserole, 109
    Moussaka, 109–10
    Oriental Beefless Casserole,
        115
    Shepherd's Pie, 120
    Simple Beefless Hash, 120
    Sour Cream Steaklet Chunks,
        121

Spaghetti Sauce Bolognaise, 149
Stuffed and Broiled Mushrooms, 125
Stuffed Peppers, 126
Turnovers, 65
thyme, 45, 49
tomatoes, 29
Cheese and Tomato Casserole, 94
Cream of Tomato Soup, 53
French Baked Eggs, 99
Fresh Tomato Sauce, 145
Gazpacho, 55
Home-made Tomato Sauce, 147
Hot Dogs and Tomatoes, 103
Pressed Egg and Tomato, 67
Ratatouille, 117–18
Stuffed Eggs and Tomato, 126
Tomato and Mushroom Sauce, 150
Tomato and Onion Sauce Italian Style, 150
Tomato Pie, 128–9
Tomato and Potato Mousse, 69
Tomato Rice, 129
Tomato Soufflé, 129
Tomatoes stuffed with Cottage Cheese and Basil, 77
Tomatoes Provençal and Mince, 130
Vegetable Burger Stew with Tomatoes, Peas and Cheese Topping, 130
turmeric, 47
turnips, 29–30
Carrot and Turnip Purée, 134
Turnip, Carrot and Split Pea Soup, 58

TVP, *see* Textured Vegetable Protein
utensils, 20–1
vegetable burgers,
Beefless Pie, 85
Beefless Rice Casserole, 86
Beefless Stew, 86
Beefless Stroganoff, 86
Burgers Chop Suey, 89
Burger Goulash, 88
Burgers Bourguignonne, 89
Burgers with Fried Onion, 91
Burgers à la King, 89
Burgers with Parsley Butter, 91
Burgers in Sour Cream and Red Wine, 91
Chili Non Carne, 94–5
Festive Roast with Savoury Stuffing, 98
Greek Beefless Stew, 100–1
Italian Burgers, 103
Lentil and Steaklets Stew, 104
Madras Onion Curry, 105
Maine Sauerkraut, 105
Meatless Balls, 106
Mexican Loaf, 108
Mince and Aubergine Casserole, 109
Moussaka, 109–10
Olive and Steaklet Bake, 115
Pasties, 65
Pepper Steaklets, 116
Peruvian Burgers, 116
Sauté Schnitzel, 119
Savoury Turnovers, 119
Schnitzel Scaloppini in White Wine, 120
Shepherd's Pie, 120
Sloppy Joes, 68
Sour Cream Steaklet Chunks, 121

Spaghetti Sauce Bolognaise, 149
Spanish Burgers, 123
Steaklets Diane, 125
Steaklets Pepper, 125
Swiss Schnitzel, 127
Swiss Steaklets, 128
Teriyaki, 128
Tomatoes Provençal and Mince, 130
Vegetable Burger Stew with Tomatoes, Peas and Cheese Topping, 130
Vegetable Burger Supreme, 130
Vegetable Burgers in White Wine, 132
Vegetables and Baked Schnitzels in White Wine, 132
vegetable frankfurters,
Hot Dogs and Tomatoes, 103
vegetable sausages,
Festive Roast with Savoury Stuffing, 98
Meatless Loaf with Herbs, 106
Sauerkraut and Veggy Dogs, 67
Sausage Rolls, 67
Sunday Breakfast, 126
vegetable schnitzels,
Festive Roast with Savoury Stuffing, 98
Sauté Schnitzel, 119
Swiss Schnitzel, 127
Vegetables and Baked Schnitzels in White Wine, 132
vegetable steaklets,
Baked Steaklets, 84
Lentil and Steaklets Stew, 104
Olive and Steaklet Bake, 115

Pepper Steaklets, 116
Sour Cream Steaklet Chunks, 121
Steaklets Diane, 125
Steaklets Pepper, 125
Swiss Steaklets, 128
vegetables, 22–30
French Fried Vegetables, 136
Rice and Vegetables in Wine, 119
Vegetables and Baked Schnitzels in White Wine, 132
Vegetable Curry, 132
Vegetable Soup, 58
Wine and Vegetable Soup, 60
vitamins, 7-8
walnuts, 34
watercress, 30
Delicious Watercress Soup, 55
Watercress and Lettuce Salad, 78
wheat, 41
wild rice, 41
wine,
Burgers in Sour Cream and Red Wine, 91
Rice and Vegetables in Wine, 119
Sauté Schnitzel, 119
Schnitzel Scaloppini in White Wine, 120
Vegetable Burgers in White Wine 132
Vegetables and Baked Schnitzels in White Wine, 132
Wine and Vegetable Soup, 60
zinc, 9
zucchini, 30
Zucchini with Apples, 142
Greek squash, 136

CONVERSION TABLES

Weight

Ounces (oz)	grams (g)
½	15
1	25
1½	45
2	55
2½	70
3	85
4	115
5	140
6	170
7	200
8	225
12	340
1lb	455
1lb 8oz	680
2lb	910

Liquids

fl.oz (pints)	millilitres (litres)
2	60
3	90
4	120
5 (¼ pint)	140
6	180
7	205
8	230
10 (½ pint)	290
12	340
14	400
15	430
20 (1 pint)	570
2 pints	1.1l
1 tablespoon	(½ fl.oz/15ml)
2 tablespoons	(1 fl.oz/30ml)
3 tablespoons	(1½ fl.oz/45ml)
4 tablespoons	(2 fl.oz/60ml)
6 tablespoons	(3 fl.oz/85ml)
8 tablespoons	(4 fl.oz/115ml)

Oven Temperatures

°F	°C	Gas Mark
275	140	1
300	150	2
325	170	3
350	180	4
375	190	5
400	200	6
425	220	7

Quick and Easy Measuring Table

Ingredient	Weight	Handy Measure
Almonds, whole	4oz/115g	1 cup
Apple, chopped	6oz/170g	1 cup
Banana, mashed	5oz/140g	1 cup
Beans		
fresh green	8oz/225g	1 cup
kidney	8oz/225g	1 cup
large, dried	6oz/170g	1 cup
small, dried	8oz/225g	1 cup
Breadcrumbs		
fresh	2oz/55g	1 cup
dried	4oz/115g	1 cup
Butter	1oz/25g	2 tablespoons
	2oz/55g	¼ cup
	3oz/85g	⅓ cup
	4oz/115g	½ cup
	8oz/225g	1 cup
Carrot, diced or shredded	6oz/170g	1 cup
Cauliflower florets	4oz/115g	1 cup